I0120719

Class Work

Class Work

Vocational Schools and China's Urban Youth

T. E. Woronov

Stanford University Press
Stanford, California

Stanford University Press
Stanford, California

© 2016 by the Board of Trustees of the Leland Stanford Junior University. All rights reserved.

No part of this book may be reproduced or transmitted in any form or by any means, electronic or mechanical, including photocopying and recording, or in any information storage or retrieval system without the prior written permission of Stanford University Press.

Printed in the United States of America on acid-free, archival-quality paper

Library of Congress Cataloging-in-Publication Data

Woronov, T. E. (Terry Ellen), author.
  Class work : vocational schools and China's urban youth / T. E. Woronov.
    pages cm
  Includes bibliographical references and index.
  ISBN 978-0-8047-9541-8 (cloth : alk. paper)—ISBN 978-0-8047-9692-7 (pbk. : alk. paper)
  1. Vocational education—China. 2. Vocational school students—China. 3. Urban youth—Education—Social aspects—China. 4. Educational sociology—China. I. Title.
  LC1047.C6W67 2015
  370.1130951—dc23
                                                                                           2015011165

  ISBN 978-0-8047-9693-4 (electronic)

Typeset by Bruce Lundquist in 10/14 Minion

Contents

Acknowledgments

This book has been a very long journey, and I can never fully express my tremendous gratitude to the many people who have offered help, support, sustenance, and kindness along the way. First, thank you to my generous funders. The research for this book was made possible by a National Academy of Education/Spencer Foundation Postdoctoral Fellowship, with additional support from the University of Arizona. Subsequent research was made possible by the China Studies Centre and the School of Social and Political Sciences at the University of Sydney.

I owe my deepest debts to the students, teachers, and administrators at the two vocational schools in Nanjing, who graciously welcomed us into their schools and their lives. I am enormously grateful for their willingness to share their time and experience and their patient efforts to explain China's complexities to a naïve foreigner. I only hope that this book can begin to do justice to them and to the challenges they face every day. None of this research could have taken place without the institutional support of Hohai University. I am extremely grateful to Professors Chen Ajiang and Shi Guoqing for their support and for making my stay in Nanjing possible. I cannot begin to thank Emma Wang Xubo, without whom the fieldwork never would have happened. I owe all the findings in this book to her help, insight, and friendship, although all the errors, of course, are my own. For their patience, diligence, and amazing fieldwork, thank you to our wonderful research assistants, Chen Tao, Liu Guoxing, Wang Wenting, and Yang Juan. Thanks, too, to colleagues Wang Shufang, Hu Liang, Wang Yijie, Gao Yan, Jin Yihong, and Fan Ke at Hohai, Nanjing, and Nanjing Normal Universities for their warm welcome, intellectual engagement with this project, and continued friendship. I owe a very special debt and the very warmest thanks to my oldest and dearest friends in China, Zhang Liang and Chen Yingfei. Anything I might possibly know today about contemporary Chinese society and culture is due to their patient help and guidance over many, many years. *Feichang ganxie.*

I am indebted to a host of people who have helped in many ways with this project from its earliest inception to the final stages of the book. Deepest thanks to Marlys Bueber and Michael Phillips for their help, support, and hospitality. Preposterously overdue thanks and gratitude to Laura Burian and Fang Ximin, and Nancy Gordon, Zwia Lipkin, and the incomparable Tian Ying. Long belated thanks to Wang Zheng at the University of Michigan, who was the one of the first supporters of the project and helped make it possible. My gratitude to the many people on several continents who have offered advice, encouragement, a critical eye, and stimulating conversation across many years: Jeremy Beckett, Jean Comaroff, Melinda Cooper, Judith Farquhar, Luis Angosto Ferrández, Martin Gibbs, Yingjie Guo, Mette Halskov Hansen, Neil Maclean, Maurizio Marinelli, Helen McCabe, Norma Mendoza-Denton, Mimi Nichter, Maryann O'Donnell, Barbara Schulte, Gary Sigley, Sonja Van Wichelen, Wang Jun, Souchou Yao, and, of course, the Boys. Special thanks to an anonymous reviewer for Stanford University Press as well as to Chen Shuxia, Cui Fangqi, and Tigger Wise for their research and editorial assistance. Special thanks to Jen Roth-Gordon for her help and encouragement all the way through.

I don't know where to begin to thank Leticia Veloso, whose intellectual and personal friendship has been invaluable from the start of this project to the finish. Every academic word I've written since the University of Chicago has been a product of our long-term collaboration and has benefited from her generosity, kindness, and keen intellect.

Portions of this book are derived, in part, from articles published in the *Journal of Contemporary China* 21 (77): 779–791, and *Comparative Education* 49 (2): 242–259. Portions of the Introduction appeared in *South Atlantic Quarterly* 111 (4): 701–719. Portions of Chapter 2 appeared in *The Handbook of Class and Social Stratification in China*, edited by Yingjie Guo (Cheltenham, UK: Edward Elgar Press) and *The China Journal* 66: 77–99.

Finally, I was able to get to China in the first place only because of the astonishing help and support of David Woronov, Michon Davies, and especially Chris and Leila Duncan. I am profoundly, deeply grateful. Still.

Class Work

Introduction

Numeric Capital

It's early afternoon, the middle of the week, early spring 2008. Although I am perched on a low stool at the far back of a large classroom among a group of second-year (eleventh-grade) vocational secondary students, I have a clear view of the blackboard at the front of the room, because almost all the students in front of me are asleep. Faces planted on the long, narrow tables that serve as desks, arms dangling, the dozing students provide me with a clear view of the teacher, who—oblivious to the students' lack of attention— lectures in an endless drone, her back to the room. Water trickles down a wall from a leak in the ceiling and puddles onto the concrete floor. The ceiling soars more than five meters above us; below it hang pipes, electrical wires, and suspended fluorescent light fixtures that flicker in the chilly, cavernous space. Earlier in the year some students hung Christmas tinsel from the ceiling pipes and taped construction-paper hearts to a bulletin board on the back wall to add some color to the drab room. Other than the teacher's droning voice, the only other sound is the occasional click of a student tapping out a text message on a mobile phone or selecting a song on an MP3 player.

SCENES LIKE THIS were depressingly common during the year I spent observing classes (2007–2008) in two secondary vocational education (VE, or voc ed) schools in Nanjing, a provincial capital in central China about 300 kilometers (185 miles) west of Shanghai. Although I spent time with the students hanging out after school, on weekends, and in their dorms and cafeterias, my overwhelming memory of a year in Nanjing was of watching the students sleep through class.

I originally went to China with several questions in mind. An earlier research project with children in elementary school (Woronov 2003) had left me interested in the educational fate of working-class youth as they moved into secondary school. When I left for China, I envisioned carrying out a study of what educators call the "school-to-work transition," or how schools—particularly vocational schools—prepare students for jobs. I arrived in Nanjing with a dog-eared copy of Paul Willis's (1977) classic *Learning to Labor: How Working Class Kids Get Working Class Jobs* tucked under my arm. My initial goal had been to go to China to ask some of the same questions Willis had raised decades ago about youth and the (re)production of working-class culture. In order to study what might constitute an urban working class in China today and how it is produced, I first had to understand who the vocational students were, how these schools were structured, how the students got there, and where they would go once they graduated. But why were they sleeping all day?

I quickly discovered two things. One was that these deceptively simple questions were remarkably difficult to answer, for reasons I address in the following chapters. I then learned that few people I knew in China seemed to share my interest in either these students or these questions. Instead, there were only stereotypes—remarkably consistent ideas at the level of naturalized common sense in China about who and what vocational schools and students are and what the school-to-work transition consists of for working-class youth. These stereotypes were clear: according to popular attitudes in China, voc ed students are failures.

This was meant both literally and metaphorically. Literally, secondary VE students are failures because they enter the vocational system in tenth grade after failing a mandatory exam called the High School Entrance Exam (HSEE, or *zhongkao*) taken at the end of ninth grade. Simply put, students who *do* pass the HSEE move into "regular" (*putong*) high schools where they prepare for the notorious University Entrance Exams (UEE, or *gaokao*) at the end of twelfth grade. The general public understanding is that the secondary voc ed system exists to mop up students who fail the high school entrance exams in ninth grade.

Metaphorically, voc ed students are failures because commonsense logic in China tends to equate exam results with an individual's moral and personal value. Because popular opinion holds that vocational students are by definition poor students, in an unquestioned leap of logic they are frequently also considered to be bad people. And their sleeping all day? This, too, was easily explained by the same stereotypes: since they were bad students, VE students must either be stupid, lazy, or both. So their sleeping all day in school was explained to me by many informants as merely a natural expression of this stupidity or laziness.

Sadly, in a year of ethnographic research on vocational education in China, I met almost no one who questioned the many assumptions at the heart of these stereotypes. Yet the bland Chinese phrase that summarizes a student's fail-ure to test from junior high school (*chuzhong*, grades 7–9) into an academic or "regular" senior high school in tenth grade—*kaobushang*, or "didn't test up"—indexes a structural, ideological, and moral system that funnels an astonish-ingly large percentage (close to 50 percent) of the nation's youth into vocational education. They are thus placed in very particular positions in China's rapidly changing job market, urban class structures, and moral economies. After talking at greater length to the students, teachers, and administrators at the two voca-tional schools I studied, I found the situation was actually much more complex than the stereotypes would indicate. The exam system was much more convo-luted, the students' decisions to enter VE were much more complicated, and the schools and the entire vocational system were many times more intricate than simply serving as holding tanks for students who had failed entry into the more desirable, regular secondary education system.

I explore these complexities, using the VE system as a lens through which to understand broader aspects of contemporary Chinese society. I am specifi-cally interested in exploring the changing regimes of value that are congealed in these schools and the bodies of these young people as they lay draped across their desks, sleeping their school days away (Ralph 2008). What constitutes value in the rapidly changing social and economic context of China today? How is it calculated? Specifically, how do commodity values and moral values intersect, overlap, and inform each other in what in China calls the "socialist market economy"?

These are students who failed one high-stakes exam, at the end of ninth grade, when they were about sixteen years old. This one failure will determine much of their future. How this happens is the subject of this book. I explore the ideologies behind the testing systems that establish these students as both academic and moral failures, as well as the administrative and bureaucratic structures of their schools, the social backgrounds of the students, the content of their daily lessons, and their job trajectories after graduation. These young people are largely invisible in daily discourse about adolescents in China, and they are rarely portrayed in studies of Chinese youth; they are neither par-ticipants in spectacularly rebellious punk subcultures (de Kloet 2010) nor the stressed and studious youth focused on exam scores and memorization (e.g., Fong 2004). Instead, they struggle to get through school and through their lives in a system that is a complex, messy combination of socialist and capitalist, old and new, within the gritty reality of working-class lives against the background of the rapid economic development of urban China.

High-Stakes Exams: Creating Vocational Students

China's high-stakes exams are notorious. An enormous amount of research—as well as daily discourse in China—focuses on the UEE, which is administered to students at the end of year 12. This exam is a rite of passage that now drives curriculum and pedagogy throughout all twelve years of Chinese education; the concomitant pressure and stress of the UEE have attracted tremendous attention both within China and among foreign scholars (Kipnis 2010). There has been growing unease in China regarding the effects that round-the-clock studying for this test has had on young people's emotional and physical health, and in the past decade there have been periodic—and so far largely unsuccessful—moves to modify the UEE to accommodate more critical and independent thinking skills (e.g., Woronov 2008). When most people think about Chinese testing regimes, the UEE is what they imagine.

Yet vocational secondary students neither prepare for nor take the UEE; in fact, for the most part they are not and will never be eligible to take this exam. Instead, students generally enroll in VE because of their poor scores on a much earlier bottleneck in the high-stakes testing system: the HSEE. All students in China who wish to continue their education past junior middle school take this exam at the end of ninth grade.

The standardized HSEE is a fairly recent invention, originating in the state's wide-scale education reform policies of the mid-1980s. In 1986, the national Ministry of Education declared that all of the nation's youth should have access to nine years of mandatory education (*jiunian yiwu jiaoyu*), and the government began to pour resources into elementary (grades 1–6) and junior middle (grades 7–9) schools to expand universal education through grade nine (Yan Hao 2010).[1]

After the 1986 reforms, more and more students completed nine years of schooling, and families pressured the state to open more secondary educational opportunities. At precisely the same time, Premier Deng Xiaoping's reforms were radically transforming China's economy and labor market, as he broadened the move to a socialist market economy. This led to a set of interconnected problems for educational policy makers: What should be done with students once they finished ninth grade? How should policy makers handle demands from families for more educational opportunities for their children? And how should the education system be structured to prepare workers for the new economy? The Ministry of Education was concerned to produce graduates for the new labor market who were neither overqualified nor undertrained. One solution was to implement a testing regime to sort the nation's youth into different educational and occupational streams: the HSEE.

The HSEE determines which students can continue on to regular academic high schools after ninth grade.[2] Regular high schools (grades 10–12) are designed to prepare students to take the university entrance exams at the end of year 12. These high schools are ranked according to their graduates' scores on the UEE and their eventual admission rates into universities, with prestigious "key" (*zhongdian*) schools at the top and local neighborhood high schools on the bottom.

Since at least 1993 the State Council and Ministry of Education's goal has been for an equivalent number of students to be enrolled in vocational secondary schools as in regular high schools (State Council 1993).[3] The overall national passing rate for the HSEE is therefore set at around 50 percent, although the specific passing rate varies from place to place and year to year, depending on the number of seats available in each district's regular high schools. Passing rates tend to be higher in large cites and lower in rural areas. In Nanjing in June 2007, the year I arrived to study vocational high schools, 52 percent of the graduating ninth-graders scored well enough on the HSEE exam to enter regular academic high schools and begin their pursuit of university admission, while 48 percent did not. Because specific passing percentages are determined by local school districts and vary annually, there are no national-level statistics available of overall passing rates on the HSEE.[4] The best available data from the Ministry of Education indicate that in 2013, 55 percent of the nation's secondary students were enrolled in regular high schools, a statistic that may serve as a proxy for national HSEE passing rates.[5] These data indicate that the Ministry is therefore approaching its goal of a statistical (50/50) balance between vocational and regular secondary enrollments nationally.

Students who fail the HSEE have a few different options. Some drop out and enter the job market as unskilled laborers. Students from wealthy families can purchase admission into an increasing number of private academic prep schools, which focus on university admission (Donald and Zheng 2008). Students who wish to stay in school but cannot afford private prep schools choose some form of vocational education. The Ministry of Education estimates that 19.6 million students were enrolled in some form of secondary vocational school around the country in 2013.[6] As I explain in Chapter 2, however, this statistic is somewhat misleading, for it excludes students in some key categories of vocational education.

Two things are important to note about this testing process. The first is that once a student fails the HSEE, his or her future is radically curtailed. Unless the student's parents are wealthy enough to pay for private school, there is no pathway to enter a regular high school. This means there is no way to take the UEE in the future and very little hope of entering a university.[7] Without a university degree, in the future these students will be locked out of white-collar occupations and therefore will be prevented from entering China's growing urban middle classes.[8] At the most basic level, their futures will always be limited as nonprofessional workers who have attained only a vocational school credential.

The second important point is that passing rates on the HSEE are set by the government. Passing rates vary by locality and are the result of complex decisions, based partly on local and national resource allocations and partly on macro-level calculations about the kinds of workers the nation needs to train to supply the changing economy. The outcome is that almost half of the students who take the HSEE *must* fail this exam, regardless of how hard they study, how well they prepare, or what their preferences are.[9] While these tests are publicly understood to be an objective measure of student performance, and public discourse blames the students for their own failure, an average of 45 percent of graduating ninth-graders in China fail the HSEE because the state determines in advance that around half of the students taking the test must fail.

This is not a secret. The Ministry of Education (2015) publishes its policies online, and municipal newspapers around the country annually announce every city's HSEE results, including the overall passing and failing rates. Although these are open policies and decisions, the government's role in managing the passing rate on the HSEE is little known in the Chinese public imaginary. The stereotype of vocational students is still that they are stupid and lazy and deserve their limited occupational futures. In the process, the structural constraints on the students and their futures are rendered invisible. The question is how and why this occurs.

Culture, Culturalism, and Values

A close look at young people who are labeled as failures so early in life raises the issue of social worth, or how society values people (Narotzky and Besnier 2014). In many accounts of education in China, the question of who holds social worth is couched in terms of "cultural values" and is addressed through what anthropologists call a culturalist argument. As many people in China were quick to tell me, this is a question of Chinese (and, more broadly, East Asian) values, which derive from China's long Confucian heritage. In this view, Chinese culture traditionally reveres education, and its people love learning (e.g., Huang 2014). Therefore, I was told, young people who reject education, study poorly, and test badly are naturally held in low social esteem, for this is simply an expression of Chinese cultural values. In the Chinese culturalist view, loving to study is normal, and desiring the best possible marks in school is culturally expected. Chinese culture, I was told, is exceptionally unified on this point: education is revered, and therefore bad students are reviled. Several people patiently explained to me when I first arrived in China that there was therefore really no need to study vocational education. Vocational students must be bad—otherwise, they wouldn't be in vocational schools in the first place. To many people I spoke with, this already explained everything there was to know.

There is, of course, a great deal of merit in culturalist arguments. As Andrew Kipnis (2010) noted, China's Confucian heritage does provide a good explanation for what he terms "educational desires," or the almost universal desire the Chinese parents he knew expressed for their children to attain the highest possible educational success. Yet discussions of Chinese education couched in terms of Chinese culture have an important shortcoming: they cannot explain educational failure or underachievement, except to pathologize failure as deviant or repugnant. If "Chinese culture" reveres education, and it is therefore normal to study and love learning, then educational failures become simply abnormal (cf. Foucault 1977). From the culturalist perspective, vocational students do not provide insight into society, its regimes of value, or changing labor formations; they provide insight only into failure and pathology. As many of my friends in China asked me, Why bother studying them?

Beyond this, however, are other concerns with the culturalist explanation. First, I noticed that while many parents and teachers were more than happy to provide China's Confucian heritage as an explanation for the widespread attitudes that disdain vocational students and schooling, I found this was often a class-based discourse, most frequently provided by white-collar and other middle-class informants.[10] Working-class families I knew seldom produced these cultural explanations. While antivocational-school attitudes definitely existed across classes, the culturalist arguments did not; working-class families I knew did not resort to arguments about traditional Chinese culture to describe their understanding of the educational system, particularly if their own children had not performed well in school. Instead, these families included more economic and social factors. Thus, disdain for vocational education was widespread across classes, but explanations for this disdain were class specific, with the cultural explanation more pronounced among middle-class informants.

Second, the popular culturalist argument is dehistoricized. Confucianism is not a monolith; it has changed radically over the past centuries, and its status within China has changed significantly even within the past fifty years. At the same time, the Confucianist argument also erases the history of the vocational system and the social and institutional logics that govern it. Some aspects of the VE system date back to the beginning of the twentieth century. Other aspects, including the high-stakes testing system that sends students into vocational schools in the first place, are only a few decades old. This history has been rendered invisible, naturalized by state discourse and market processes. The fact that the recent history of the educational system has been rendered invisible, however, does not mean that the system is a natural product of ancient or traditional culture.

Third, the culturalist argument posits China (and Confucian-influenced East Asia) as a global exception, a contemporary product of ancient traditions. This tends to erase the ways that some aspects of education in China are quite similar to those of the rest of the world. This similarity is not accidental. In some cases, China is intentionally modeling its educational policies and practices on other nations'; in others, it is under the same kinds of pressures that other advanced industrial nations are facing. Changing pressures and ideologies about youth and education today are very similar in China to those in many other parts of the industrialized world. To understand education in China as simply a reflex of traditional Chinese culture is to neglect these larger global processes.

This book is therefore intended as a political economy of vocational education, one that brackets off China's Confucian heritage in favor of exploring the social, economic, and historical setting of vocational schools. I do this not simply to look at VE from a different angle or to reject culturalist arguments as a form of Orientalism (see Kipnis 2010). Instead, I argue that vocational students and their schools provide privileged insight into the social transformations of China's reform era, specifically the nascent formation of a new urban working class. Focusing on culture and tradition and on voc ed students as pathologized failures neglects the wider social and economic processes that produce social outcomes of failure. I address these concerns—historical transformations, class formations, and the status of Chinese youth compared with their age-mates elsewhere in the world—in order to place urban vocational education, and the value of vocational students, in context.

Regimes of Value:
Development, Economism, and Human Capital

Anthropologists working in societies undergoing rapid, wide-scale transformations have noted that times of transition from one form of objectification to another—for example, from subsistence agriculture to wage labor (Taussig

1980), or from socialism to capitalism (Dunn 2004; Patico 2008)—are particularly interesting moments to study regimes of value. During these moments of transition, the question of who and what hold social worth is actively debated, as are the qualities that constitute a moral person. Conditions of rapid social change also generate explicit debate about the temporalities of the life course: What should be done today so that young people will become the right kinds of adults in the future (Narotzky and Besnier 2014; Weiss 2002)?

The same has been true in China, as the nation has undergone unprecedented development and a wide-scale yet incomplete transformation from socialist to capitalist modes of production. To understand how and why vocational students hold little social value in this context requires understanding how their structural and moral status is linked with the political, economic, and ideological transformations of China's reform era.

The reform era dates from Deng Xiaoping's "reform and opening" policies in the late 1970s, when China's leaders began a shift in economic logic to what in China is called a socialist market economy (Meisner 1996; Schram 1984). Since then, China's modernity has been understood to be based in economics and economic development rather than in revolution and progress toward an egalitarian, communist future (Meisner 1996). Starting in the early 1980s, the state began to transform China's economy through development policies and projects, including forming special economic export zones, privatizing large segments of the state-owned industrial sector, undertaking large-scale urbanization, and increasing reliance on export-oriented manufacturing.

As these policies were implemented, "development" as both economic policy and guiding state ideology was presented to the Chinese people as a politically neutral way to move the nation away from the turmoil of the revolutionary past and to overturn a decade of radical, Cultural Revolution–era policies (see Baum 1994; Meisner 1996). Economics and economic development became commonly understood in China as based in rational, scientific principles, a change from the previous Cultural Revolution decade (ca. 1966–1976), which reform-era politicians framed as guided by irrational revolutionary political fervor. Development policies, the leadership argued, can and should be evaluated by objective, empirical data, such as statistics and rates of economic return, rather than through subjective demonstrations of political zeal. The ideology of economic development in China is thus linked to science and rationality, which carry a strongly positive moral valence (Greenhalgh and Winckler 2005; Hoffman 2010; Rofel 2007; Sigley 2009). This rationality was condensed in a new reform-era slogan, "economics in command," which displaced the slogan "politics in command" that had dominated the political landscape during the Cultural Revolution (Schram 1984).

In 1992 Deng Xiaoping formally stated that class struggle in China had come to an end and then accelerated the reforms with the statement "to get rich is glorious" (Meisner 1996). Since then, as part of the focus on economic rationality and getting rich, money has become the rationale for China's development policies, and wealth has become the measure of development for both the nation and individuals. Economics and finance have thus increasingly become a model for all levels of social life: the nation, the family, and the individual. The language and concepts of finance and economics have become the language of daily life (Hertz 1998; Shao 2006). Terms like "investment," "yield," "growth rates," and "profit and loss" now dominate Chinese discourse across a range of social domains and increasingly form the ways people describe their daily lives and motivations. Social scientists call this trend "economism," or the reduction of social process to economic dimensions.[11]

Economism, by definition, is not restricted to the economy writ large. It also reaches into the level of families and individuals, where it is effected through the concept and policies of "human capital," a global theory that was imported to China from American economic theory in the 1980s and is now widely embraced there—as in many (or perhaps most) parts of the world—as common sense. Human capital theory transposes economics—the language and concepts of cost-benefit analyses, rational investment, speculation, and future yield on investment—from the level of the national economy to individual families and children via formal education.

The concept of human capital is fairly simple. It refers to "the set of skills that an individual can acquire thanks to investments in his or her education or training, and its primary purpose was to measure the rates of return that investments in education produce or, to put it simply, the impact on future incomes that can be expected from schooling and other forms of training" (Feher 2009, 25). In other words, theories of human capital were designed to measure the ways that investments in education, skills, and training will improve an individual's ability to perform labor and thus generate income.

The theory was originally propounded by postwar economists and was most fully elaborated by University of Chicago economist Gary Becker in the book *Human Capital* (1964), and he was awarded a Nobel Prize in 1992 for his groundbreaking work on the topic. Originally, the concept was based on the argument that human capital was a form of the means of production, similar to other kinds of capital equipment (such as factory equipment) in which increased investment would produce increased rates of return. It was thus premised on a Fordist (and capitalist) model that understands the human life course as metonymic of factory production. Although it measures accumulated education and training, human capital theory at its heart is modeled on labor. Like that of factory workers, young people's time is essential; they should continuously spend their time in productive activity, doing tasks that accumulate value. Their time is their accumulative investment, although the payoff for their investments will not be realized until an unknown future date.

Since midcentury, economists, developmental economists, educational experts, and specialists in a wide range of disciplines have extended and expanded the concepts and tools of human capital analysis, and the term has entered mainstream discourse around the world. Indeed, CEOs of major corporations today regularly refer to their employees as their company's "human capital." The United Nations Development Programme (2013) has enshrined a comparative human capital evaluation in its annual human development reports, which are statistical measurements that partly correlate national development with human capital accumulation. These statistics are based on the premise that "economic growth and social progress are historically strongly correlated with development of human capital" (Dahlman 2001, 69). Politicians across the globe speak of increasing investments in human capital domestically and internationally.

For most Western and Chinese readers, the notion of human capital accumulation seems very commonsensical, in several domains. One is at the level of national policy, where investment in education is a long-term strategy of national development around the globe. Most readers might naturally agree that education is a resource that needs to be budgeted in any nation's economy. National policy makers consider questions such as these: What percentage of a nation's resources should be allocated to education? Should more students be funneled into tertiary education or into vocational or skills training? Should more resources be directed toward elementary or secondary education? At another level, human capital is also understood as a resource accumulated and allocated at the familial level. How much of each family's resources should be allocated to education? Should an individual borrow money to further education? If so, what kinds of degrees are worth going into debt for? It is assumed that these decisions are made rationally, according to cost-benefit analyses, and that the same kinds of questions about capital investments and potential returns should be raised at the level of the individual, the family, and the state.

Because national, familial, and individual levels of decision making about investments in human capital are metonymic of each other, Michel Foucault (2008) argued convincingly that the concept of human capital accumulation brought economism and the idea of economic modeling into our everyday lives. Human capital, in Foucault's analysis, represented two processes: first, "the extension of economic analysis into a previously unexplored domain, and second, on the basis of this the possibility of giving a strictly economic interpretation of a whole domain previously thought to be non-economic" (2008, 219). Then, as a result of applying these cost-benefit analyses to decisions about education, people learn to think of their skills and abilities as something they own and to conceptualize the self and the future as sites of investment. This, too, seems natural in capitalist societies.

Time, Investment, and Human Capital Accumulation

China embraced the ideology of human capital accumulation wholeheartedly as part of the reform-era ethos of economism, scientific rationalism, and economic development. As a result, the language and concepts of economic modeling have slid from the financial world into the daily world of families, as children are increasingly understood as an essential site of investment for the future.

The temporalities associated with human capital accumulation—planning for an unknown future by investing in education today—have transformed the normative life course for youth, as well as the prescribed pace of human development. As China's economic development has proceeded at an unprecedented rate, the race to the future has left little time for loitering, and the metonymic discourse of human development pressures young people to achieve academic and economic accomplishments as quickly as possible (Zhang Z. 2000). Just as national development is predicated on rational management, capital investment (particularly in high technology) and producing high-quality commodities for export, human development models increasingly call for parents to raise their children using methods proven by scientific experts, invest in capital equipment such as computers, and orient their children's developmental goals to the foreign market. Students today are expected to experience much of childhood and youth as a massive project of delayed gratification, where they are promised that all work and no play in the present will eventually pay off in higher dividends (i.e., salary earned from a good job gained as an eventual result of high test scores) in an unspecified distant future. Parents experience the present as an increasingly anxiety-ridden gamble, where they are exhorted to invest a huge amount of their time, energy, and money into their child's education, with only a vague sense of what kinds of opportunities the future may hold (Katz 2008, 2011). Like other investments in the futures market, families must nervously wait to see if their investment will pay off.[12]

These pressures on young people to spend their time studying and to accumulate human capital are thus not simply a reflex of traditional Chinese culture. Instead, they mirror China's current savings economy, which is a legacy of both the recent socialist redistributive economy and of the Fordist logic of productive work as a form of investment for the future. The human capital model links the subjectivation of the nation's youth with the macroeconomic condition of China as the world's saver and producer (R. Martin 2002). The regime of value where children are a form of accumulation strategy cannot be divorced from China's current multiple modes of production. At the same time, it is important to note that human capital accumulation—as both an ideology and set of policies based in Fordist labor models—is by no means confined to China. Many of the pressures on Chinese children to use every minute of their time productively and continually accumulate education are similar to those faced by youth in other advanced industrial societies. For example, geographer Cindi Katz (2008, 2011) has written extensively about how conceptualizing children and youth as accumulation strategies among families in the affluent West has led to "hothouse" and "helicopter" parenting and how this has produced hypervigilance around middle- and upper-class children.

Numeric Capital and Commodity Fetishism

In China, test scores play an essential role in the model of human capital accumulation. Because of the tremendous pressures on families and children to accumulate ever-higher amounts of human capital, test scores have become more than just a quantitative expression of educational achievement; they condense and represent social value. In another kind of metonymy, young people increasingly *are* their test scores.

In the Chinese popular imaginary, the primary activity of young people today—their only approved activity, really—is studying. Normative behavior for urban Chinese adolescents today is exceptionally narrow: they labor at their school work (Qvortrup 1995). The product of this labor is exam scores, which represent both children's academic labor and congealed family investment. In the future, this activity (studying) and parental investments that support their child's studying will ideally be repaid in the form of dividends generated in a new (moral) economy, where value accrues to high grades and good test scores, which then purportedly generate high-paying jobs, prestige, face, and connections (*guanxi*) for the ongoing reproduction of the family as the means of producing the future. It is therefore possible to conceptualize China's youth both as laborers, who toil long and arduously to produce test scores, and in some ways as commodities, whose value is objectified and condensed in a test score that is eventually converted to income in the job market. Numbers—test scores—are where value is expressed and represented.[13]

While young people in China are not literally bought and sold as commodities, the human capital model as it has been implemented in daily life economizes human beings, reducing them to numbers that are then assumed to have a particular kind of value that is realized in the job market. More saliently, it erases the person, who is replaced with a number. Increasingly, social value adheres to the numbers themselves. I call this "numeric capital," the regime of value that measures the accumulation of young people's exam scores that embody and represent social value, an economism that is sedimented within the bodies of the nation's youth.

In China today, this focus on *numbers*, value congealed in youth as exam scores, is a form of fetish, in Marx's sense, whereby a number comes to stand in for a person, for what the person is worth as a human being, including his or her moral value. This refers to Marx's famous discussion of the commodity fetish, where he introduces the commodity as "a very queer thing, abounding in metaphysical subtleties and theological niceties" (Marx [1867] 1978, 294). Marx explains that the commodity as a fetishized object hides the conditions of its own production; value accrues to products not at the moment of production but only when they are exchanged. At that time, value *seems* to be a quality of objects themselves, when in fact it is a congealed form of the labor required to produce the objects. In other words, commodities are fetishized as containing value in themselves rather than as physical objects that incorporate "material relations between persons and social relations between things" (ibid). According to anthropologist Michael Taussig, commodification "requires an abstraction: the essential qualities of human beings and their products are converted into commodities, into things for buying and selling on the market" (1980, 4). Commodity fetishism is thus a kind of conjuring, whereby the human labor and social relations required to produce commodities are erased, and value is magically assumed to adhere to products themselves.

The fetish of the number in China produces value in the dual sense of the word. First, it represents value in the mathematical sense: how many points are required to enter this school, or that course, or to get this job, this income, this ranking. And it produces value in the sense of what is meaningful, worthy, and socially deserving. The fetish of the number generates a regime of value whereby human beings (individual young people) are reduced to the value of their test scores. The fetishized value of these numbers conceals both the labor of the child (and his or her family) that was required to produce them and the entire social structure of the testing regimes.

Although the human capital model is derived from capitalist and Fordist modes of accumulation, in China this model is applied in conditions that are much more complex. Today, numeric capital as value and as fetish mediates between several modes of objectifying the human condition: late socialist, capitalist, industrial, and postindustrial. Although today's reform era is understood in China as a rupture with the past, it is actually in many ways a mirror of the socialist period. Like socialism, the reform era is a utopian project, positing a teleology into a better future. The future is no longer defined by socialism or communism, as the Chinese Communist Party (CCP) imagined until the late 1970s, but today it is instead a future of national development marked by wealth and power. Young people embody this future and must prepare for it by ever-increasing investment, for what makes this future better is not the radical egalitarianism of communism but consumption, wealth, and money.

The future thus progresses today through the logic of the commodity: the more a person has, the better off he or she is. The progressiveness of consumption and the commodity make this imagination of the future concrete: people's lives get progressively better as they consume more commodities. The moral value of this form of progress is unquestioned, for it is demonstrated mathematically, by numbers that prove progress, including increased living standards, profits, and annual growth. Youth and their families are again metonymic of the nation: as national wealth and living standards are measured and counted, so, too, do individual youth progress by accruing measurable numeric capital. And just as the utopian project of communism was never achieved, the promise of development may be speculative for some; investment may not pay off until an unknown future date, when value that is imagined now is made real.

In the following study, vocational education serves as my "case study" to illuminate some of the regimes of value underlying the new forms of capitalism and late socialism that are coexisting, intersecting, and competing in China today (Hubbert 2006). The old logics of industrial socialism and the new logics of late-industrial capitalism are both at work as the values of numeric capital emerge in different ways around the figure of the vocational student, their schools, their teachers, and the job market. My goal is to try to understand the students' experience of life in their schools within these changing and overlapping modes of production by exploring what life is like for those who have low numeric capital, who have invested poorly, and who are moving out into the new job market with little or nothing to offer in the way of skills or value. I seek to understand how schools structure these students' lives and what they are able to make of their schooling and limited opportunities after they have been forced onto a particular life path at about age sixteen.

Human Capital, Human Quality

The term "numeric capital" is not intended to expand on Bourdieu's taxonomy of various forms of capital (social, cultural, etc.; Bourdieu and Passeron 1977). Not that this is not useful. These categories are common sense in China; in fact, because of the ways economism has pervaded everyday life, people I knew frequently used the language of finance to talk about their children's lives and education in terms of capital and investment. Connections (*guanxi*) as a kind of social capital are an essential part of life in China, and students and teachers were forthright in discussing how "connections" could be exchanged for economic capital in the form of jobs. My concern, however, is not to use commonsense categories as analytic ones or simply to document how various forms of capital circulate and are exchanged for one another. Instead, I seek to understand what constitutes social value, and what are its sources.

I approach this question by studying a group who are considered to be failures: students who did not invest the appropriate time, energy, and diligence into their studies and, as a result, have not accrued the numeric capital necessary to advance in the educational system, market themselves for well-paid jobs, or garner social esteem.

These students are, of course, by no means the only (or the most) marginalized group in China, nor are they only ones blamed for their own predicament. By 2007, when I arrived in China to study vocational schools, there was a growing sense that it was their own fault that many people or places had been left out of the country's huge growth in wealth over the previous decade (Anagnost 1997; L. Jeffery 2000; Shao 2006). In the past two decades there have been many studies of rural migrants, the urban unemployed, the rural poor, and China's ethnic minorities (e.g., Jacka and Sargeson 2011; Solinger 2012; Zhang L. 2001). These groups have been left out of China's race to development; they are the backward (*luohou*) populations against whom the progressive, developed urban middle classes are defining themselves. They take on the blame and become the other against which the developed of China are defined (Anagnost 1997).

Many of these studies have focused on a recent social category developed by the Chinese state called "population quality" (*renkou suzhi*). The term *suzhi* or "quality" was popularized in the late 1980s, concurrent with the economic reforms and spread of the theory of human capital accumulation (Anagnost 2004; Greenhalgh and Winckler 2005; Hoffman 2010; Hsu 2007). Although the term "quality" has been notoriously difficult to define, over the past twenty years it has been fundamental to creating new forms of social hierarchy in China, as the state used the discourse of *suzhi* to divide the Chinese population into differing strata of high- and low-quality people. A decade ago I called *suzhi* a "keyword" to indicate the many ways the term was widely used in the late 1990s to distinguish between the right—and wrong—kinds of people for the new Chinese economy (Woronov 2003; see also Kipnis 2007). Since then many scholars have looked at how aspects of *suzhi* discourse have been applied to differentiate between high- and low-quality people, including studies of population policy and the One-Child Only policies (Greenhalgh and Winckler 2005), disability (Kohrman 2005), laid-off workers (Hsu 2007), the new middle classes (Tomba 2009), and migrant workers (Sun 2009; Yan Hairong 2008). My own work looked at efforts by the Ministry of Education in 1999 to implement a set of education reforms called "education for quality" that were intended to transform China's children into "higher-quality" youth who would bring China into its long-awaited destiny of wealth and power on the international stage (Woronov 2003, 2004, 2008, 2009).

In fact, I initially selected vocational secondary schools to study in 2007 because I was interested in understanding how the kinds of children who had been identified as "low quality" in my earlier research were faring as they reached high school age. I hypothesized that vocational schools might be a good place to look at "low-*suzhi*" youth. Yet when I arrived at the two schools in Nanjing in 2007, I almost never heard the term *suzhi* used at all. Unlike my previous stay in China in 1999–2001, I never saw the word written on the school bulletin boards or anywhere on the school grounds. Other than one conversation, when one of the senior teachers referred sotto voce to his students as "those low-quality [*suzhi*] kids," I never heard the word spoken in or around the schools.

I suspect the reason was that by 2007–2008, the concept of quality was so thoroughly taken for granted that it no longer needed to be discussed. Why bother referring to the VE students as "low quality" when this was already commonly understood? My overwhelming sense was that by the time I was studying vocational education, *suzhi* discourse was no longer as important in the social field as it had been in 1999–2000 and that it no longer seemed relevant to the questions I found important to ask. State discourse about quality seemed far less important in the lives of voc ed students than the social and political structures that positioned them in vocational education in the first place.

Rather than focus on a state discourse that had little ethnographic purchase in my field sites, I therefore approach vocational education through the lens of numeric capital, a concept I use to encapsulate both the state discourse that demonizes youth who fail to invest appropriately in their future through studying, and the state structures—such as the high-stakes exam system—that stream some students into working-class futures.

Vocational students are positioned where they are in the urban hierarchy not only through state discourse and ideology but also through structures including exams, specific kinds of schools, and the labor market. These structural forces cannot be fully captured through discursive analyses like *suzhi*. Additionally, focusing on the ways the vocational students' marginality is produced through the hierarchical discourse of low *suzhi* confines them in an analytic framework of Chinese exceptionalism. Yet the vocational students have much in common with their age-mates around the world, and these commonalities are significant to understanding who they are.

In 2004, Ann Anagnost suggested that the Chinese state was using *suzhi* as a way to displace talking about social class. I agree. By the time I finished my fieldwork in 2008, I could no longer justify using an analysis of the state's *suzhi* discourse to displace an analysis based on class. Therefore I move away from an approach based on government discourses of quality and instead focus on political economy and the cultural politics of class and class formation.

New Class Formations

Taking on the issue of class formation, especially the formation of a segment of the urban working class through the lens of a subject group like vocational students, means addressing several thorny problems in the existing scholarship on contemporary China. Class is a problematic topic in China today (see, e.g., Anagnost 2008a; Guo 2012). There has been considerable attention to the rise of what has been called the "new rich" or the "new middle classes" (e.g., Goodman 2008; Osburg 2013; Tomba 2004; Zhang L. 2010). Some scholars have also begun to study the new urban poor at the other end of the socioeconomic spectrum (e.g., Solinger 2009; Gold et al. 2009), while Pun Ngai and her colleagues have devoted significant attention to new industrial working class they argue is forming in China's export factories (e.g., Pun and Smith 2007; Pun and Lu 2010). The plight of China's migrant workers, the tens of millions of people who have moved from impoverished rural areas to seek jobs in China's growing cities and peri-urban areas, has also been the subject or tremendous interest by anthropologists (e.g., Jacka 2006; Pun 2005; Yan Hairong 2008; Zhang L. 2001). Relatively little attention, however, has focused so far on the current status of the urban working class.[14] Yet not long ago this group was considered the backbone of the nation: during the Mao era, urban factory workers constituted China's proletariat and were socially and ideologically the nation's privileged class.

Central to my argument is that counterintuitively, in China's major cities the industrial sector is vanishing. In the largest cities, the majority of factories have either closed or relocated to export zones, industrial parks, or to the rapidly growing peri-urban areas on the city's outskirts. As the factories have moved, so, too, have industrial jobs. Unlike their parents' or grandparents' generations, young people leaving vocational school in China's largest cities can no longer find factory work.[15] These youth are therefore entering a new, largely postindustrial economy and find jobs in the service or tertiary sector (*di san chanye*).

This tertiary sector of the economy is growing very rapidly, guided by government policy, and barely existed more than fifteen years ago. In its Twelfth Five-Year Plan (2011–2015), the Chinese government formally announced its focus on the service sector and stated its intention to convert the economy from its reliance on manufacturing-based exports to a service-based economy driven by domestic consumption (State Council 2012). As a result, the state has put tremendous effort into developing the upper echelons of this sector in the past decade, including building the finance, media, IT, and biotech industries. Yet as urban sociologists note (Sassen 2012), the service sector is highly stratified, and highly paid service occupations generate job growth in the form of lower-level service work that supports the higher tiers. Thus, in China, as the entire tertiary sector grows, vocational school graduates in major cities are moving into jobs at the lower ends of this new economy. They are finding jobs working in the retail and hospitality industries, repairing computers and mobile phones, or staffing call centers and doing data entry. This is a broad transformation in the nature of labor from that of their parents' generation.

These transformations are not unique to China, for the service-sector formations underway in Chinese cities are similar in some ways to those occurring in other parts of the industrialized world. Researchers who study the tertiary sector note that increasing numbers of young people are working in lower-end tertiary-sector occupations around the globe, particularly in part-time or short-term work. There has been a notable rise in these kinds of jobs in postindustrial economies across the globe. The Nanjing vocational graduates' futures in uncertain service-sector jobs links the vocational graduates to youth in other parts of the postindustrial world who have sometimes been called the new "precariat" (Allison 2012; Bourdieu 1998; Cross 2010; Mitropoulos 2006; Molé 2010; Muehlebach 2012; Neilson and Rossiter 2008; Southwood 2011; Standing 2011). Today the term is generally used to describe a growing group of mostly young workers, largely in Europe, who work in low-skilled, frequently part-time jobs with few benefits, little security, and no future. This kind of work is spreading globally, among young people with relatively low levels of education who, in a previous generation, would have entered factory work (McDowell 2012). Although China as a whole is still an industrial nation, the urban vocational school graduates in China's largest cities are in many ways joining their global age-mates in Europe and Japan in facing a postindustrial economy where factory jobs are scarce, replaced instead by relatively short-term, low-end, low-paid service-sector work.

This book is a close description of the daily lives of a small group of students enrolled in two vocational schools in Nanjing, China, in 2007–2008. In the larger sense, however, it is in intended as an ethnography of class formation. The story of the vocational schools illustrates how a new segment of the urban working class, a service-sector class, is forming in China's larger cities today. The lives of these students will demonstrate how this class formation is a social and cultural process as well as an economic one.

Research in Nanjing and Chapter Outlines

This research took place in Nanjing, the capital of prosperous Jiangsu Province. A city of around seven million, Nanjing ("southern capital" in Chinese) is considered a "second-tier" city in the Chinese system that ranks municipalities by size and population. Nanjing was a very interesting place to study education in 2007–2008. Located west of Shanghai, it is an important regional hub of the Yangtze delta. Nanjing was the imperial capital several times during China's dynastic history and again most recently during the Nationalist (Republic of China) era (1927–1937).[16] For centuries Nanjing had a reputation as a cultivated center of learning, literature, and the arts. Once the heart of China's thriving Jiangnan literati culture, today Nanjing has one of the largest concentrations of universities in the country.

Yet the city's glittering imperial past and close geographic proximity to Shanghai are belied by its relative sleepiness today. Life in Nanjing does not have the frantic pace of its neighbors Shanghai, Suzhou, and Hangzhou. It is slower, quieter, and far less Westernized or developed than these nearby cities. Although it is not a backwater, neither is Nanjing at the forefront of the nation's development. It is now renowned as a conservative city that is slow to change. While cities across China were being demolished and remade at break-neck speed in the 1990s and 2000s, when I arrived in Nanjing for this project in 2007, I was stunned to see how little seemed to have changed since I had last lived in the city almost a decade earlier (1998–1999). This made Nanjing a particularly interesting place from which to observe the transformations taking place across China in 2007–2008, right before the global financial crisis. At the time, China was investing in massive urban development projects in preparation for the 2008 Olympics, although this frenetic development seemed largely to elude Nanjing. The pre-Olympic patriotic frenzy reported on daily TV felt more like a local Beijing spectacle than daily reality for us in Nanjing; the vocational students I knew followed the unavoidable news stories about the Olympics, but without much ardor.

During my research I was affiliated with the Sociology Department at Hohai University. Although Hohai is a second-tier (*erben*) university that specializes in engineering, my friend Chen Ajiang, the chair of the Sociology Department, had gathered a group of extremely bright, ambitious, and unorthodox thinkers to his department, who used their position slightly outside the spotlight of the top-ranked universities to do innovative social research.[17] They were quickly building an international reputation for their qualitative research, particularly on social issues related to migration and the environment. I could not have had a better group of interlocutors and partners for my research. Professor Chen assigned one of the department's lecturers, Emma Wang Xubo, as my research partner. A native of China's far northeast, Emma was unusually tall, thin, and elegant among her southern Chinese colleagues. Her soft voice and cultivated Mandarin accent hid a lightning-fast wit and wickedly playful sense of humor. With her characteristic insightful intellect and willingness to tackle new questions and problems, Emma took on the challenge of locating two schools that would be willing to host a foreign researcher in the politically fraught year leading up to the Olympics. She was unusually open-minded about data gathering and analysis in the methodologically fuzzy world of participant observation. Together we hired four extremely bright, open-minded, and conscientious master's degree students in the Sociology Department as our research assistants: Chen Tao, Liu Guoxing, Wang Wenting, and Yang Juan. Emma and these four graduate students were immediately popular among the VE students and teachers. They visited the schools several times a week, took notes, visited classes, and generally hung out with teachers and students. In the following text I often use "we" rather than "I" to indicate that many of the field notes and observations were recorded collaboratively with Emma and our research assistants.

The following chapters explore changing regimes of value in contemporary China and processes of new class formation through a study of two vocational schools in Nanjing. To protect their anonymity, I refer to these two schools as the Bridge and Canal Schools and use pseudonyms for the teachers, students, and administrators we met there. I am profoundly grateful to these schools for so generously allowing access to a foreign researcher, particularly at the moment right before the 2008 Olympics, when the Chinese government was extremely sensitive to how it was being portrayed.

Most ethnographies include a page or two at this point describing the book's field sites before getting on to the "real" anthropology later in the text. My argument about numeric capital and class formation, however, is predicated on the structure of the vocational education system. Chapter 1 is therefore devoted to a detailed description of the two field sites in historical context. It begins with a brief introduction of the history of vocational education in China, showing how the current system continues to be influenced by its historical antecedents. I discuss the ways the vocational system was established in Republican-era China both to raise the skill level of China's industrial workers and to limit the aspirations of the urban working class (Schulte 2013). After the founding of the People's Republic of China (PRC) in 1949, ideological battles over the nature of education, known as the "red vs. expert" debates, cemented vocational schools' reputation as places where students learned to "love labor" rather than learning. Yet the historical legacies extended beyond ideology. One type of secondary schooling, originally established as part of urban China's "iron rice bowl" labor allocation system, continues to operate today.

I describe how the Bridge School was positioned within the socialist labor system, rather than the educational bureaucracy, and the implications this had for students, teachers, and the students' eventual job postings. In contrast, the Canal School operated on an entirely capitalist logic. Managed by a large, provincial-level university, the Canal School was founded to meet increasing student demand for more secondary vocational options and provided a new educational "product" (a "3+2" secondary degree) that was supposed to make the school more marketable to students, and the students more marketable to employers. Yet these same profit-seeking motives had led the school's owners to wind down the school's operations after the campus was sold to developers. I argue that the ways the structures of the two schools were predicated on socialist and capitalist models had far-reaching implications for the education they provided.

Chapter 2 introduces the students at the two schools, highlighting the so-cial diversity represented in the vocational school classrooms. Although the students were all from the working classes, they came from a very wide range of backgrounds, including rural, urban working-class, and second-generation migrant families. Within their classrooms, the students' social relations chal-lenged some common assumptions about social categories in China today, for their friendship groups crossed social and legal boundaries, including *hukou* (residence permit), and the urban-rural divide. And just as they confounded normative social categories, the students also belied the popular stereotypes about them. Rather than the immorality that is commonly ascribed to vo-cational students, many of the students were filial youth who had entered vocational school out of obedience or consideration to parents who were liv-ing in poverty or constant migration. The students' family backgrounds are described to show how their decisions to enter voc ed were often linked to family hardship.

I also argue that the HSEE, the high-stakes exam that placed the students in vocational schools in the first place, serves as a form of class sorting in China today (Slater 2010), which occurs in two ways. First, although there are no statistical data on the class constitution of students in VE, vocational schools seem to educate working-class students. Evidence suggests that wealthy urban students who fail the HSEE enter private academic secondary schools instead. Vocational education is thus an option for the working classes, not necessar-ily because they are they only students who test into this stream, but rather because they do not have the means to buy their way out of it. Second, after graduation, young people who hold vocational credentials are significantly limited in their career prospects. A vocational degree locks these graduates out of future white-collar jobs, which therefore destines them for a future in the urban working classes.

The two schools were not merely places of learning, however, for like all schools they were also places of employment. Although teaching in China is always described as a moral activity, Chapter 3 discusses teachers and teaching in terms of the teachers' contractual obligations. The two vocational schools managed two different categories of employees. One group of teachers held "iron rice bowl" jobs in the socialist state sector and, because their jobs were permanent, were supervised through moral authority. The others were tempo-rary, "flexible" employees, who worked according to a capitalist logic. Rather than the moral "love" teachers are expected to have for their students, these teachers modeled short-term, commodified labor relations for their students.

Chapter 3 also looks closely at curriculum and assessment at the two schools and returns to the question that opened the book: Why do the students sleep all day in class? I argue that both schools "devocationalized" their curricula or retreated from teaching specific job-related skills. The Bridge School classes moved away from vocational skills by teaching high theory rather than vocational skills, little of which was comprehensible or applicable to the students. The Canal School moved in the opposite direction, where teaching focused on embodied disciplines rather than job skills. While neither approach prepared students for future skilled labor, these pedagogies and curricula did help explain the students' behavior in class, for, in Slater's (2010) term, the schools lack a "coherent center" that gives the students a reason to stay awake. Extending the discussion about class sorting and class formation, I examine how the two schools were (and were not) preparing the students specifically for future service-sector jobs. By focusing on language standardization, I look at how both schools sought to create better employees for the service economy by teaching classes in standard Mandarin, to little effect.

Chapters 1–3 describe the structure of the schools and the education system, showing the ways that both the Canal and Bridge Schools were linked in complex ways to the socialist and capitalist systems in China today. Chapter 4 changes focus to look at some of the ways the students think about themselves. This opens the challenging question of the students' identities. I argue that rather than assume that the students all "had" an identity and that I simply had to "give them a voice," the students' subjectivities had to be actively produced in the two schools. I look at teachers' efforts to require the students to express their dreams and desires, in order to incite them to become "choosing" and "desiring" subjects (Farquhar 2002; Hoffman 2010; Rofel 2007) who propel themselves into the future through accumulation. The students, however, resisted these efforts and instead expressed future desires simply for happiness. This created significant tension in the schools. I argue that the construction of the vocational students' identities was rife with paradoxes, including contradictory pressures on them to both express themselves and restrain their self-expression. Although they did not state their identities outright, they did construct themselves as moral and filial youth, partly through the ways they confounded their teachers' expectations and desires. There were several domains around which "identity" was neither a smooth nor seamless process for the students, including their use of spoken dialect, their patriotic sentiments in the months leading up to the Beijing Olympics, and their tentative allegiances to localities. I explore these domains and how these contradictions were linked to the students' working-class status.

Chapter 5 looks at the school-to-work transition and describes some of the vocational students' experiences in the job market. I follow the students as they attended internships, training classes to prepare for job interviews, job fairs, and as they began their first jobs. The discussion begins at a private weekend training course, where a growing new industry uses American self-help materials to teach confidence and self-promotion to China's insecure youth. From there, I discuss the mandatory internships all the students were expected to complete during their final year of school. I follow some of the graduating students to internships on a construction site in Nanjing, where they discovered firsthand two discouraging facts about the changing urban job market: their vocational secondary degrees may not be enough to distinguish these students from rural migrant workers in the future, and family connections are more useful for employment than anything they may learn at school.

Chapter 5 continues with a description of the job fairs several of the graduating Canal School students attended and how the students had to learn to market themselves to employers. Initially breaking into the job market was difficult, for it required learning how to narrate a story of themselves as marketable for employers, but by the time they graduated from the Canal School in the spring, they had mastered the intricacies of the job search and had "jumped" to multiple jobs. Yet while they had seemingly limitless opportunities to change jobs, they had very limited vertical mobility and constrained their choices to continuous entry-level work.

The Conclusion picks up several years later to see how some of the vocational students were faring in their work and personal lives. I summarize their experiences as new members of the urban working class and compare the vocational school graduates with some of their age-mates around the world. Arguing that they are forming a new Chinese "precariat," I position the students and their lives as young adults within a global framework of service workers in short-term, low-paid, tenuous work. I also explore the thorny question of class consciousness among this new segment of the working class. Although several factors seem to constrain the emergence of working-class consciousness among this group of new service-sector workers, their history of passive resistance in school and their creative approaches to the challenges of adult life may open the possibility of new identities and new forms of collective consciousness in the future. Their lives have just begun.

1 Vocational Schools

The taxi ground to a halt in the pouring rain. The bus behind us honked frantically. "Out! Get out now!" the taxi driver shouted. Emma Wang and I piled out of the aging taxi and landed in ankle-deep mud. Although this was the main street in this part of Nanjing, parts of the road were unpaved and not much wider than a single lane; buses, taxis, pedestrians, and carts selling fruit, snacks, and household items jostled for space on the narrow road. It was only a twenty-minute taxi ride from the genteel part of the city where our university was located, but we had arrived in the middle of an impoverished, working-class neighborhood, essentially a Nanjing slum. On one side of the street, narrow alleyways were lined with crumbling, six-story concrete housing blocks, typical of shoddy, 1970s socialist-era urban work-unit (*danwei*) architecture. Towering above everything on the opposite side of the street loomed one of China's engineering marvels: the massive bridge across the Changjiang (Yangtze) River. Our first research site was a school located almost directly beneath the pylons of this bridge, which marks one of the symbolic passages between north and south China. Acknowledging its location, we called this the Bridge School.

I HAVE OUTLINED THE IDEOLOGIES of numeric capital, economism, and human capital accumulation that constitute elements of education during China's current reform era. These ideologies about youth and education are inextricably linked to China's efforts to modernize its economy and society and connect China to the rest of the world. I now focus on how the two schools where we conducted research articulate with and explicate different aspects of contemporary Chinese life: educational and industrial, socialist and capitalist. A description of these schools highlights the ways multiple systems continue to coexist and intersect in China today.

A brief discussion of the history of vocational education in China highlights the ways that VE has long been a site of negotiation of some of the paradoxes and tensions of China's transitions to different kinds of modernities—industrial, socialist, and capitalist-style reform era. For over a century, vocational schools in China have been debated, promoted, and resisted as vocational education has been variously deployed as the skills-training sector of the educational system and a means to potentially solve myriad national problems. At different times, VE has been called upon to build the nation's industrial capacity, raise the skill level of the nation's labor force, and meet increasing demands by families for additional educational opportunities for their children. Vocational education was first introduced almost a century ago as a way to "save China" (Schulte 2013; Schwintzer 1992); it began as a means to mold generations of youth into the right kinds of (moral) subjects for the nation's (industrial) labor needs. Some of the issues first raised in the early twentieth century, when VE was introduced to China, continue to be relevant today. Many of the structural systems put in place to implement vocational training during the Republican and revolutionary eras are also still in place and continue to influence the ways that voc ed is carried out on a daily basis.

Because of these continuities with the past, vocational education highlights the regimes of value, within competing logics of production, that operate in China today. VE is a particularly interesting place to see how the fetish of the number mediates between (late) socialist and capitalist logics. One reason is that students are placed in voc ed, like in all schools in China, through the high-stakes testing regimes of hierarchical ranking systems established and managed by the state. But unlike the academic educational sector, some parts of the vocational system still feed directly into the former *danwei* system and the new urban service sector. The VE school-to-work transition thus illuminates the transition and overlaps from the (socialist) form of production to a newly precarious labor market, based in the growing urban service sector.

A Brief History of Vocational Education: Foundations in the Early Twentieth Century

China was rapidly industrializing in the early twentieth century at the start of the Republican era (1911–1949). China's leaders at the time struggled with the dual problem of how to raise the quantity and quality of China's industrial products in order to compete in the global marketplace and how to educate a new generation of modern subjects who would increase the nation's wealth and power through industrial production (Bailey 1990; Schwintzer 1992). As historians have noted, intertwined questions of citizenship, morality, class formation, and the nature of labor were at the center of multiple political debates at the time (Culp 2007).

Educational policy and industrial development were both further complicated during the Republican era because of large-scale movements of people from rural to urban areas to work in China's newly industrializing cities. After migrant laborers arrived in the cities, social relations were quite different from traditional rural social formations, and factory-based workers' groups began to form a nascent urban proletariat (Yeh 2008). An ongoing problem for the state was how to manage this new, potentially revolutionary group of workers. One possibility promoted by the more conservative national leaders in the ruling Guomindang (Nationalist Party) government was vocational education, which was seen as a way to raise both individuals' industrial skills and their moral probity. Vocational trainees could thus simultaneously be educated to increase national productivity and to understand their essential role in building the nation. For this reason, as historian Barbara Schulte notes, two popular slogans in the early twentieth century, "education for saving the country" (*jiaoyu jiuguo*) and "industry for saving the country" (*shiye jiuguo*), were successfully combined into "vocational education for saving the country" (*zhijiao jiuguo*) (2013, 227; see also Schwintzer 1992).

One prominent Republican-era educational reformer, Huang Yanpei, founded the Chinese Society for Vocational Education (Zhonghua zhiye jiaoyu she) in 1917 to promote training in industrial skills. Influenced by John Dewey's concept of "pragmatic education" and vocational education programs he had observed during visits to the United States and Germany, Huang stated that the original motto of the voc ed movement was "to give work to the unemployed and to give joy to those working" (Huang Yanpei, 1931, cited in Schulte 2013, 143). However, as Schulte notes, this joy was:

> less about individual fulfilment than about the joy to serve society. Vocational education was to provide a solution to the "social question"—to provide for the massive numbers of those who could not continue their education after primary school (or who should not continue lest they become graduates with useless degrees) and who were then graduated into unemployment. (2013, 230)

In addition, Historian Yeh Wen-hsin (2008) points out that China's elites identified several "problems" among the working classes around this time, including such traits as a general unwillingness to take on manual labor, too much interest in accruing educational credentials (rather than in gaining skills training that would improve China's industrial production), and an inability to tolerate the hardships associated with manual and industrial labor. VE was supposed to help overcome all these problems (Yeh 2008, 43). Vocational education in the Republican era was thus designed specifically as a way to tackle the social problem of the working classes by managing their aspirations for additional education and upward mobility (Schulte 2013; Yeh 2008). The "joy" that Huang Yanpei sought to create among the working classes increasingly became a goal of producing "happy" workers, content with their station in life. According to Schulte, voc ed was formed to "safely and productively store away the masses who aspired to climb up the social ladder through education in an increasingly non-agrarian economy" (2013, 230). The early days of vocational education were thus explicitly decoupled from revolutionary change and designed to train a quiescent industrial labor force.[1]

Several aspects of vocational education dating from the system's foundations in Republican-era China are still relevant today. VE was established not only as a place to train skilled workers for the industrial economy but as a sector where national development goals were formulated and met and where individuals were supposed to learn how to slot into a national plan. Second, although there were moves at the time to develop rural vocational training, the origins of the voc ed system were clearly urban and industrial; it was a system modeled on and designed for industrial production. Third, vocational schools were developed in response to and in order to manage large-scale social transformations and dislocations, specifically rural migration to the cities. Finally, and most important, vocational schools were designed as places to manage working-class aspirations. Specifically, VE acted to dampen the aspirations of the working classes for more education and to manage their desires for upward mobility out of the industrial sector.

Revolutionary Era

China had no unified, national system of vocational education during the Maoist era (ca. 1949–1976), and, like all aspects of Chinese education, voc ed underwent many changes during this period. Rather than outline the many twists and turns the educational system took during these years,[2] I focus instead on two interrelated aspects of vocational education established between the 1950s and 1970s that continue to have important repercussions today. One was the question of the vocational curriculum, which was part of the larger ideological struggle known to historians as the "red vs. expert" debates. The second was the question of the school-to-work transition, or how urban students moved into jobs after graduation, which was a function of the urban *danwei* system.

Structurally, by the early 1950s several different kinds of technical and vocational middle and secondary schools existed in China, as part of an enormous expansion of secondary education in the years following the founding of the PRC in 1949 (Pepper 1996; Thøgersen 1990). From the 1950s through the start of the Cultural Revolution in the mid-1960s, secondary education was divided into two tracks. On one track, academically talented students were funneled through an extremely competitive secondary system, then into limited university places, and from there into technical and professional jobs (Thøgersen 1990). On the other, the vocational system produced midlevel technical experts for the growing industrial and government sectors (Luo 2013).

The vocational schools affiliated with the Ministry of Education remained virtually intact from the prerevolutionary Republican era. Starting in the mid-1950s, however, new "workers' training schools" became popular in urban areas. Designed on a Soviet model, these schools were administered by local governments and trained workers for specific industries. Many factories, hospitals, government bureaus, and other large work units opened their own worker training schools to train skilled workers, midlevel managers, and midlevel party cadres (Luo 2013; Thøgersen 1990; Unger 1982).

These schools were embedded in the *danwei* system, which was the primary form of social organization in urban China. A work unit was simultaneously an employer and the delivery system for a range of socialist welfare benefits. Urban Chinese were employed by and received a packet of social benefits from their *danwei*, which might include housing, food subsidies, children's day care, retirement pensions, and potentially others, depending on the size and relative wealth of the *danwei* (Bray 2005). A *danwei* could be a very large institution employing thousands of people, such as a factory, government agency, hospital, or university. They were often self-contained small societies within walled compounds. By the late 1970s, virtually all urban Chinese were affiliated with a work unit, which provided them with lifelong employment security. This was known as the "iron rice bowl" employment system, since the workers' livelihood, or "rice bowl," could not be broken over the course of their lifetime.

Throughout this era, graduates of *danwei*-affiliated vocational worker training schools were automatically assigned to lifelong jobs in their schools' work units. Graduates had no choice of work assignment; jobs were allocated by the work unit, and workers generally stayed at their units through retirement. Because virtually all urban residents were affiliated with work units and urban employment was managed by the danwei system, until the 1980s there was no private labor market where school graduates could sell their services. Because each of these workers' training schools was operated by the individual *danwei* and trained workers for the specific unit, the schools were operated and managed locally. National oversight was managed by the central Ministry of Labor rather than the Ministry of Education, which managed the regular, academic secondary schools. Some of these schools still exist today in an updated form.

Although school leavers were assigned jobs upon graduation, the question of the curriculum in vocational education—and indeed in all schools—loomed large in educational policy throughout the Mao era. The issue of the relation between labor and learning was central to Mao-era educational policy and ideology. The primary question was whether the role of education was to further the cause of class struggle or to develop and strengthen the nation (primarily by building China's industrial capacity). This question, debated at the highest levels of the Communist Party leadership, was part of what has become known as the "red vs. expert" debates, a set of ideological battles and power struggles that were partly fought over educational ideology and policy (Andreas 2009; Hoffman 2010).

The "expert" faction among the government leadership advocated for an educational system that could support and develop China's industrial infrastructure. The "red" faction argued that active, hands-on participation in production was an essential aspect of the learning process. The latter position was based on a statement by Mao Zedong: "Knowledge depends on activity in material production" (cited in Thøgersen 1990, 95; see also Hoffman 2010). Under red faction ascendency, students were sent to factories and farms to engage in productive labor to learn to love the party and not feel superior to workers and peasants. This, in turn, was supposed to eliminate the "three great differences" that still caused social fissures in China after liberation: between industry and agriculture, city and country, and mental and manual labor (Thøgersen 1990, 96).

Unger (1982), a noted scholar of education during the Cultural Revolution (1966–1976), argues that the Cultural Revolution was partly fought so that schools could actively transform, rather than merely reproduce, the nation's class structure. To do so, knowledge was geared toward the tangible and practical and directly linked to labor. This, he points out, was done both by vocationalizing the entirety of the education system and "moralizing education so that it was less technical, more practical, and more focused on character development through studying Mao Zedong Thought" (1982, 141).

In a move eerily reminiscent of the Republican era, by performing labor as part of their schooling, students not only prepared for the work they would do for the rest of their lives but were also supposed to be learning to accept their roles as part of the proletariat. The leftist leaders at the time felt this was essential to transform the political consciousness of the nation's (urban) youth and level their aspirations to upward mobility. Skills training was bourgeois and led to class divisions; those who performed "mental" work were positioned above the laboring masses of the workers and peasants. By removing education as a pathway to upward mobility, "they would be better positioned to reorient achievement-minded youth away from the 'corrupting' personal ambition they had absorbed from their parents" (Unger 1982, 142). "The radicals felt that by removing the educational ladder's reinforcement of the concept that there were 'higher' and 'lower' vocations, the virtues of working-class occupations could be better appreciated by students" (143). Schools were thus reoriented to remove academic competition among students and to focus instead on gaining practical skills linked to proletarian consciousness.[3]

This was short-lived. After a decade of leftist ascendancy, at the end of the 1970s the red faction was overturned and the expert faction, led by Deng Xiaoping, took over China's leadership. One of the first ways they repudiated the Cultural Revolution was to overturn the leftists' educational policies. An essential first step was the 1977 reinstatement of the high-stakes UEE, which symbolized the state's revalorization of "expertise." The UEE brought academic competition back into education as well as the association of numbers (marks) with science and rationality. But, like those of the earlier Republican era, several legacies of the Cultural Revolution era continue to resonate in vocational education today. One of the holdovers from both these eras is the current association of vocational education with limited job aspirations, working-class futures, and poor pathways to upward mobility.

Early Reform Era (1980s–1990s)

One of the first moves the Chinese leadership made after the Cultural Revolution was to reform education and reward technical knowledge. Students were no longer urged to "love labor" but instead to gain specific technical skills to build industry that would, in turn, develop the nation. In March 1978, Deng Xiaoping delivered the opening address at a National Symposium on Science and Technology in Beijing. He reiterated that the role of education was no longer to level class differences, and focused on the importance of science and technology for economic modernization, stating: "The basis for training science and technology talent rests in education" (Hannum 2005,11).

As historian of education Mun Tsang notes, after the start of the reform era China's educational leaders were once again concerned with managing students' expectations about social mobility, but their goals were different than during the Cultural Revolution. After 1978, the party leadership saw education's purpose as contributing to economic development through training skilled personnel (Tsang 2000). The leadership believed that education should be stratified rather than egalitarian, training different people at different skill levels, and then allocating them to different roles in an increasingly stratified labor market. Education reforms were implemented to resegregate students into vocational and academic streams at the secondary level, with the explicit goal of sorting those who would become experts in the new economy from those who would remain as workers. Starting in the late 1970s China's leadership greatly expanded the vocational sector, and, in an important move, the VE system was one of the first educational sectors to experiment with decoupling graduates from the iron rice bowl job allocation system (Tsang 2000).[4]

In 1986, a wide-scale Education Reform Law expanded universal education through grade 9 across China and called for further expansion of the secondary vocational sector. This law also codified the leadership's goal that vocational students should rely on "market mechanisms" for job allocations after graduation. In theory, this marked the beginning of the end of the state's job allocation program, removing vocational graduates from the *danwei* system and forcing them into the newly created open labor market to seek jobs (Lewin and Xu 1989).

In practice, however, it is very hard to categorize vocational training nationally throughout the 1980s and 1990s, as policies changed rapidly and were carried out unevenly across the country. Lewin and Xu (1989) note, for example, that some regular high schools were rapidly converted to vocational schools to meet the state's demands to increase enrollment in voc ed, then were converted back again when this experiment failed. However, a few key items stand out. One is that from the early 1990s on, most vocational graduates were not allocated jobs in the state sector. They were thus pioneers of the private labor market, for they were among the first school leavers in China to find jobs on their own, a practice known as "entering self employment" (Hoffman 2010).

Second, because of all the various policy prescriptions from the central government, the system became increasingly complex (Biermann 1999; Whiteside and Zhang 1992). For example, along with the new VE schools, former worker training schools still existed:

> Most of the skilled workers' training schools operate under the responsibility
> of the Ministry of Labor, while the typical senior vocational middle schools are
> managed by the local Education Commission. The technical schools include

non-academic professions in the domain of medical training, educational professions, business administration and commerce, and technology. These schools are often under the responsibility of branch ministries or umbrella organizations in sectors such as trade, energy, and transportation. Furthermore, large enterprises run their own schools. (Biermann 1999, 31)

In 1996, a new Vocational Education Law sought further expansion of voc ed. One stated goal of this policy was that half of all secondary students should be enrolled in vocational or technical programs, which was justified as the best way to meet the nation's technical and engineering needs (Shi 2013). Since then in 2005, 2008, and 2010, the State Council has issued Decisions to Vigorously Promote the Development of Vocational Education in China at different levels, including secondary, tertiary, and adult education. These decisions both expanded vocational education and made its various segments even more complex. Today, because so many different kinds of schools are called vocational or technical schools, it is difficult to conceptualize a vocational education system that holds together with any overall coherency. We saw firsthand how this complexity worked out on the ground at our field sites in Nanjing.

The Bridge School

The Bridge School was harder to locate than most secondary schools in China, which usually are easily marked off spatially and architecturally from their surrounding neighborhoods by walls, signs, and a distinctive building style. The first day we visited, Emma Wang and I walked up and down the narrow main road of the neighborhood in the pouring rain several times before we found a small sign with the school's name on it at the entrance of a long, winding alleyway. We followed the alley for two blocks until we reached a very large, four-story, industrial-looking building at the edge of the enormous, muddy Chiangjiang River. We later learned that the size of the building was misleading, for the school occupied only one small wing of the structure; the rest of the building was taken up by a wastewater treatment facility and the city's municipal wastewater management offices.

The Bridge School's physical plant was thus highly unusual by the architectural standards of Chinese secondary schools. Its location at the river's edge meant the classrooms were chilly and damp, except on Nanjing's hottest days. Many of the classrooms were cavernous spaces with soaring ceilings, beneath which hung pipes and electrical wires. As described previously, the school resembled a hastily converted industrial space, and the students' efforts to make the classrooms appear more cheerful and youthful, such as draping the pipes in Christmas tinsel or hanging colorful origami cranes from the light fixtures, only seemed to highlight the factory-like feeling of the buildings. The profound irony of the school's location was not lost on us as we got to know the teachers and students better over the course of the school year. The ways that the vocational students were a form of social waste matter that the school processed for three academic years could not have been better illustrated than by the school's out-of-the-way location in this converted industrial facility.

Although the school was attached to an industrial plant and municipal office, there was minimal traffic between the different wings of the building. Monday-morning school assemblies and flag-raising ceremonies, which are held in schools across China, were conducted on the windswept grounds outside the management offices, facing the river. Occasionally, student groups would use one of the large foyers in the adjoining building to hold meetings or rehearse songs for a class performance, but generally the school was kept separate.

The school building was four stories high, facing an open cement area at the entrance that served as a basketball court and space for gym classes. Next to this main building was a small outhouse that supplemented the inadequate bathrooms inside the building; some of the male students hid behind this outhouse for cigarette breaks between classes. The ground floor of the main building consisted of one large room that held several dilapidated Ping-Pong tables for the students, plus a few long tables where the teachers ate lunch. There was also a tiny concession stand (*xiaomaibu*) in one corner of the room that sold small packaged snacks and drinks to the students during class breaks and at lunchtime. The second floor, divided by a long hallway, had several long, narrow rooms used as teacher and administrator offices along the left and classrooms along the right. Windows in the teachers' offices faced across a courtyard into the municipal offices, while the classroom windows looked out onto the traffic on-ramp of the massive Changjiang Bridge. Directly beneath these windows, against the school's exterior wall, was a recycling yard, where a small army of rural migrant workers (*min'gong*) sorted rubbish and recycled material from across the city. Watching the ever-changing mountain of plastic bottles, tires, scrap metal, and old cloth move through the yards below was a popular distraction for bored students during the seemingly endless school day.

The third floor of the building was devoted to classroom space, while student dorms took up the fourth floor. Entrance to this floor was barred by a locked metal gate across the stairwell, which prevented students from reentering the dorms during school hours. Our research team never saw the dorms, since entrance was strictly regulated, but students reported that there were up to eighteen students per room, housed in bunk beds stacked three beds high. Some of the students laughed when I expressed shock at living in such crowded conditions; they assured me that cramming so many students in each room kept the high-ceilinged rooms warmer in winter.

In spite of these large classrooms and the four stories of space, the school wing seemed too small to accommodate the six hundred enrolled students. We later learned that only students in the first two years of their three-year programs were actually on campus; third-year (graduating twelfth-grade; *biyeban*) students did not take classes but were instead supposed to spend the entire school year completing course-related internships and were therefore not on campus.

Bridge School Structure

The Bridge School was founded by the Nanjing Municipal Engineering Office in the early 1970s and was originally set up to train midlevel technicians for the city's infrastructure projects under the socialist *danwei* system. The Bridge School has long offered a three-year secondary vocational certificate, called a *zhongzhuan* degree. Over the years, the school has trained technicians, supervisors, and staff for road and highway projects, sewers and wastewater treatment plants, bridge construction, and land reclamation. The school has moved to different locations around the city over the decades; its current location is only the most recent campus. The school also maintained a second, smaller satellite campus across town, which we did not visit.

As the training branch of one part of the municipal government, the Bridge School was not under the auspices of the local, provincial, or national educational authorities (cf. Biermann 1999). When the school was founded during the Mao era, it was relatively common for large work units (including municipal governments) to set up their own worker training schools (Biermann 1999; Luo 2013; Thøgersen 1990). The Bridge School was one of these specialized schools:

> [Specialized secondary schools] can be divided into those providing education and training for positions such as technicians and primary school teachers, and those providing training for skilled workers, nurses and public health workers. They are controlled and administered by *different government departments* and obtain their finance from these departments rather than from local education authorities. The technical and skill courses provided are closely related to the needs of the various departments and reflect developments in the local economy. (Whiteside and Zhang 1992, 288, emphasis added)

Because it was administered by the Municipal Engineering Office, the Bridge School was entirely autonomous from the local Nanjing Education Commission (*Jiaowei*) and its higher administrative authority, the provincial and national Ministries of Education. This had several repercussions. One is that administratively, students enrolled at the Bridge School and other schools like it are not captured in either local or national statistics for vocational education; they are, in effect, invisible to the larger educational system. Students who enter vocational schools located within different bureaucratic and administrative systems simply fall off the larger educational radar. We discussed the question of the Bridge School's administrative status with a senior official at the Jiangsu Provincial Department of Education. When we asked about the oversight of schools that are outside the Department of Education's mandate, he confirmed: "Oh yes, we're aware that there are some schools that still exist in this category, but we don't pay any attention to them. They're irrelevant to us."[5] For the same reason, because they are under the auspices of a different bureaucratic system, these students do not appear in Ministry of Education statistics that measure postsecondary-school employment rates; there is no way to know how they fare in the aggregate as they seek jobs after they finish school. Thus, the national Ministry of Education statistics on VE enrollment, HSEE scores, graduation rates, and employment rates do not count the students at the Bridge School or others like it across China.

Second, for the same reasons, none of the school's finances, management, and oversight are directed by the government's educational institutional structure, nor is curriculum, teaching quality, or hiring practice. This can be an advantage, as places like the Bridge School can be quite flexible in how they run their schools, but this results in a wide range in quality of their educational programs.

Finally, the Bridge School provides a particularly good example of how different kinds of systems exist simultaneously in China, working toward similar ends in similar ways but without overlapping. The Bridge School is a holdover from an older *danwei* system, where urban residents were assigned lifelong jobs in state-owned industries, some of which were large and complex enough to train their own technicians and managers. Since it was established originally as a worker training school by a state-owned *danwei*, the Bridge School initially existed as part of the labor allocation system, not the education system. Although it is clearly a school and confers a diploma recognized by the state and employers, even today it is still not part of the educational bureaucracy. It is thus a very good example of how vocational education is linked to multiple complex systems in China today: capitalist and socialist, public and private, old and new, intertwined and overlapping.

Tuition at the Bridge School for the 2007–2008 school year was approximately 3,000 RMB, plus an additional 700 RMB for dormitory space for boarding students.[6] Because it was subsidized by the city government, this was fairly inexpensive by the standards of secondary education in Nanjing at the time and was considered a good deal by the students.[7] Principal Huang, however, thought that the school would not be able to underwrite the same level of tuition in the future; indeed, he did not foresee that the school had much of a future at all. In his estimation, the government will likely increasingly shift its focus and resources into vocational schools administrated by the Ministry of Education, not those organized by other ministries. He shook his head sadly, predicting that that within the next twenty years, former workers' training schools like his would be phased out entirely.

Courses, Programs, and Job Allocations

The Bridge School's links to the municipal government and the state sector were a particular lure for incoming students, for every year the school promised that at least a few of its graduates would be assigned (*fenpei*) secure iron rice bowl jobs in the public sector. Before the reform era, all graduates would have been assigned jobs in this way. Today, however, this differentiates the Bridge School from the Canal School and most other vocational secondary schools, where all students have to find their own jobs in the private labor market upon graduation. Thus, somewhat ironically, the Bridge School was able to sell its programs to incoming ninth-grade graduates by promising that at least some would *not* have to sell themselves in the future labor market.

Graduates' assignments to municipal government jobs varied by year. The year we observed classes, these permanent jobs were in Nanjing's new subway system. Places in the two classes that funneled the top students into subway system jobs after graduation were very competitive; students in the Bridge School's two "subway prep" courses had the highest entrance exam (HSEE) scores coming in to the school and were at the top of the school's moral hierarchy. The logic behind this ranking system was that in three years' time, when the students were ready to graduate, the municipal subway system would contact the school to hire a certain number of graduates. The majority of the available jobs—about 70 percent—would be allocated to the top students in the Subway 1 Prep class, which had the highest entering score requirement. The remaining 30 percent of available jobs would be allocated to the top graduates of the Subway 2 Prep class, which had slightly lower entrance exam scores—even though both classes studied an identical curriculum. Students assigned to work in the subway system could look forward to a lifetime of low pay and probably fairly menial work, in exchange for total job security and a generous packet of benefits associated with paternalistic, socialist-sector government jobs (Walder 1986).

Like most vocational secondary schools, this program and the Bridge School's other course offerings changed annually to meet perceived projected demand in the job market (Donald 2009). In 2007–2008, along with the two subway prep classes, the school offered courses in landscaping, tourism, construction site management, and gas company employment. In recent years, the school had run courses in policing and security, computer technology, horticulture, highway construction, and wastewater management.

Additionally, as part of the government's growing concern for the education of the nation's poorer children, for several years the municipal government had funded the school to run a special course for students from "disadvantaged households" (*kunnan hu*, a euphemism for impoverished families). The year we observed classes, this was a special landscaping arts course for students from a rural area on the outskirts of Nanjing that had been incorporated into Nanjing municipality in 2001. Students in this class received free tuition, room, and board and were also guaranteed secure jobs after graduation as groundskeepers in the city's growing public park system. When we met the students in this class, however, we were struck by how similar they seemed to all the other students in the school; they had the same clothes, mobile phones, and MP3 players as everyone else. The landscaping arts students laughed at this observation and confessed that they entered the program after their parents had bribed local county officials to endorse *kunnan hu* certificates that made them eligible for admission into the course. They all thought that getting a free education with a guaranteed public-sector job after graduating was a terrific deal, one worth the slight disdain with which the other students treated them as being from the "poor students" class.

The Canal School

The second school we observed was located near a newly opened park along Nanjing's Qinhuai River, so we called it the Canal School. It was one of a number of vocational secondary schools that had been opened by one of the many branches of the distance-learning universities (*Dianda*) in the province to meet growing demands for more secondary education. *Dianda* systems exist at multiple levels in China (provincial, municipal, urban district, rural). They were established to provide distance-learning programs, mostly delivered through television, to students who were unable to access more formal tertiary institutions. The various *Dianda* systems across China tend to be enormous institutions of tens of thousands of students, with programs including adult education, professional certification programs, and a wide range of online degree and nondegree programs (Donald 2009). Because of their low cost, low barriers to admission, and extensive rural education offerings, studying at one of the distance learning universities holds very low prestige in China.

Secondary vocational education is a relatively recent addition to *Dianda*'s educational options. Because *Dianda* is a tertiary institution, the Canal School offered a higher level of credentials, which it used as a marketing strategy to attract incoming tenth-graders. Unlike most vocational secondary schools that offered a three-year *zhongzhuan* diploma, the Canal School added two additional years for what it called a five-year *dazhuan* degree. This was more than slightly disingenuous, however, for a *dazhuan* degree is generally awarded to students who graduate from three-year technical colleges that they attend after completing three years of regular senior high school. To clarify that theirs is just a secondary degree, the *Dianda* program was referred to as a "3+2" (*san jia er*) credential, which, in theory, combined the three years of secondary vocational education with two additional years of more advanced training. This additional training, students were assured, would make them more attractive in the job market when they graduated. In practice, however, neither the more advanced training nor the job market advantages ever materialized for the students enrolled in this program. (See Figure 1 for an outline of how students progress through different educational options.)

Along with selling their more "advanced" training, one of the Canal School's marketing strategies to attract incoming students was to sell the prestige of the word "university" to graduating ninth-graders. Because the school was part of the *Dianda* system, entering students could—and did—call themselves "university students" (*daxuesheng*) even though they were only in tenth grade. During the year we heard teachers use this as a disciplining strategy, admonishing students to better behavior by reminding them that university students should be better behaved and more mature.

The Canal School's physical plant was in much worse condition than the Bridge School's. Two years before we arrived, the *Dianda* campus that owned the school determined that the land the building stood on was worth far more than they were earning by selling vocational education, so they decided to demolish the school and sell the property. The administration had therefore

```
          ┌─────────────────────┐
          │  Elementary school  │
          │      years 1–6      │
          │     (xiaoxue)       │
          └─────────────────────┘
                    │
          ┌─────────────────────┐
          │ Junior middle school│
          │      years 7–9      │
          │     (chuzhong)      │
          └─────────────────────┘
                    │
          ┌─────────────────────┐
          │    HIGH SCHOOL      │
          │  ENTRANCE EXAM      │
          │ (HSEE) (zhongkao)   │
          └─────────────────────┘
```

Pass: Approx. 52% (urban areas; rate is lower in rural areas)	Fail: Approx. 48%		
Regular high school years 10–12 (putong gaozhong)	Technical school (mostly rural, jishu xuexiao)	Vocational secondary school (zhiye xuexiao)	Dropouts approx. 5%
UNIVERSITY ENTRANCE EXAM (UEE) (gaokao)	3 years (zhongzhuan) educational ministry	3 years (zhongzhuan) noneducational ministry	5 years (dazhuan), 3+2
(Pass UEE) University four-year degree (BA)	(Fail UEE) Vocational tertiary degree (dazhuan)		

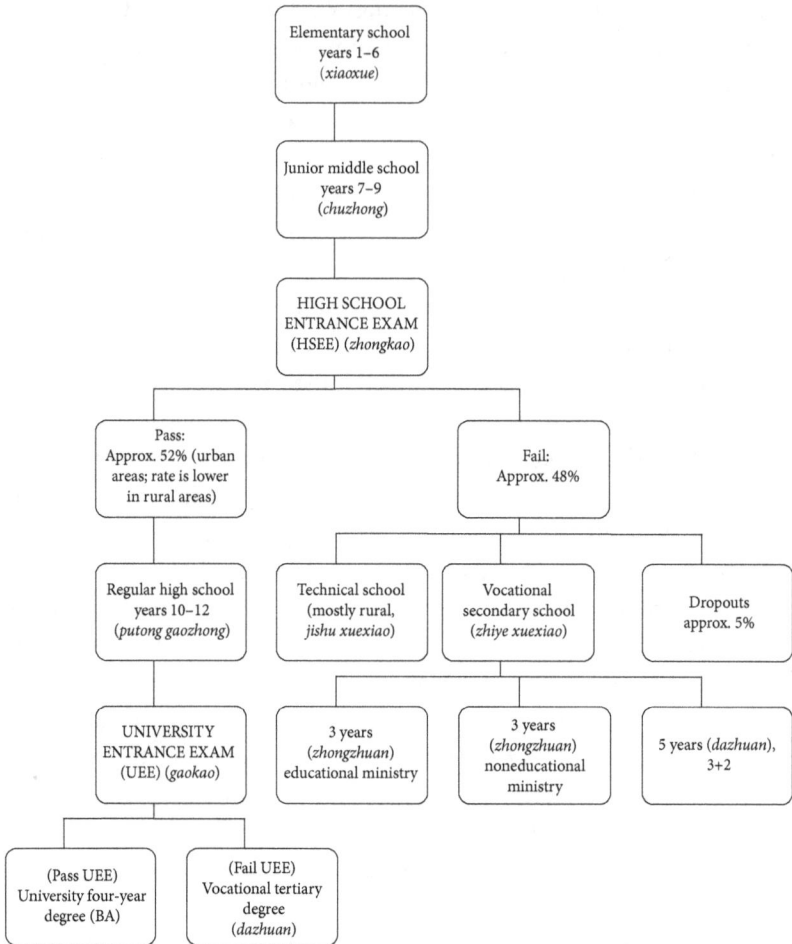

Figure 1. Students' progression from elementary to tertiary education, based on students in Nanjing, Jiangsu Province, 2007–2008 academic year.

ceased all maintenance on the campus, and, as students graduated, classrooms and dorm rooms were closed off by plywood nailed across the windows. The remaining students rattled around the half-empty building, winding their way through weeds and rubble to get to classes. The Canal School's campus was thus just as symbolic in its own way as the Bridge School's, as unwanted vocational students wandered through the remnants of an unwanted campus.

Because the campus was about to close, the year we were there the school offered only a few courses; although there were several on-site, we knew of only three: computer technology, accounting (*kuaiji*, which I refer to as the bookkeeping class), and auto repair. Unlike those of the Bridge School, the Canal School administrators were reluctant to have a foreign researcher in their midst. The party secretary who served as the principal on-site allowed Emma Wang and our graduate research assistants relatively free access to the students and classrooms, while restricting my presence on school property. Although I was able to observe some classes at the Canal School, I spent more time with the students during their lunch breaks, after school, and on weekends.

Like the Bridge School, the Canal School was administratively unusual. Its educational programs did fall under the broad purview of the Ministry of Education's vast bureaucracy. However, because of the unusual 3+2 degree program, the Office of Secondary Education technically had oversight of the students' first three years of school, while their final two years of study were under the purview of the Tertiary Office. In practice, however, because of this bifurcated oversight, the students fell between the cracks of both offices and were counted by the statistics of neither bureau; like the Bridge School students (but for entirely different reasons), the Canal School students were in a liminal state, unseen by the supposedly totalizing surveillance of Chinese bureaucratic systems.

Yet unlike the Bridge School, which assigned some of its graduates to iron rice bowl jobs in the socialist state sector, the Canal School was entirely based on capitalist logic. None of the Canal graduates were assigned jobs after graduation; all would have to find their own jobs in the private job market. Without future secure jobs to lure potential students, the Canal School had to promise incoming students that the new 3+2 degree would be highly marketable after graduation, and that students, by buying this educational product, would become better commodities for employers to hire five years in the future. The school thus commodified speculation on the future of young people as potentially "hot" commodities. However, Canal School graduates learned the hard way that their 3+2 degrees were not necessarily better investments than any other kind of vocational education, and that they were no more valuable as commodities on the job market than those with three-year *zhongzhuan* diplomas.

Conclusion: Vocational School Students, Working-Class Youth

Since the start of the reform era in the early 1980s, China's Ministry of Education has placed increasing emphasis on vocational education. A series of educational reform decrees over the past thirty years have all stressed the ways that VE can help produce a better-trained, better-prepared workforce, ready to meet the challenges of the socialist market economy. Indeed, in 2011 the Ministry of Education claimed that vocational education is key to China's goal of "promoting long-term stable and rapid economic development and social harmony and stability."

These policies cannot be divorced from either the history of the vocational system or the broader ideological system that frames contemporary education. As a result, there is a kind of double disconnect today between policy and reality. The Ministry of Education presents its plans for VE as a key aspect of China's "evolving knowledge economy" and improved "technological innovation" (Ministry of Education 2011; Schulte 2013, 227), yet the structure of vocational schools is still firmly rooted in the industrial system for which they originally were designed. In spite of the Ministry's promises of voc ed's role in preparing youth for the exciting new knowledge economy, the schools are grounded in industrial models, while acting as funnels into the lower ends of the service sector. At the same time, while most VE students were at the cutting edge of the reform-era transformation that released them from the protection of the state's *danwei* system and the security of iron rice bowl jobs and moved them out into the new private labor market, some students are still embedded in the socialist *danwei* system, competing for assignments to secure, state-sector employment.

Regardless of where they stand in relation to the job market, all the vocational students today are positioned in the moral economy of numeric capital, which structures them as failures relative to their more successful age-mates who test into regular, academic high schools. As the ideology of human capital expanded after the Cultural Revolution, stimulating "educational desires" across China (Kipnis 2010), VE became a site to manage the "surplus" of that ideology. In this regard, the two schools we studied—and the Chinese Ministry of Education—face a problem long familiar to educational leaders in China: how to use VE to convince the working classes to be happy with their lot in life and remain content with working-class jobs. The ideology of numeric capital helps accomplish the historical goal of managing the aspirations of the working classes in a new way, partly by blaming the students for their own failure, and partly by erasing the role of the state in sorting almost half of the nation's youth into VE.

In Chapter 2, I look more closely at the students themselves, specifically at the ways their aspirations are managed through vocational education. A close look at who they are, where they come from, and how they ended up in these two schools confounds any simple understanding of vocational students as a group of failures and leads to a new conceptualization of both their value and of the new urban working classes.

2   Vocational Students

In July 2007, as I was preparing to leave for a year of fieldwork research in Nanjing, a friend in China, a professor at a major university, called. My friend reminded me that the Beijing Olympics were due to start in almost exactly a year (August 2008) and that the government was nervous about possible negative reporting and research about China. The previous week the internationally respected China Development Brief had been suddenly shut down for conducting "unauthorized surveys,"[1] and the Chinese government had warned offices across the country to restrict foreigners' access to research data. My friends in China were concerned about me. Could I possibly postpone my trip for a year, until after the Olympics?

No, I couldn't. I was due to leave in less than a week, and there was no way to change my plans at that point. My friend sighed deeply. "In that case," she replied, "could you just do historical research instead and work with archives and documents?" "No, sorry," I reminded her, "I'm an anthropologist. We do participant observation research, so I have to work directly with people, talking with them, and observing their lives." To my surprise, my friend was cheered by this. "That's great!" she said. "As long as you don't do any surveys or collect any statistical data, it'll look like you aren't doing real research. In that case you should be okay." She then asked me to remind her what I was planning to study. There was a brief moment of silence. "Vocational schools? Really?" She laughed. "Well, you should be fine then. No one cares about them, so no one should pay much attention to you or your work."

My friend, a canny observer of the Chinese system, was right on both counts. In the end I was able to operate under the radar of the Chinese state. Although there were some limitations placed on my research, I was mostly able to observe classes and hang out with students at the two secondary vocational schools in Nanjing. And as she predicted, none of my Chinese contacts initially had much interest at all in my research on vocational education. In fact, when I first arrived in Nanjing, my academic and middle-class friends there were incredulous about my research topic. "Vocational schools?" they asked, aghast. "Really, who cares? Why don't you study young people who actually deserve to be studied, like all those poor unemployed university graduates?" "But I want to understand youth culture," I replied. "Youth culture?" they responded, with roars of laughter. "You're kidding! There's no such thing as 'youth culture' in China. All kids do here is study for exams!"

IN DISCUSSING THE STUDENTS THEMSELVES and their backgrounds, my goal is to challenge the stereotypes of vocational students as both bad students and immoral youth by showing that their stories and backgrounds are far more complex than that they are simply poor students who failed to study. In the process, I also seek to challenge some of the taken-for-granted social categories used to analyze urban Chinese society today, for the Bridge and Canal Schools bring together groups of youth who cross social categories that are usually understood and analyzed separately. The question of the students' backgrounds also opens up the important issue of class in contemporary China under today's conditions of very rapid economic change. Vocational secondary schools serve as a new form of class sorting; as urban vocational secondary students prepare to enter China's new service economy, they are forming a new section of the urban working class.

Because I was in China in the months leading up to the 2008 Beijing Olympics, there were some restrictions placed on my research. I was not allowed to ask the students or their parents to complete any questionnaires or surveys, nor was I able to speak to any of the students' parents. All of the following information about the students' family backgrounds is therefore based on what the students themselves reported.

Bridge School Students

Because Principal Huang at the Bridge School welcomed us to spend several days a week at the school, visiting whichever classes we wished, we got to meet many more students than we did at the Canal School, but we did not get to know individual students as well.

Bridge School students generally fell into two broad categories: those from Nanjing, who commuted to school each day by bus, and students from the surrounding countryside and farther afield, who boarded in the school's fourth-floor dormitory. There were finer distinctions, however, within the broad categories of commuter and boarding students. Many of the commuting students were originally from Nanjing and held a city household registration permit (*hukou*).[2]

These students came from a wide range of working-class backgrounds. We met students whose parents worked for the city bus company and others whose fathers drove cabs and whose mothers sold produce in local wet markets.[3] One student told us his father loaded gas canisters in a liquid gas factory. Several said they had one parent who had been laid off (*xiagang*) from formerly state-owned factories; these families were quite poor and struggled to make ends meet (Gold et al. 2009). We did not meet any students whose parents did white-collar work.

Others among the commuting students were what are known in China as "second-generation migrant children" (*min'gong di'er dai*). This refers to the children of people who migrated to cities from China's rural hinterlands. Many of these youth were born and raised in cities, but because of China's legal restrictions on converting rural to urban residence permits, they still held a rural residence permit from their parents' original homes. These young people are still a poorly understood social group about whom little research has yet been done.[4] Many Bridge School students reported their parents were migrant workers. They most commonly told us that their fathers were construction workers in sites around Nanjing, while their mothers worked in restaurants, as hotel maids, and at cleaning jobs.

Among the boarding students, there was an even greater mix of occupational family backgrounds. The largest group came from the two suburban counties, Jiangning and Liuhe, that bordered Nanjing city to the north and south. These formerly rural areas had been incorporated into Nanjing Municipality in 2001 and since then have been the site of massive transformations, including rapid industrialization and vast new housing construction for urban commuters. These are linked to national development policies called the New Socialist Countryside that have transformed agricultural and rural communities (Bray 2013). A few of these boarding students came from families that were still farming the land, but most reported that their parents were working in factories that had relocated from the city to these newly industrialized areas or as construction workers. Others' families had been forced off their family agricultural plots by recent development programs and were now living in the run-down, cheap housing units built to accommodate rural residents who were dislocated to enable the construction of new apartment blocks for urban commuters (Bray 2013). These families struggled to make ends meet, with parents often finding work such as security guards or street cleaners. Students from these two counties usually returned home to their families every weekend, since their homes were relatively close to the city.

Other boarding students were from more distant locales and could return home only during school vacations. Some students came from migrant-worker families based in larger cities, including Shanghai, Suzhou, and Beijing. These students saw their families infrequently and had a range of different experiences settling in at the Bridge School. For example, one student had been sent to the Bridge School by her divorced mother whose work as a hotel maid caused her to move frequently around China's larger tourist cities, including Hangzhou, Suzhou, and Shanghai. She sent her daughter to Nanjing because the mother considered it a "safe" and "cultured" city for education. As a recent arrival, this student neither spoke nor understood the local Nanjing dialect and felt isolated and lonely.

This student, however, was a very rare exception; the others we met seemed to get along tremendously well regardless of family background, place of origin, or home dialect. Because all the students in each vocational course took all their classes together, they formed friendship groups within programs that crossed *hukou* divisions, family background, gender, and native dialect. Within courses, commuters befriended dorm residents; local Nanjing residents became friends with rural kids and the children of migrant workers. Because urban and rural residents are generally considered to be very different kinds of people in China, these friendship groupings were unexpected; Bridge School classrooms were in some sense the Chinese equivalent of melting pots. I discuss this in more detail in Chapter 5, which focuses on the question of students' identities.

Canal School Students

During the school year when we observed classes at the Canal School, we got to know two classes of students quite well. One was the second-year (eleventh grade) bookkeeping class of forty-one students (thirty-nine girls and two boys). Approximately half of these students lived in Nanjing and commuted by bus. The other half were from farther away and boarded in the school's rudimentary dorm facilities. Like their counterparts at the Bridge School, most of these students came from Jiangning and Liuhe Counties. Some of the boarding students, however, lived farther away. For example, Zhang Zhigang, one of the two boys in the class, was originally from rural northern Jiangsu Province, but his father now worked as a security guard at an apartment building in Beijing; he saw his parents only once a year. His classmate Lu Xue's family had relocated from rural Jiangsu to Shanghai, where her father headed a construction crew. She visited her parents only on school holidays.

As they were for the Bridge School students, the family backgrounds of the Canal School bookkeeping students were quite diverse, and their parents' livelihoods represented the ever-broadening range of work possibilities at the lower ends of the new Chinese economy. Many of these students, too, were second-generation migrants from rural areas. Song Mengwei's parents, for example, had migrated to Nanjing from Anhui shortly after she was born. They now owned a prosperous car repair business in the city and, by buying property in the city, had converted their rural *hukou* to urban ones. Most of the other second-generation migrant students, however, still held a rural *hukou*, even though they had spent their entire lives in the city.

Among the commuting students, most held a Nanjing city *hukou*, and their parents were all members of the urban working class. We met some students whose parents worked in the few factories that remained in the city, while several had parents who had been laid off from the industrial state sector. One student's mother was a cook in an elementary school cafeteria on the city's south side. Another's father was a manager at a branch of the large local supermarket chain, and her mother was a cashier at the same store. Several had fathers working as security guards.

We also worked closely with the students in the fifth year (graduating, *biyeban*) computer technology class at the Canal School. Unlike their slightly younger classmates in the bookkeeping course, most of the forty-five computer tech students came from Nanjing. None lived in the school dormitories. The students whose homes were too far from Nanjing to commute either lived with their classmates' families or rented rooms somewhere in the city, preferring this to the poor quality of the school's dorms.

Like the bookkeeping students, the computer tech students came from urban working-class or second-generation migrant-worker backgrounds. The class president was Xu Wenjuan; her father worked at a local prison, and her mother had been laid off from a factory. Xu's boyfriend was Su Xiaogang, whose father was a technician in a factory; his mother, too, was unemployed. Xu's friend Wang Shui's father was disabled and had been laid off years earlier from his job at a state-owned factory. Wang's mother supported the family by selling vegetables at a local market. Other students told similar stories: Qian Ling's parents, migrants from rural Anhui Province, made and sold tofu in another local wet market. Tang Limei's parents used to work in a state-owned factory at the edge of the city. When it closed down, they moved to central Nanjing to start their own small business. Wei Ren's parents had both worked in a state-owned textile factory that was still operating; her mother had retired, but her father still worked there as an electrician. Like their counterparts at the Bridge School, none of the Canal School students came from middle-class families or had parents who held white-collar jobs.

Questioning Stereotypes of Vocational Students

The students at both schools were thus very diverse. Although they were all from similar class backgrounds, they came from social categories that are generally considered discrete in China. Classrooms combined groups of rural and urban *hukou* holders; first- and second-generation migrants; and students from the city, neighboring counties, surrounding countryside, and even distant provinces. Yet vocational students are generally understood as being all the same: educational failures. They are seen as lazy students, morally suspect youth who deserve their own fate. We therefore tried to learn more about them, to understand if their diversity merely masked a fundamental similarity. Were they really all the same? We asked, How *did* they get to their schools? What were their test scores? What kinds of moral youth were they, and how did they see themselves? Perhaps not surprisingly, the answers we received were much more complex than the stereotypes might have led us to believe.

Failing and Passing the HSEE: Recasting Morality

Many of the students at both schools openly admitted that they had indeed entered vocational school because they were mediocre students in junior middle school who hated studying and had not prepared for the HSEE. But a few had interesting explanations for this. Some said that given the competitiveness of the exam system, they felt that there was simply no point in studying. For example, Canal School student Lu Xue just stopped studying in ninth grade, when she heard how difficult senior high school would be. "Why bother?" she reported thinking to herself. "I don't really like studying and don't want to work that hard. I'll just take whatever score I can get on the HSEE and will go to vocational school." Her classmate Li Ping's father made this decision for her. "I did alright in junior high school," she told me. "But then my dad reminded me that it's really stressful to study so hard. He thought that it would be too difficult for me to keep that up all through senior high school, so he just signed me up for this bookkeeping course."

Others told us that they were too busy helping their families to study for the exams. Canal School computer tech student Qian Ling told us that her father got up at 3:30 every morning to prepare tofu for sale, which her mother brought to the market every day at 5:00 a.m. They worked seven days a week, and except for an annual break during Spring Festival (Chinese New Year), they never took a single day off. By age seven she was helping them prepare tofu and staffing their market stall whenever they needed her. She attributed her poor test results to the ways her time and attention had always been divided between helping her parents at their grueling schedule and trying to get her school work done. Her classmate Wang Shui told an even sadder story about working in a local vegetable market, contributing additional labor to support her family as her father's disability grew worse as he aged. Her studies, too, suffered as she awakened earlier and earlier every morning to help her parents and as she did more of the housework to help her mother.

Along with these stories, we also learned that many of the Bridge and Canal School students actually *did* pass the HSEE and chose to attend voc ed to save their working-class parents the risk and cost of tuition at a regular high school. Several informed us that they had decided not to attend regular high schools as an act of filial piety, out of concern to protect their struggling parents from higher tuition bills and the risk of an uncertain future. "I did quite well on the HSEE," said Du Jian in the Bridge School subway prep class. "But when I realized that I could use my score to get into the subway prep course and that after only three years I could be assigned a good, secure job with the city, it would have been selfish of me to ask my parents to pay for a regular high school. After all, after three years at a regular high school, I would then have to take the UEE, which is so much riskier. And then university is even more expensive!" This is a story we heard repeated surprisingly often, of students who reported that they foreclosed their own futures to protect their parents. They had chosen to attend VE as a safer route, to save their parents future tuition expenses and to enter the job market sooner, and to help their parents avoid the anxiety and insecurity of facing the UEE after twelfth grade.

Others were aided in this decision by their parents, for better or worse. The Canal School's Dai Jingyi, for example, scored well enough on the HSEE to attend a regular high school, but her mother decided to send her to vocational school instead. "My parents were worried about wasting money," she told me. "If I spent three years in high school and then didn't test into university, then those three years would be wasted. If I did test into university, they'd have to figure out how to pay for another four years of college. This way, at the Canal School, they'll only have to pay for five years and I'll be ready for a job right away." Dai was fine with this decision, which made perfect sense to her. Wei Ren's parents, however, forced her to attend the Canal School against her wishes. Her score on the HSEE was also high enough to enter a regular senior high school, but she had only scored well enough to enter a mediocre high school near her family's home. Her father refused to pay tuition there, saying that since she could not attend a key school that would prepare her to test into a good university, her only alternative was vocational education. Five years later, as she prepared to graduate from the Canal School computer course, Wei was resigned but still slightly bitter about this decision her father had made on her behalf.

Counter to the widely held stereotypes of vocational students as immoral youth, many of the students thus saw themselves as even *more* moral than students enrolled in regular high schools, for they had chosen to curtail their own educational ambitions to attend to their parents' needs and wishes. The exam system is therefore not nearly as simple as the general ideology holds it to be: a meritocracy where the smart, diligent, and moral students rise to the top and the bad, lazy, immoral students sink to the bottom (vocational schools). Instead, the students, their lives, and the system as a whole are much more complex, as some students relinquished their own ambitions to take their families' needs into account.

Given this complexity, we were also curious: Once it was clear that they were going to enter the vocational stream, how did the students decide which school to attend and which vocational course to choose? After all, in theory their vocational course would determine their future, since students enter vocational school expecting to train for their eventual profession. How did they make the important decision of what their future profession would be?

Many students told us that they personally had not given any thought at all to which school they would attend or which course to take, for this decision had been made for them entirely by their parents or other relatives. Students reported that family members made these decisions based on a range of factors. For some, the decision was entirely gendered. For example, many of the Canal School students told us that a parent or other family member selected the bookkeeping course because this was "a good career for girls." Most of the students we asked about this just shrugged and accepted it at face value, while a few elaborated. "If I can get a job as a cashier, then I'll be able to work indoors all day, and can even probably sit down at work," Wang Xinyi told me. "My parents thought that this was important for a girl." Her classmate Meng Rong agreed, adding, "Bookkeepers and cashiers don't have to be out on a sales floor, talking to strangers. And we won't have to travel for business. So it's a safer job than sales, which is a better job for men. We can stay safely in one place with this job, so it's better for girls." They both said they were happy with their families' decisions to send them to the Canal School.

Other students—and their families—made the important decision about which vocational school to attend and which course to study with what seemed to us to be remarkably little forethought, research, or information. Several of the Canal School students told us they had been impressed by a brochure for

Dianda that was circulating at their middle schools; photos of the campus looked impressive, with up-to-date classrooms, labs, and facilities. Only after they enrolled did they realize that the brochures pictured a different campus than the one they would actually attend, a bait-and-switch they were still upset about years later. In another example, bookkeeping student Yang Minglu's mother, who worked on the janitorial staff at a local university, asked one of the university professors for advice on which vocational school to select for her daughter. That person suggested *Dianda*, so Yang was sent to the Canal School.

Bridge School students told us similar stories. Subway prep course student Fan Li's mother, a bus driver, learned of the Bridge School when she attended a job-related training course sponsored by the Nanjing Engineering Bureau. She sent her daughter to the Bridge School as a way into the subway system, a job with the same kind of lifelong security as her own work in the city bus system. Li Hujuan's middle school received an advertising flyer for the Bridge School, which recruited heavily in her hometown in semi-rural Liuhe County. Her parents thought the flyer promised a future of good city jobs for Bridge School graduates, so they sent their daughter there.

Other students told us that they had selected their schools and courses themselves, without input from parents. Tang Limei, for example, chose the Canal School because the girl sitting next to her in middle school had selected it. She thought the school's affiliation with *Dianda* sounded prestigious and decided to attend without any additional information. Her father, a migrant laborer on construction sites around Nanjing, agreed with her decision. Her classmate Qian Ling wanted to study to be a day-care teacher and chose the Canal School herself because it offered this as a course option. When she went to register, however, she learned that the school was running only a computer tech class her year. Because the Canal School offered her a full scholarship, she reluctantly signed up for the computer course, and discovered only after classes started that she actually loathes computers, programming, and everything to do with electronics.

Sometimes the teachers repeated these kinds of stories to us as well, yet rather than see these stories as examples of how well the students and their families had coped with a complex and changing situation, the teachers used these as examples of how poorly informed the parents and the students were. Indeed, these stories can serve as indicators of how little cultural and social capital the students' parents had and how difficult it was for them to understand the tremendous complexities of the Chinese secondary education system. Even middle-class parents I knew in China complained about the complexity of the system, the amount of time and effort it took to learn about the different secondary educational options available, the changing regulations in place every year, and the best ways to negotiate the system. Parents who work seven days a week or are scrubbing floors or selling tofu in a wet market have neither the time nor the resources to research school options. They are blamed for poor parenting, when many, in fact, are merely poor.

At the same time, it is important to note that several students stressed that from their perspective, the economic situation in China was changing so quickly that excessive planning for the future may not be the best approach after all. As bookkeeping student Liu Rui told me, "Look, I'm just a lazy student. If you go to a regular high school, you have to study every day of the week. Here at the Canal School we have weekends off. It's great!" When I asked her about the future, she merely shrugged. "A lot of things can change in a few years," she replied. "Who knows? My parents don't have any strong opinions. They aren't too worried, so I'm not either." This, of course, is a radically different approach from that of stressed-out parents and students who are frantically investing in human capital, speculating on one particular vision of the national future. Yet given the rate at which the job market was changing when Liu Rui told us this story, perhaps a more laissez-faire approach to planning for the future—and to human capital accumulation—is not as irrational as it might seem. Educational policy changes all the time in China; even the 3+2 degree offered at the Canal School had existed only a few years, and most of the teachers and administrators believed that it would probably be phased out in the future. Liu's approach, shocking as it was to her teachers, may ironically end up being the most rational of all in the rapidly changing Chinese economy.

Parental Pressures and Poverty

These stories of family background raise the question of parental pressures on children and youth. Within China, public discourse equates normative youth with studying; young people are simply assumed to spend all their time preparing for exams (see Fong 2004). A significant part of parenting—especially mothering—is assumed to consist of managing children's studying.

This is thus an area where public discourse and teachers condemn vocational students' families for bad parenting; from their perspective, if students have tested badly, it is obviously because parents must not have applied the appropriate guidance or pressure. But rather than the stresses of cram schools, homework, and exam pressures faced by "normal" youth in China, we found that the young people we knew in the vocational schools often faced the pressures of lives lived in poverty and migration. Yet like so much of the lives of the vocational students, these kinds of stresses were entirely invisible in the broader discourse of youth and parenting in China.

As indicated previously, at least some of the VE students were balancing multiple responsibilities, and filial piety for them involved far more than obediently studying for exams and accruing numeric capital. Some of their stories give a sense of what their daily lives were like, far from the typical pressures of homework, memorization, and cramming for exams. For example, Canal School student Tang Limei's mother died when Tang was in third grade. Afterward, she moved around Jiangsu Province to live with various relatives and changed schools frequently. Starting in middle school, she followed her migrant-worker father to Nanjing as he found work on construction sites; while he lived in rudimentary housing at his work sites, she stayed with her classmates' families whenever she could.

Bookkeeping student Zhang Zhigang had never lived with his migrant-worker parents, who left him as a baby with his elderly grandmother in the countryside. When she died, he moved among various relatives' homes until he began boarding at the Canal School. We didn't understand how alone he was in the world until Emma Wang, my research partner, received a call from him one Sunday afternoon. The seventeen-year-old had cut his finger badly playing basketball and was concerned it might be infected; he had no other adult in his life he could think of to call to ask what he should do. Thus, some of these students faced significant pressures of working-class life, of living alone, of urban poverty, and of making their own decisions, rather than the normative pressures of studying. These are not the stressed-out youth represented in the Chinese media or in the culturalist discourse of "tiger mothers" in the West. But the particular pressures of working-class life are invisible in the discourse of normative Chinese youth.

Yet it is also important to note that life for these young people is more than simply stress and strain. The vocational school students *were* pressured by their parents to succeed, but their definitions of "success" were not the same as the middle-class definitions. Like their peers across China (and around the world), the Bridge and Canal School parents set expectations for their children based on their desires for the next generation to lead a better life. The differences from middle-class discourse are the ways these parents define what a "better life" may be. If a vocational secondary degree can guarantee their offspring a lifetime of employment indoors, out of the elements, or sitting down in front of a desk, then the VE youth are on a path of upward mobility. Compared to their parents' lives of manual labor or farming, exposed to the elements and backbreaking work, the students' future urban jobs as cashiers, computer technicians, or subway station guards were indeed an improvement over their parents' work; vocational school was a stepping-stone to occupational mobility. The students and parents therefore did not necessarily see vocational schools as a debased form of schooling, but as a means out of agricultural or migrant labor and into the urban working classes.

Thus, for many of the students, attending a vocational school indexes far more than merely failure, laziness, or immorality. In the same vein, while some of the students did describe themselves as lazy or disinterested in study, many were in vocational education not simply because they were failures but because they and their parents made strategic decisions about maximizing opportunities and minimizing risks. Attending a regular high school is a significant risk, with relatively high costs financially, extremely high costs emotionally, and very high risks of not getting into a university. Sending a child to vocational school may be perfectly rational, not merely a sign of a child's poor study habits or immorality.

In this way, the vocational students and their families serve as an important counterpoint to the hegemonic ideology about children, families, and the pressures on students in China today, which is conveyed in the discourse of "all Chinese kids do is study." The experiences of the Canal and Bridge School students indicate that researchers need to look at youth from a broader range of social backgrounds, across different educational settings, and learn more about their daily lives, for much of what is generated as normative Chinese youth is actually a *middle-class* discourse. This raises the important question of social class and the new forms of social inequalities being (re)produced in and through these schools.

Vocational Secondary Education and/as Class Sorting

There is tremendous interest in China's "emerging middle classes" (Li Cheng 2010) and the new rich (Goodman 2008; Osburg 2013), but ironically, the word "class" (*jingji jieceng*) is rarely used in China today. As scholars have noted, Mao Zedong used "class struggle" (*jieji douzheng*) as the organizing principle of the Cultural Revolution (Anagnost 2008a; Dutton 1998; Meisner 1996). After the end of the Cultural Revolution, the term "class" therefore carried connotations of social unrest and conflict. In 1978 Deng Xiaoping declared that class struggle in China had come to an end, and with it the term "class" faded from daily use. In its place, by the early 1990s "social strata" (*shihui jiceng*) began to be used to describe differences in income and social status.

This new terminology does more than simply change vocabulary. As Anagnost (2008a) points out, the use of the term "social strata" erases the Cultural Revolution from historical memory, depoliticizes social hierarchy, and removes the possibility of using social class as an analytic category (see also Guo 2012). As a result, the concept of classes as structural social categories inexorably in conflict with each other, as in Maoist social theory, has now been replaced with a neoliberal concept of individual responsibility, so each person is individually responsible for his or her own "social status" (Anagnost 2008a; Ren 2013; Tomba 2009). Larger social forces are no longer accountable for an individual's destiny; individuals are expected to take control of their lives and their futures and seize new opportunities to get rich. Many scholars who study new forms of governmentality in China have noted this process, whereby responsibility has devolved from the state to the individual (Foucault 1991; Greenhalgh and Winckler 2005; Jeffreys and Sigley 2006; Sigley 2009; Woronov 2009; Zhang and Ong 2008). This process is not confined to China; scholars around the world have noted that this phenomenon, which sometimes carries the inelegant term "responsibilization," is taking place around the globe as part of the neoliberal transformations (see, e.g., Anagnost 2013; Gordon 1991; and Lemke 2002 for a discussion of these processes).

In education, the question of responsibilization is, again, linked to the ideology of numeric capital, where *individual* youth and their families are expected to be responsible for their exam scores and, as a result, their futures. This appears in daily Chinese discourse in multiple and overlapping ways. It appears in the ideology of the exam system as a meritocracy that naturally rewards clever, hardworking students; in the stereotypes of vocational students as stupid and lazy individuals who deserve to be relegated to dead-end vocational schools; and in a moral discourse that equates bad test scores with immorality.

Yet it is essential to remember that in spite of the widespread notion that any individual student is in charge of his or her own destiny just by studying hard enough, the overall passing and failure rates on the HSEE are determined by the government, not by individual students' diligence. How hard any individual ninth-grader prepares for this test may ultimately be less relevant than the fact that across China, approximately 45 percent of youth will fail this exam. This is government policy. The ideology of numeric capital assigns value and responsibility to individuals, but the exams are a systemic, not individual, problem. To study the students as a *group* requires understanding how the entire high-stakes exam and indeed the entire educational system are linked to class reproduction, not only to the morality, quality (*suzhi*), diligence, or intellect of individuals.

If I had asked the Canal or Bridge School students directly, they almost certainly would have resisted a class-based analysis of their lives. Although they were well aware of growing income disparities between rich and poor across China, they did not use a language of class to describe their own situations. Yet vocational schools are part of a wider system of urban class sorting (Slater 2010). This should not be a surprising claim, for social scientists have long noted that schools around the world are important structures for (re)producing class distinctions (e.g., Bourdieu and Passerson 1977; Kahn 2011; Slater 2010; P. Willis 1977).[5]

I argue that this class-sorting process takes place at two points in the voc ed process: upon entry into the vocational stream, and after graduation from vocational school. First, however, it is important to note that there are no available statistical data on the class composition of vocational school students overall, nor have there been any large-scale studies to look at the correlation between social class and HSEE results. Once students fail the HSEE, they may fall out of the Chinese statistical systems and be uncounted; to my knowledge there are therefore no aggregate data on the secondary vocational system that include the schools under the oversight of different ministries. One recent study (Song, Loyalka, and Wei 2013) examined the family backgrounds, incomes, and grades of a random sample of graduating ninth-graders in an impoverished county in rural western China. The authors found a strong correlation between the students' success on the HSEE and family income; students from wealthier families did better on the exam and entered regular high schools at higher rates than did those from poorer families.[6] I know of no similar studies of students in urban areas.

My research was based entirely on qualitative rather than quantitative data. However, in our research we never met even one student from the growing Chinese middle classes at either of the two vocational schools we studied, nor did we meet a single student whose parents did any kind of white-collar work. Although our sample size was very small, every student we met in both schools came from either urban working-class or rural migrant families. They came from families from both the industrial and service sectors of the urban working class, second-generation rural migrant workers, and displaced rural families in peri-urban areas on the outskirts of the city. In statistical terms, within our small sample, 100 percent of the students were from working-class backgrounds.

We discovered that there is likely a straightforward reason for this. It is *not* necessarily simply the case that students from wealthy families do well on the HSEE, while students from poorer families test badly. Rather, we understood that urban families who can afford to do so prefer to send a child who tests badly on the HSEE to private academic high schools. In other words, families that can afford an alternative option generally do not choose to send their children to vocational secondary high schools. Although we know this only anecdotally, we understand that voc ed is an option for low-scoring urban students whose families cannot afford to purchase an alternative, private education.[7] The vocational system today is therefore a system for the working classes—less because they are the ones who test into the system (although that may be true) than because they generally cannot afford to buy their way out of it. Much more research is still necessary to confirm this claim, for it is very important to understand more about the class background of the students who enter vocational education in both urban and rural areas.

Just as pertinent, I suggest, is what happens to the Bridge and Canal School students after they graduate from vocational school. Graduates of these vocational schools are locked out of future white-collar and middle-class jobs. These students' futures are radically limited because they failed the HSEE; they will be able to enter only working-class jobs after they graduate. China's wealth may be increasing rapidly, but white-collar jobs require university degrees—or at the very least academic (regular) high school diplomas. Membership in the middle classes requires fairly high academic credentials (Li Chunling 2010). The vocational school students are therefore locked out of futures in the middle classes before they are even seventeen years old.

A few lucky voc ed graduates in China may have the chance to become entrepreneurs in the future, and some may even become quite wealthy, but the opportunities for poorly educated youth to get rich in the current economy is limited to only a very few exceptional individuals (Osburg 2013).[8] People I spoke with in China almost always mentioned a few well-publicized examples from the Chinese media of VE graduates who have gained entrepreneurial wealth as cases that proved that vocational school can be a path to riches, but this is by no means true for the vast majority. The possibility that a few individual voc ed graduates may strike it rich does not disprove the structural barriers faced by most.

Thus, even though state ideology argues that the exam system is a meritocracy, the testing system (re)produces class divisions, such that the HSEE sorts approximately 45 percent of the nation's graduating ninth-graders into the working class. This, however, is not a widely noticed social issue in China. I suspect that a segment of the working class being sorted out of the education system before high school is not considered a social problem because the middle classes generally *do* continue to progress through the education system. As long as the middle classes continue to be (re)produced, the fate of the working classes is usually not considered a social issue. The best analysis of how and why this occurs comes from Bourdieu and Passeron (1977), who suggested that as long as an education system continues to reproduce the *middle* classes and enables this group to keep its privileged status in society, there will be little resistance to that system. Additionally, they argued, in this case there will also be ongoing support to maintain ideologies that the education system does *not* reproduce class divisions.

In China, the idea that the exam system produces a meritocracy—and the associated reproduction of the middle classes—is instituted and maintained through the ideology of numeric capital. This is partly reproduced through a range of daily practices that demonize academic failures (Slater 2010). For example, many university and graduate students (i.e., academically successful students) in China have told me that their parents used the threat of vocational school to frighten them into studying harder when they were in elementary school. Even today, many middle-class urban parents I know in China bully their young children by threatening, "If you don't get better marks now, you'll have to go to vocational high school!" Indeed, the well-known pressures on youth to study hard to enter the right kinds of high schools and then the right kinds of elite universities are themselves a reflection of class anxieties: worries about class status start as early as kindergarten, when middle-class parents begin to pressure children to study hard, partly as a way of expressing their fears about their family's future class position (Anagnost 2004, 2008b).

Mette Halskov Hansen's recent study of a mixed vocational and academic secondary school in rural Zhejiang Province is another chilling example of this demonization. She found that when parents in the local community learned that classes for the academic and vocational streams were being held in the same building, they protested vigorously. Parents of students in the academic stream insisted that the vocational students be moved into a different wing of the building so they would not "infect" the students in the "regular" secondary stream (Hansen 2014; Hansen and Woronov 2013).[9] The perceived "contagion" by VE students is a kind of meta-commentary on class (Slater 2010) by rural parents, who are desperate for their children to be able to seize the narrow window of educational opportunity for potential future class mobility, and who fear anything that might drag their offspring back into a future of agricultural drudgery.

This same concern was present in the two vocational schools I studied, where all the teachers adamantly agreed that they would never choose to send their own children to the schools in which they worked. The mere suggestion was met with horror in the teachers' rooms in both schools. A good example occurred when I first arrived at the Bridge School. At my very first meeting with patient and soft-spoken Principal Huang, he told me his daughter was in ninth grade and studying for the HSEE. He mentioned that he hoped she could meet me, because she had never met a foreigner and wanted to practice her English with a native speaker. I agreed immediately and tried to set up a time to get together with her for dinner or tea. Yet Principal Huang kept postponing this meeting because his daughter was too busy to meet, even though she was not scheduled to take the exam for several months; every evening and weekend were taken up with tutors, cram schools, study sessions, and practice tests. She could not arrange even a single evening to meet me until two weeks after the HSEE exams were finished. We eventually met in July, within days of my departure from Nanjing. By then it was clear that she had tested well enough to enter an excellent regular high school and would safely avoid a future of studying in her father's school.

Conclusion: Numeric Capital in Students' Lives

I have described a group of young people in Nanjing who were sorted out of the regular academic educational stream at the end of year 9. In the popular imaginary they are unlike "normal" Chinese youth, who supposedly spend all their time studying. They are morally suspect as lazy students who did not study hard enough to succeed at the high school entrance exams—indeed, they are so morally suspect that they do not deserve to be studied, nor would their own teachers consider sending their own children into their own classrooms. Their schools are bureaucratically and architecturally unusual, placing students in waste treatment centers and among boarded-up buildings, and some of the students are invisible to the state's surveillance regimes. Yet many see themselves as moral and filial youth and work hard to contribute to families that are struggling daily to get by. Many are upwardly mobile compared to their family backgrounds and are working to improve their lives.

They come from a wide range of backgrounds, including urban, rural, and peri-urban; they are from urban working-class and first- and second-generation migrant families. They carry household registrations from Nanjing, the suburbs, rural Jiangsu Province, and rural areas across China. A lucky few will be assigned to lifelong jobs in the state sector, while others will be precariously employed in the rapidly changing tertiary economy. They will all work in the lower ends of the urban service sector as computer technicians, supermarket cashiers, and subway platform security guards. These are youth who face significant daily pressures—but not from studying and memorizing for exams. They see them-selves as filial children and sometimes express their filial piety by intentionally choosing this debased educational stream.

Thus, in spite of the simplistic stereotypes that categorize them in stark black-and-white terms, close ethnographic research shows they are a complex group of young people who are difficult to categorize. We need, in other words, a finer-grained analysis of young people in China to understand what life is like for the millions of the nation's urban youth who are sorted out of the academic stream by the state's high-stakes testing policies and who are demonized as bad and immoral youth.

At the same time, these students demonstrate that the social categories gen-erally used to analyze contemporary urban Chinese society may no longer be entirely relevant to describe this new generation. Sociological studies of China, both domestically and around the world, tend to assume a priori that urban Chi-nese people fall into two broad categories: urban residents (urban *hukou* hold-ers), and nonresidents (rural migrants). This is perfectly reasonable, since these are also legal categories in China that describe how the Chinese state catego-rizes the population for purposes of policy, surveillance, and allocation of state benefits. Yet at the level of lived experience, the vocational school classrooms demonstrate that *hukou* status is not necessarily a relevant basis for individual identity. The students do not organize themselves as city residents, migrants, and second-generation migrants; these state and legal categories do not constitute their identities, nor will these categories necessarily significantly influence their future life chances.

In the previous chapter I described the high-stakes testing system in year 9, the HSEE, that shuts almost half of China's youth out of the academic stream. The ideology of numeric capital then blames the students who fail this exam for their own failed future possibilities. I have extended this argument by claiming that through the mechanism of this exam, urban vocational secondary schools are a form of class sorting in China today, whereby a new segment of the urban work-ing class is being formed. Students who are sorted by the HSEE out of the regular academic stream are locked out of middle-class, white-collar futures. Families of poorly performing children who have sufficient economic capital may buy their way out of this fate by purchasing places in private academic high schools; vocational secondary schools remain as an option for students from the urban working classes, those from rural areas, and the children of migrant workers.

The students I knew in Nanjing would probably not describe themselves or their schools in terms of a class-sorting process. This is not surprising; young people in many parts of the world do not generally speak of their lives this way (Bettie 2003), for class-based analyses have increasingly given way to more individualized and depoliticized notions of social causality. Some Western scholars have even argued class is therefore no longer relevant as a way to analyze young people's lives (see McDowell 2012 for a review and critique). Yet it is impossible to understand vocational secondary education in China without understanding the class ramifications of the sorting system that places students there.

From a more macroeconomic perspective, even with the tremendous growth in the Chinese economy and the government's efforts to move away from manufacturing-based exports and into a "knowledge-based" economy (see State Council 2012), the state still needs to sort and socialize some young people into lower-tier jobs. This is true around the world (Bourdieu and Passeron 1977; Slater 2010), although the mechanisms used to sort and socialize young people across different social classes vary geographically and historically. The vocational sector in China was originally created as a way to train a new industrial working class at the start of the twentieth century—and to teach those young people to be happy with their (working-)class position. This same function—social sorting into class streams—was partly the basis for overturning the entire educational system during the Cultural Revolution. Just because the word "class" is not used in China today to discuss social hierarchy does not mean that these problems and issues no longer exist. And just because the VE graduates are now seeking jobs in the private labor market does not mean that the state is not deeply implicated in the sorting into different educational streams—and eventually into different class positions.

Today the ideology of numeric capital is a particularly effective sorting system, for it is a moral system that supports a structural one. It places the responsibility for the students' position in vocational education—and their paths to their futures—on students' own shoulders; it is their own responsibility that they ended up in vocational school. If they had studied better and tested better, they would not be in voc ed and would have a different trajectory into the future. In this ideology causality is seen as located within individuals rather than in a system that requires almost half of the students to fail, regardless of their effort.

China, of course, is by no means the only place this occurs. As Paul Willis wrote more than thirty years ago to describe capitalism in the West:

> Opportunities are created only by the upward pull of the economy, and then
> only in relatively small numbers for the working class. The whole nature of

Western capitalism is also such that classes are structured and persistent so that even relatively high rates of individual mobility make no difference to the existence or position of the working class. No conceivable number of certificates amongst the working class will make for a classless society, or convince industrialists and employers—even if they were able—to create more jobs. . . . It is quite illusory to picture the labor market as open to determination from the pool of skills and capacities amongst young workers. Young people [have no] meaningful power over the occupational market. (1977, 127)

Although he was writing about England at the end of its industrial era, his insights are resonant in China today. The symbolism of the Bridge and Canal Schools, of unwanted and wasted students attending school in crumbling buildings, treated as waste matter, shows how little investment the state is making in the human capital of its future service workers, regardless of its rhetoric. Although these young people will enter the largest segment of China's future economy, the work they will do—as cashiers, retail clerks, security guards, ticket sellers, and computer technicians—is not what the government means when it trumpets its plans to "build the service economy" (State Council 2012). When the Chinese government talks about moving away from manufacturing and into a service economy, as it did specifically in the recent Twelfth Five-Year Plan (2011–2015), it intends to focus on development of the financial sector, science and technology, consulting, and engineering (State Council 2012). Even here, the nation's vocational students and their class position as a new service sector are largely invisible.

I have explored the structural positioning of the students and their schools, but they are not merely victims of the state's class sorting process. In Chapter 3, I describe the various creative ways they managed their time and energy in school every day, including sleeping through class as a reasonable response to the ways the curriculum and teaching were structured. I later explore some of the ways the students think about their own lives and their identities—as vocational students, as urbanites, and as future service workers—and how they are produced as new subjects for China's new global economy.

3 Teachers, Teaching, and Curricula

It's quite early, just before 9:00 a.m. on a Sunday morning, not long after the end of the Spring Festival holiday in 2008. I have met Song Guangling, the sole early riser living in the Canal School dormitory, in front of the local Carrefours supermarket near the school. She and I have arranged to buy some snacks for an outing later that morning with some of the bookkeeping students; we've planned to visit some of the nearby historical sites, and then we'll all go out for lunch. The enormous two-story Carrefours is almost empty, for the hordes of weekend shoppers have not yet arrived at this early hour.

A sweet, thoughtful sixteen-year-old, Song is from a village about two hours north of Nanjing, an area that is rapidly industrializing under the government's New Socialist Countryside reforms. Her parents both live in Shanghai as migrant workers. Song's gentle, considerate nature and serious demeanor have earned her a reputation among her slightly more cosmopolitan classmates as a bit of a country bumpkin (*tubaozi*), a reputation she does not deserve.

As we stroll up and down the long aisles and towering displays of food, Song slips her arm through mine to chat, common among female friends in China. "Teacher Wu,"[1] she says, "Can I ask you something?" "Of course," I reply. "What's it like to live in a capitalist country?" she asks. I turn to see if she's teasing me. She isn't. Stunned at the students' unerring ability to ask unanswerable questions, I decide to ask her one in reply. Gesturing at the commodities all around us in the massive French-owned supermarket, I ask, "What would you call this?" She stops and thinks for a moment. "It's socialism," she replies. "Really?" I ask, genuinely surprised. "Why do you say that?" "Well, in our politics class [*zhengzhi ke*] the teacher tells us that China is a socialist country [*Zhongguo shi yigi shehuizhuyi de guojia*]. So this has to be socialism, right?"

THE TWO SCHOOLS were not only places for instruction. They were, of course, also places of employment (Connell 2009; Whiteside and Zhang 1992). As employers, both schools also mixed the socialist *danwei* system and the private market economy and as such reflected an interesting—and fairly common— employment situation in China today (Otis 2011). The strengths and weaknesses of both forms of work contract, as well as the many tensions between them, influenced the kinds of education the schools offered, the modes of pedagogy they delivered, and the overall life of both schools. Teachers and their work also served as models to the students. To understand vocational education in China, it is necessary to understand the content of the classes (curriculum), the ways it is delivered (pedagogy), and the ways in which the schools modeled employment to students via the ways they managed teachers as employees. Just as the schools needed to accommodate different categories of students (rural, urban, migrant, second-generation migrant); so, too, did they need to manage different categories of employees (state and private, permanent and temporary). These different categories and different modes of management constituted a complex, ongoing form of mediation, where the schools tacked back and forth between two kinds of logics—capitalist and socialist—two kinds of labor disciplines, and two kinds of teaching methods. But I argue that these logics were encapsulated in a system that was missing an overarching educational logic because of a curricular process known as "devocationalization." To return to the question raised in the Introduction about why students spend hours and days sleeping in class, I argue that both schools lack what anthropologist David Slater called a coherent center, a "pattern of legitimate governance" and "reason to be in school" (2010, 155) that makes school life meaningful and, in the case of the VE students in Nanjing, that gives them a reason to stay awake in class.

The Labor of Teaching:
Capitalist and Socialist Labor Disciplines

The teachers, school administrators, and middle-class parents I knew in China liked to use very high-minded language to talk about teaching as a moral activity. I was often told by a wide range of informants that the principles of education in China originate in the Confucian classics, are an extremely important aspect of a culture that reveres learning, and are grounded in students' respect for teachers and teachers' love for students.

In practice, however, I quickly discovered that like most jobs, teaching in China is actually governed by the contractual relationship between teachers and the schools that employ them. Teachers at the Bridge School were hired on two different kinds of contracts: permanent (*bianzhi*) and temporary (*feibianzhi*), a distinction the teachers themselves mentioned whenever we first met and which mapped precisely onto the different categories of employment for which the Bridge School students were preparing. The school thus also mirrored the mix of state and private employment that exists in many Chinese workplaces: public (state sector, *danwei*) and private (contractual) employees working side by side in the same institution or physical location, often receiving different sets of benefits and rates of pay and subject to entirely different workplace disciplines.

The Bridge School's permanent teachers worked for the state sector and held iron rice bowl positions with the Nanjing Municipal Infrastructure Bureau, like the city's bus drivers, sewer workers, and highway construction engineers; these positions were the structural equivalent of the subway system jobs where some of the students hoped to be assigned after graduation. All of the school's administrators and several of the most senior teachers held these permanent positions, many of whom had several decades of teaching experience. Most of these people were in their fifties and approaching retirement; most taught basic classes (Chinese, math, politics) rather than the particular vocational skills classes that varied each year.[2]

Like most employees in the Chinese state sector, these teachers were able to retain their jobs regardless of performance, a situation the Bridge School's Principal Huang mentioned ruefully whenever we discussed teaching and teachers. "The students fill out teacher evaluation forms every semester," he said. "And we take them very seriously. If permanent teachers are not teaching well, I can't fire them or ask them not to teach. All I can do is try to supervise them better and urge them to be more conscientious in their teaching. This can be extremely difficult." He did acknowledge, however, "Many of our permanent teachers have university degrees in education and care a lot about the students. And they're here at the school all day, every day. They communicate with the students and get to know them well, which is very important for good teaching."

In contrast, the contract teachers, who formed the majority of the teaching staff, were hired from outside and were paid 30 RMB per fifty-minute class.[3] Vice Principal Wu explained that these contract teachers had some advantages over the permanent staff: "They don't have to come to school every day and actually make more money per class. For the permanent teachers, we have to get to school at 8:00 every day and leave at 4:00. If you average it out, we make only about 8 RMB per class, much less than they do." The major disadvantage for contract teachers was the precariousness of their work: they were assessed on their performance every semester and could be terminated at any time.

The permanent teachers received a bundle of socialist-era-type benefits from the city (their *danwei*), including free lunches every day,[4] gifts of cooking oil and other foodstuffs at Chinese New Year and other major holidays, housing allowances, and guaranteed pension benefits (Walder 1986). The promise of the socialist redistributive economy still held for these workers. In exchange for their low salaries, the permanent staff had exceptionally stable jobs and futures. Because they could not be fired, these teachers could be disciplined only through moral authority, via a Mao-era paternalistic relationship; the principal managed them through appeals to doing the right thing and exhortations to be good role models for the youth in their care.

The contract teachers, however, were different. In exchange for their higher wages, these teachers were subject to market disciplines and the constant possibility of being fired. Many were also on the constant lookout for better jobs and better pay and had no loyalty to the school. For many of these instructors, teaching was merely the source of an hourly wage rather than a moral obligation. Although morality was ideologically constituted as being at the heart of teachers' relationships with students, for many teachers, the teacher-student relationship was entirely commodified.

This produced an interesting tension in the teachers' rooms at both schools. One group of employees' work was entirely disciplined as a moral project, because there were no alternative forms of discipline available. For the other group, however, morality was largely considered irrelevant for their job performance. Principal Huang therefore had to manage two different kinds of employees, and every fifty minutes the students bounced between two different kinds of teachers and instructional logics. One set of teachers was employed following a radically noneconomistic logic; they saw teaching as a moral process and related to their students as moral objects, in need of nurturing, pastoral care, and guidance. The other set followed an (almost) entirely economist logic, where students and classes were units, assessed through an instrumental cost-benefit analysis. They maximized their marginal utility through minimal class preparation time, contact with students, and teaching effort. The two systems existed in a kind of parallel universe. They shared the same physical space, and students sat in the same seats all day as teachers rotated in and out of the rooms over the course of the day, while the quality of this space rotated between socialist and capitalist logics. There were individual exceptions, of course; a few of the permanent teachers were terrible teachers, while some of the contract teachers were highly effective educators who were very popular with the students.

Occasionally, the principals at both schools resorted to making culturally based appeals to the contract teachers, especially in the middle of the semester, when these teachers could not be replaced easily if they quit or had to be fired for incompetence. These appeals were couched in highly formulaic culturalist language, such as, "Remember, here in China we teachers love our students, are diligent in our teaching, and are good role models for our students." A few of the contract teachers were quite susceptible to these kinds of pleas and worked harder to improve the quality of their instruction, but most of the poor-quality contract teachers did little to change their teaching practices when approached with these arguments. They were in their jobs only for the money and were planning to quit anyway as soon as a better opportunity arose.

Flexible Teachers, Flexible Workers

Teachers not only instructed students in work-related subjects; they also served as models for different forms of labor. The Bridge School and Canal School teachers, operating in very different environments, presented different kinds of models for their students.

The Bridge School

A few of the homeroom teachers (*banzhuren*) at the Bridge School were assigned from among the school's permanent staff. *Banzhuren* are an important educational category in China throughout primary and secondary education. They are the most important teachers in a Chinese child's life from first grade until the end of secondary school, for they have responsibility and oversight for each students' overall behavior, educational achievement, and even their social lives. *Banzhuren* liaise with parents and school administration about any problems with students' grades or behavior in any subject, handle daily discipline, and are in charge of the overall marking for students.[5]

Most of the Bridge School's *banzhuren* were contract staff hired from among a pool of retired former elementary school teachers. Since state-employed women in China generally retire at age fifty-five, most of the *banzhuren* were middle-aged women who had spent a lifetime in the *danwei* system and were working to supplement their state pensions. Several of these women had decades of experience as elementary school teachers, administrators, or party secretaries, and they often were assigned to teach the school's mandatory classes in politics, morality, or Chinese literature along with their homeroom duties. These women commanded great authority in their classrooms because of their age, experience, and the cultural status accorded to the position of the *banzhuren*. But as lifelong teachers of much younger children, many had some trouble adjusting to working with high school students. They generally received grudging respect from their students, who at the same time tended to chafe at what they saw as their teachers' tendency to infantilize them. The students did a lot of eye rolling behind these teachers' backs but never dared to confront them directly.

These women were at the top of the contract teacher hierarchy at the Bridge School, because as *banzhuren* they were generally on campus all day, every day. And although they were structurally part of the contract work system, they were lifelong products of the socialist *danwei* system. As both retired professional educators and homeroom teachers, they were completely fluent in the same language of morality, nurturance, and discipline as the permanent teaching staff and deployed this language—and forms of morality-based discipline—with the same ease as the full-time teachers. Except for their formal contract status, they were indistinguishable from the permanent teachers.

Most of the other contract teachers were much younger, and many were master's degree or PhD candidates at one of Nanjing's many universities. They were generally hired to teach part-time in one of the school's specialized vocational courses. Some of these teachers were so young that the only way to distinguish them from their students was that they were standing up in front of the classroom. These teachers were largely very inexperienced and tended to have few, if any, pedagogical skills. We noticed that many of the technical classes these teachers taught at the Bridge School followed a similar pattern: the teachers raced into the classroom moments before the bell rang, turned their backs to the students to face the blackboard, lectured nonstop for fifty minutes mostly with their backs to the students, then raced out the moment the class ended. For these teachers, who were paid only for the fifty minutes of the actual class period, time spent engaging with students outside class was time wasted. They were economic rationalists, maximizing their marginal utility by minimizing their time commitments to the students and the school. These teachers were also frequent no-shows, skipping class to attend interviews for better jobs or quitting midsemester because they had found better work. The students reported that they largely disliked these classes, finding them less comprehensible and more boring than any others.

For example, we spent one long day observing the gas company technical classes taught by Teacher Pei, a stern woman in her early thirties. Teacher Pei, we learned, was a professional engineer who was inexplicably moonlighting at the Bridge School one day a week for extra income; to accommodate her schedule, the administration had scheduled all of the students' gas company-related technical classes back-to-back on the same day. The students therefore sat through six straight hours of Teacher Pei's lectures without, one student assured me, understanding a single word. Teacher Pei was notorious for teaching from a particularly dense textbook that none of the students had bothered to purchase. It was full of charts and graphs and formulas; the content was entirely beyond my comprehension, and the students I asked all simply shrugged when I asked for help. Several of the students later told me that the material was vaguely related to topics such as designing gas-powered appliances, building natural gas tunnels, and the workings of the internal-combustion engine.

I later learned that different students in the class had worked out quite elaborate strategies to make it through the weekly six-hour Teacher Pei marathon (generally held every Friday). For example, some of the young men had arranged an all-night poker game in the boys' dorm every Thursday night, so they arrive in class exhausted on Friday morning, which would then facilitate their sleeping in class all day. Another young man, who appeared to be studying diligently, had worked out a special rental agreement with a local bookstore: every Friday morning he would stop at the store and rent a science fiction pot-boiler for fifty cents (*wu mao*), read it all day propped up behind a notebook, then return it on his way home. Other students had worked out a very elaborate folding system to turn their school uniform jackets into fairly comfortable pillows, a kind of fabric origami they had figured out in the classroom.

Teacher Pei's class was an extreme example, but the Bridge School students generally seemed to use the technical class periods as opportunities to catch up on their sleeping, texting, listening to (pirated) music downloads, and reading novels and comic books/manga. We also found that there was a fair amount of movement between classes during these class periods; because many of the contract teachers made little effort to learn the students' names or recognize their faces, some of the students would simply leave and wander into other classrooms during those class times to chat with friends.

The contract teachers thus provided an interesting model for the students. The school principals lamented the ways that the contract teachers displayed little "love" for their students and were poor role models of the traditional Chinese educators' virtues of patience, diligence, and loyalty, all qualities that were indeed generally demonstrated by the full-time staff. Yet the contact teachers, as employees, much more closely resembled the kinds of laborers that most of the students would become upon graduation: hourly workers in the service economy. These teachers were flexible workers (Harvey 1990; E. Martin 1994) who had to manage their time, energy, and resources carefully; they were always on the lookout for better opportunities and had little loyalty to their employers. The students understood that these teachers "jumped feeding troughs" to better jobs,[6] sometimes for better teaching gigs, sometimes to entirely different industries (many, after all, had highly portable technical and engineering skills). Although the students were frequently bored to tears in these classes, they also appreciated the flexibility of their contract teachers and the model of flexible labor they unwittingly provided.

The Canal School

Unlike those at the Bridge School, the teachers we met at the Canal School were all on temporary contracts. The sole exception was the acting principal, Secretary Ji, who, as his title indicates, was one of the Communist Party secretaries within the *Dianda* Secondary Vocational Education division. Ji, notably, was a bureaucrat rather than a professional educator, a midlevel employee in the enormous state bureaucracy of *Dianda*. His job entailed overseeing both the daily operation and the closing down of the Canal School, as well as the ongoing operation of at least one other *Dianda*-owned vocational school in Nanjing (we never learned how many other schools he was responsible for).

An affable and popular man among the students, Secretary Ji, like many midlevel career bureaucrats, was naturally conservative (Weber 1978); he was leery of making any possibly controversial decisions, particularly in the months leading up to the Beijing Olympics. Although he was not on campus every day, Secretary Ji was the reason for my limited access to students and classes at the Canal School, for he decided it was safest to restrict my presence in the school during school hours. He did allow me to hang out with the bookkeeping and computer tech students on weekends and after school. The graduate student assistants observed classes (and I observed some), and Secretary Ji and I met for occasional lunches together off campus. Because the campus was about to close, there were few classes actually held at the Canal School, and, unlike at the Bridge School, we met relatively few teachers there.

Because Secretary Ji, the Canal School's only administrator, was not always present on campus, daily authority at the school resided in each class's *banzhuren*. These homeroom teachers therefore had much more authority at the Canal School than their counterparts did at the Bridge School. Teacher Zheng, the bookkeeping course *banzhuren*, was thus much more prominent in the lives of the Canal School bookkeeping students than any of the equivalent Bridge School homeroom teachers. A retired former clerical employee of China's vast National Railway system, Teacher Zheng had worked for the Canal School for only a few months when we first met her.

A stout woman in her late fifties with frizzy, permed hair, Zheng had taken the part-time bookkeeping course *banzhuren* job to supplement her state pension after her mandatory retirement from her state-sector job. Somewhat to our surprise, we found that the Canal School saw Zheng's lack of educational credentials as an advantage rather than an impediment when they hired her to run the bookkeeping class. Her decades of experience in the conservative state railroad bureaucracy had made her a firm believer in the power of rules and discipline, in the moral systems elaborated by the Chinese Communist Party, and in unquestioned obedience to institutional hierarchies. She was, in effect, a bit of an anachronism: a proud product of the socialist era who firmly believed in the moral virtues of the socialist system and the Communist Party and who fully intended to drill these beliefs into her young charges. The seventeen-year-old students in the Canal School bookkeeping course, perhaps not surprisingly, loathed her.

Teacher Zheng had been hired to replace a much younger man who had served as the homeroom teacher for the bookkeeping class during their previous, freshman year.[7] During that previous spring semester one of the young women in the class, who had been living in the school dorm at the time, began a flirtation with a man she had met online and then agreed to run off with him. "He was a lot older," one of the students told us later in a delighted, scandalized whisper. "He was almost twenty-two! And he was a *society* [*shehui qingnian*] guy!"[8] The student was gone from the dorm for several days before any of the dorm managers or her homeroom or other teachers noticed her absence; her parents were informed, and they then called the police. The young woman was located a few days later in a city not far from Nanjing and returned to her family. She was expelled from the Canal School, and the dorm manager and the *banzhuren* teacher, both contract employees, were fired. Teacher Zheng was brought in at the start of the following school year to restore discipline, order, and morality to the girls of the bookkeeping class, a task she took on with alacrity. After all, Zheng reminded us, the bookkeeping girls still had four more years of study before they graduated, and she was planning on staying with them—and keeping her supplementary income—for that entire time. She therefore had plenty of time to whip them back into moral shape, correcting any potential corruption that may have been caused by their proximity to a debased classmate the previous year.

Teacher Zheng accomplished this by focusing her pedagogic efforts on managing the students' bodies (Foucault 1977). She began the school year by posting a list of class rules, including a policy of "no makeup, no jewelry, no nail polish, no high heels, no short skirts, no shorts, no permed hair." She lined the students up every morning to inspect their nails and clothes for cleanliness and neatness. Students who were caught swearing or misbehaving in class were required to write self-criticisms, a classic socialist-era technique intended to teach miscreants to reflect on the errors of their ways and how they affect the collective group (Judd 2002). Although she did not teach any of her own classes, Zheng stood outside the classroom watching the students through the doorway during their regular classes, glowering if they sprawled in their seats, crossed their legs, or played with their mobile phones during class. One of my graduate student assistants unknowingly referenced Foucault's (1977) panopticon when she marveled at this level of surveillance in her field notes, writing: "Teacher Zheng reminds me of a jailer."

After school the students howled in frustration at this treatment; ranting about Teacher Zheng was one of their favorite after-school and online chat room topics. Zheng, however, staunchly defended her approach when we spoke with her outside class. First, she reasoned, the class enrolled thirty-nine girls and only two boys. Girls, she informed us, are much harder to manage than boys, because if left to their own devices, they can get into terrible trouble. They therefore require strong guidance and discipline. Although she never said so directly, Zheng was of course implying that girls can cause sexual trouble, referring to the possibility of their finding boyfriends or even running off with one, as their classmate had done the previous year. The Canal School girls were especially in need of management, she said, because their parents are lax: "Many come from broken homes or are living in the dorms far from their families, and it's up to me to keep an eye on them." Along with serving in loco parentis, Zheng felt that their future work as bookkeepers required special moral training: "These girls will get jobs handling other people's money. They have to be much more moral than the average person. If I don't discipline them now, they could get in a lot of trouble later." Although we specifically asked, Teacher Zheng never elaborated on the logic that tied her moral argument together: how her forbidding makeup and crossing legs at the knee somehow inculcated a financial probity that would help these students in the future, when they would most likely work as cashiers (cf. Otis 2011).[9]

Surprisingly, in spite of their animosity to Teacher Zheng, the students agreed with her on this point and echoed her reasoning: because they literally were going to handle other people's money, bookkeepers (or in reality, cashiers, the job they were most likely to get after graduation) must be more moral than the average person. Their problem was with the grooming aspect of Zheng's logic, for they did not agree that wearing mascara or earrings necessarily led down a slippery slope to possible immoral financial behavior on the job. Born in the 1990s, they did not agree with her unquestioned logic that connected consumption and simple displays of fashion with lack of control in all domains and thus immorality and "easy" sexuality. This tension between Teacher Zheng and her students around perceived embodied displays of (im)morality continued all year.

Other contract teachers in the Canal School bookkeeping course tended to be a revolving door; the students frequently never knew if a class would be held or not, which teacher would show up, or if the scheduled teacher had quit and a replacement had been hired. The exceptions were the few retirees on contract, like Teacher Zheng and Teacher Meng, their Chinese teacher. Like many of the Bridge School instructors, Teacher Meng was a retired middle school teacher who was supplementing his pension by teaching Chinese (*yuwen*) in several vocational schools around Nanjing for 30 RMB per hour. A gentle man in his mid-sixties, Teacher Meng was a former sent-down youth.[10] He had spent many years in the countryside during the Cultural Revolution and had only returned to his native Nanjing in the mid-1980s. In spite of his many years of teaching experience, Teacher Meng had terrible trouble controlling the bookkeeping students, who took advantage of his sweet nature to turn their Chinese class into a free-for-all. The students explained their chatter in class, back talk to the teacher, and general rowdiness as signs of affection for Teacher Meng. Whenever he stopped class, frustrated with their behavior, the students clamored to tell him that they were only back talking and teasing him because they liked him.

They had no such explanation for their behavior in their other classes, where they tended at best to ignore and at worst to taunt their other teachers, who constituted an ever-changing parade of new faces during the school year. The bookkeeping students urged my graduate research assistants to attend their math and English classes so they could see for themselves that these teachers raced into and out of class and taught with little attention to the students or the material. At one point the bookkeeping students actually bet two of my graduate assistants that several of the teachers were so unfamiliar with the composition of their classes that they would never even notice that the grad students were in attendance, a bet that the grad students indeed lost when they sat in on the Canal School's math, geography, and English classes. The students made a game out of how bad the quality of teaching could get.

Curricula, Teaching, and the
Problem of "Devocationalization"

Along with coping with several different styles of teaching and teachers, the VE students at both schools had to tack back and forth between attending very different types of classes every day. But only after spending several months observing classes did we come to understand that the students' boredom and their concomitant sleeping through class every day was not just an outcome of poor teaching skills. It was also built into the curriculum.

We clarified this when we spoke one day with contract Teacher Dai, a master's degree student in electrical engineering at Nanjing Normal University who taught the engineering principles class to the Bridge School's construction management students. Unusual for a contract teacher, he was willing to hang around after his class one day to explain to us how his class worked: "The students here are using the same textbooks I used as a third-year university undergrad majoring in engineering," he said. "I thought the books were hard then, and I'd already graduated from regular high school and was halfway through my undergrad studies. And the material only made sense to me after I had done years of classes on the topic, *and* after I got a job working on a construction site and seeing how these principles were actually used in putting together buildings. There's no way these kids are going to understand this stuff."

Among educators, the technical term for this problem is "devocationalization" (Schulte 2013; see also Gewurtz 1978). It means "moving aims and motivations not directly related to professional training to the fore" (Schulte 2013, 9) and is intended to make VE classes more academic and less focused on vocational training. Generally, the goal is to make voc ed less vocational and therefore more attractive to students, parents, and society as a whole, because academic study is considered more desirable than vocational training. This is by no means a problem confined to the Bridge School, or indeed even to China, nor is it a recent problem in Chinese vocational education. Schulte and Gewurtz both note a similar tendency among early advocates of vocational education in China, who even as early as the start of the twentieth century found a tendency for vocational schools to skew their curricula away from practical courses and skills training toward theory and academic content to appease students and parents who wanted more academic training and less focus on strictly job-related skills (Gewurtz 1978; Schulte 2013).

We noticed that devocationalization took place in different ways at both schools. At the Bridge School, highly technical material was taught entirely through theory, without any labs or hands-on components. For example, the construction management program was trying to teach electronics and circuitry without any actual electronics; students learned entirely from diagrams. The teacher admitted that she herself would never have been able to learn any of the material she was teaching without practicing it at the same time in a lab, but no such hands-on material existed at the school. Some VE schools, she explained, either have the resources for on-site labs or have agreements with factories to bring the students in to observe the equipment in use, but the Bridge School did not have any such agreements in place.

Additionally, the material taught in the Bridge School vocational classes did not appear to be linked to the jobs the students were going to be hired to do, and the material was pitched at a level far beyond the actual technical requirements of the students' eventual job descriptions. For example, students in the gas company preparation course studied the design and construction of natural gas pipelines, gas-powered appliances, and engine design. Upon graduation, however, the young men in the course typically got jobs delivering gas canisters for the small, local gas companies found in every Nanjing neighborhood, while the young women were employed as receptionists and clerks at these same small shops. These disconnects—between vocational training and eventual job placements—held across the Bridge School curriculum. The subway prep students studied the design of subway cars, the design and construction of subway tunnels, and the logistics of subway line scheduling. After graduating, the male students were generally assigned jobs as platform and station guards, while the female students sold tickets and cleaned the stations. A few might eventually gain jobs as subway car drivers or find clerical work in the municipal transit system, but none could aspire to the kinds of technical/engineering jobs their training included, for those jobs were reserved for university graduates with engineering degrees.

This was also true for students in the less technical courses. Students in the Bridge School's tourism course, for example, spent their vocational class time memorizing tour books about well-known tourist destinations in Nanjing. Although the students and one of their teachers visited some of these sites once or twice a year, their training as tour guides was based entirely on their ability to recite verbatim the content of the tour books. Their teachers hoped that after graduation a few would know enough about the sites to pass a standardized exam to become official tour guides; most graduates, the teachers conceded, would instead find jobs as sales clerks at shops near tourist locations. The content of their classes was thus exceptionally academic—devocationalized—but poorly linked to preparation for actual vocational needs.

Devocationalization also took place at the Canal School, although on a different register. Because the Canal School granted a five-year *dazhuan* (3+2) degree, we—and the Canal School students—assumed it would offer its students a stronger curriculum and more training than the three-year *zhongzhuan* Bridge School vocational programs; we were surprised at how little actual content was imparted to the students, particularly in the bookkeeping course that we observed closely over the school year.[11]

Although the course was titled "accounting" (*kuaiji*), during the year we observed classes, the students did not seem to study any accounting or bookkeeping principles or practices. Rather than upscale their technical training to make it more theoretical and academic, as at the Bridge School, Teacher Zheng and the other Canal School teachers devocationalized this course by downscaling the vocational skills and knowledge and focusing instead on embodied disciplines. The vocational training we observed consisted of teaching students how to use the abacus and how to speed-count large stacks of bills. Both skills were equally outmoded in Chinese businesses in 2008; abacuses had long been replaced by calculators, cash registers, and computers, and although businesses may have to deal in very large amounts of cash,[12] most businesses used special cash-counting machines for large transactions. We were thus struck by how much of their technical training was spent raising their speed at outdated technology that required little cognitive effort or skill; their vocational education was instead focused on raising their dexterity.

The students were tested regularly on both their abacus and cash-counting skills; their speed and accuracy were measured according to standard exams and preparations for district- and city-wide competitions. Other than performing at competitions, the single benefit of improved speed at these tasks was to help them pass standardized speed tests administered by a state licensing agency,[13] but the students and teachers all frankly admitted that passing these tests conferred no advantages to students in the job market. Good scores on the abacus and cash-counting tests were therefore largely meaningless to potential employers; they were merely more numbers that accrued as additional forms of numeric capital in China's endless system of counting and ranking. Not only were the students disciplined according to particular gender norms, but teaching regimes were reduced to forms of surveillance, and the vocational training they received was predicated on an embodied form. Unlike the Bridge School, where technical training was devocationalized in the form of advanced theoretical learning without any hands-on training, the Canal School bookkeeping course moved in the opposite direction by stripping vocational training of both theory and marketable skills and focused instead on manual dexterity in archaic technologies.

Holes in the Center:
Classroom Behavior and Teachers' Authority

Devocationalization is a particular problem because it leaves a vacuum at the center of the students' education: where skills teaching should occur, students were learning little that is useful. Yet this was not the only vacuum in their learning. Another significant hole was assessment and exams. The regime of numeric capital means that exam scores motivate most K–12 education in China. All levels of schooling in China, from primary school through junior middle school, and especially regular senior high school, is driven by exams. But once students have failed the HSEE and entered vocational schools, exams are largely irrelevant. Although there were various internal (classroom and school-wide) exams at both the Bridge and Canal Schools and students did receive class marks, these grades did not seem to count for anything. As far as we could tell, no student ever flunked out of either of the schools, regardless of how poor their performance was in class.

My favorite example of how little relevance test scores held for vocational students was at lunch one weekend with the bookkeeping students. Zhang Zhigang casually mentioned that the previous week he had scored a 9 on a math test. "Really? Out of 10?" I asked. "No, out of 100," he replied with a shrug. He told us that he was contemplating taking a make-up test to improve his score but that it might be too much trouble (*tai mafan*) and he would perhaps not bother.

Students who test poorly on the schools' internal exams may stand to lose their teachers' recommendations for future internships and jobs, but since these counted for less and less every year, students were increasingly unconcerned about their academic performance. Thus, similar to Slater's (2010) findings in his incisive study of a working-class high school in Tokyo, between the problem of devocationalized content and the lack of exams as motivating factor, there was little left in the two vocational schools to motivate studying.

Language Skills and Standardization: Learning to Serve

Some of the teachers recognized that the service jobs for which the students were training required particular kinds of skills that differed from the technical skills (purportedly) taught in the vocational courses in the school's various streams, but the question of what those skills were and how to impart them was an ongoing problem. Interestingly, this question came up in relation to language, not to specific technical skills.

The Bridge School

About halfway through the academic year, the Bridge School started a special Mandarin (*Putonghua*) class for the students in the two subway prep courses. Teacher Yang, a retired former elementary school teacher who was also the homeroom teacher of the construction management course, was assigned to teach. She explained that the Nanjing Transit Office, which managed the Nanjing subway system and would be the eventual iron rice bowl employer of the top students in these two classes, had directed the school to offer a Mandarin class, because Transit Office officials felt that school's graduates' Mandarin was not standard (*biaozhun*) enough. This surprised me, since I spoke *Putonghua* with the students every day. I asked Teacher Yang for clarification. "Some of the subway class students are going to be hired by the city subway system as service workers, and they have to have a high level of civility [*wenming*], but their Mandarin is far from standard," she explained. "This is especially a problem among the rural students, who have heavy rural accents."

Yang was implying that the students' supposedly uncouth rural backgrounds were embodied in their accents, which had to be corrected before they could be ready to work among the urban public who would be the future customers of Nanjing's showcase subway system. The city could dress these students in nice uniforms and train them to perform their service jobs, but, she implied, if their accents were still rough and grating to urban residents' dainty sensibilities, it would reflect badly on their employer, the city government. If the school wanted to continue to guarantee iron rice bowl employment for its graduates, it had to produce students with the skills the city demanded. The city now demanded language standardization as a way to deemphasize the students' rural backgrounds, increase their "civility," and thus make them more palatable for interactions with urban commuters (Anagnost 1997; Dong 2009).

In fact, the two subway prep classes did have an unusually high percentage of students from rural areas, particularly from the rural areas immediately surrounding Nanjing. Students, teachers, and Bridge School administrators all attributed this to rural students' tendencies to study harder and score better on standardized admission tests (in this case, the HSEE) than urban students (Kipnis 2001). But as is common across urban China, rural youth are also all naturally assumed to be lower quality (*suzhi*) than urban youth and to have lower "civility" (*wenming*) levels (Anagnost 1997, 2004; Judd 2002; Woronov

2004; Yan Hairong 2008). I was surprised to find that both the school and the Nanjing Transit Office subscribed to a stereotyped language ideology that also simply assumed that rural students had low "quality," which would then be reflected and embodied in poorer Mandarin skills (Dong 2009).[14]

Once the Mandarin classes started, however, I was even more surprised to find that Teacher Yang focused less on the students' pronunciation than on their fluency. Each student had purchased a standard *Putonghua* textbook for the class, yet Yang did not spend any time using it or on focusing on the specific phonemic areas that marked the students as nonstandard speakers, as ruralites, or as natives of Jiangsu Province. Instead, Teacher Yang made them talk, fast. All her teaching and grading was done on the students' ability to give very fast three-minute speeches about themselves, their hobbies, and their interests. I spent excruciating hours listening to students stand up in front of the room and give stopwatch-timed talks in *Putonghua* about the NBA (the boys' favorite topic), local shopping centers (the girls' favorite topic), and Taiwanese pop star Jay Chou (Zhou Jielun, everyone's favorite). Yang mercilessly corrected their "um's" and "uh's," their rambling sentences, and their going off on tangents. "This is important," she said when I questioned her pedagogic focus; "this is what makes them good Mandarin speakers." For Teacher Yang, Mandarin ability was defined as narrative fluency, not as standard pronunciation, linguistic rhythm, or clearly pronouncing tones—all of which were the content stressed in the students' textbooks. Her directives to the students were clear as she barked out orders: Stop saying "um" and "er." Stop repeating yourself. Say everything in the right order. Tell a story. Say something about yourself. Be original. Don't repeat yourself. Faster. Faster. Faster.

"What about all the other students?" I asked. "Shouldn't they get Mandarin classes, too?" Yang scoffed in reply. "The transit students are going to be service workers [*fuwu hangye*]. All the other classes are just workers [*gongren*]. It doesn't matter if they can speak standard Mandarin or not."

Actually, Teacher Yang put her finger on something very important about the relationship between vocational education and employment. In fact, *all* the Bridge School graduates will be service workers in the sense that they will not be industrial or agricultural workers; virtually all of them will find tertiary-sector jobs that require interacting in some way with the public. But the vast majority will not *serve* customers in the sense that Otis (2011) explains in her excellent study of the labor disciplines at an international luxury hotel in Beijing.

Otis describes the ways that employers in internationally managed luxury hotels have to train Chinese employees in the Western, capitalist concept of service; none of the employees began work at the hotel already knowing the feminized so-called soft skills of service: smiling, making eye contact, anticipating customers' needs, and the exquisitely fine-grained attention to customers' desires that high-end global service work now requires. Service workers have to be carefully and explicitly trained to "physically enact new modes of comportment, expressions and perception" (Otis 2011, 80); this is not a natural part of the culture or history of the Chinese working class, nor does it go unchallenged at work by local embodied practices (cf. Hanser 2008). For Teacher Yang and the Nanjing Transit Office who mandated this language class, standard Mandarin was a proxy for an entire service mentality. The ability to narrate a story of the self, quickly, smoothly, and in the standard form of the national dialect is training in a technology of the self, a form of the conduct of conduct (Foucault 1991) specific to those who will be serving Nanjing's middle-class clientele (cf. Hoffman 2010).

The remaining students were not seen as requiring this kind of training because, according to Teacher Yang, they will graduate and become "workers." Her choice of the word *gongren* is extremely telling, although in some ways her use of the term was sociologically and historically inaccurate. *Gongren* does mean "worker," and the Bridge School students will become workers after they graduate, rather than bosses, professionals, or even farmers. But historically in China *gongren* has referred to workers in the sense of the industrial proletariat who were the ideological and political backbone of the Chinese revolution and the Communist Party. But when Teacher Yang said that most of the Bridge School students will be future *gongren*, she did not mean they will be the future proletariat of China, and by no means did she imply that they will have a privileged relationship with the ruling party after they graduate. Instead, she meant that they will be precarious workers and have jobs with all the precariousness of the service economy. Those students who were not assigned permanent, secure work in the state sector, as the subway class graduates would be, were just workers in the sense that they would merely labor at a job; they would not *serve* a clientele.

All of the remaining Bridge School students (those not in the two subway prep classes) will eventually seek work in the private job market, but without having received any training in how to become an actual service worker in Otis's sense of the term—they were not be trained in how to "serve" others, how to present themselves as service deliverers, to anticipate needs, to smile and emote appropriately (Hanser 2008; Hochschild 2003; Otis 2011). Nor would they become workers in the Marxist/Maoist sense of the working class, the proletariat with consciousness, an industrial base, and the leadership of the nation. For

Teacher Yang, the word *gongren* ironically became the term for those who were released to find their own way on the bottom rungs of the privatized urban economy; for her, "service" workers were those in the protected socialist sector.

As I observed additional classes at the Bridge School, I noticed that there were no other efforts made to teach the students how to serve in the sense of providing the kinds of service Otis (2011) described. Instead, preparations for entering the service sector were entirely restricted to skills training as defined by the technical skills of the vocational courses, which was devocationalized. One particularly interesting example where I thought the students might have been taught some service-related skills was in the Bridge School's construction management course's English class, which used a textbook called *English for the Service Industry*. When I observed this class, however, I found the students using a ten-year-old textbook that defined "service" as confrontation and conflict escalation, an approach straight out of the socialist-era definition of service provision, just as Hanser described among the service workers she knew in a socialist-sector department store in Harbin. As Hanser (2008) notes, during the Mao era, service work was considered bourgeois, and employees in service-type jobs (such as counter staff in the retail sector) were as a result hostile and aggressive to their customers.

The textbook required students to memorize helpful English-language sentences, including "We are going to have to charge you extra for that," "That is not included in the price," and "No, we will not give you a refund." One day I watched two students act out an English-language dialogue from the textbook. A student posing as a restaurant patron complained: "This wine is corky." The waiter replied: "No, it's not. You're not used to drinking wine that is so dry." Clearly the concept of "the customer is always right," central in the training of service workers in contemporary Western capitalism, had not yet reached the English as Second Language (ESL) textbook industry for vocational students. In fact, this dialogue is the precise opposite of the content taught to service workers at the five-star international hotel Otis studied in Beijing (2011, 82), where managers use similar English-language skits and dialogues to train service workers to manage customers' dissatisfaction by catering to the hotel clients' every whim.

When I asked the students what they thought about this content, they merely shrugged. "We like learning English," the construction management students told me, "but it's way too hard. We can never remember any of this stuff anyway." Their kind and dedicated teacher, Teacher Chen, shook her head in frustration. "This book is so out of date. I'd like to teach them something they'd enjoy learning, but this text is what the school mandates. They're not getting anything out of it." "What about learning Mandarin?" I asked these students. "The subway students are learning it; shouldn't you?" I was met with looks of bewilderment. "Why should we bother? What use would that be?" the students replied with a shrug.

The Canal School

Like the Bridge School, the Canal School also added a special class in Mandarin halfway through the academic year; unlike the Bridge School, however, this class was not justified as important for the students' job skills. Instead, according to Secretary Ji, Mandarin was an important part of a project designed to make all of China more "civilized" (*wenming*) in preparation for the Olympics (Anagnost 1997). Speaking good Mandarin, he told me, would enable everyone to communicate universally across China. He intended that the Mandarin class would include training in "how to behave properly, including how to gesture, how to behave on the streets, and how to give foreigners a good impression when they're in China for the Olympics." He clearly saw standard Mandarin as a proxy for an entire habitus, linked to preparation for the global audience that would materialize for the upcoming Olympics (Bourdieu 1991). Somewhat to my surprise, Secretary Ji welcomed me to observe these classes myself.

The Canal School hired a young man in his early twenties to teach the weekly Mandarin class. Teacher Zhu was finishing a master's degree in journalism at Nanjing University and had scored very high on the national Mandarin Pronunciation Exam; he was therefore deemed eligible to teach the class in spite of having no teaching experience or credentials. The bookkeeping students were delighted to meet him, because in spite of his relatively short stature (he was about 5 feet 4 inches/164.5 cm), Teacher Zhu was quite good looking. The young women in the class teased him mercilessly. Teacher Zhu, however, was not amused.

"Student Number 4, stand up and read the first paragraph on page 6," Teacher Zhu would bark, addressing the students, unusually, by number rather than name. In response one of the other students would yell out in Nanjing dialect, "Teacher Zhu, do you have a girlfriend?" He ignored the comments and tried again. "Speak loudly and clearly. Don't forget to distinguish your 'l's' and 'n's.' Student 15, it's your turn." Another student would shout out, again in Nanjing dialect: "Teacher Zhu, when are you going to get married?" Eventually Teacher Zhu himself reverted to Nanjing dialect and would plead with the students to get back on task.

Zhu continued this method—calling students by number, having them read aloud, stopping them every few words to correct them, then nagging them in Nanjing dialect to stay on task—every week. The students thought this was hilarious, and they talked about their Mandarin class frequently when we got together for lunch and on weekends—partly because Teacher Zhu was so cute and so easily flustered by their teasing and partly because it was a class Secretary Ji allowed me to attend, which gave us something fun to talk about. "Teacher Wu, you can have free Mandarin lessons with us!" they shouted to me with excitement. "Do *you* think he's cute or that he's too short?" Interestingly, the students—who tended to speak only Nanjing dialect with each other—used only Mandarin for these conversations for me (it was, after all, our only common language). Yet they steadfastly refused to speak Mandarin with Teacher Zhu during their *Putonghua* class, feigning inability and lack of understanding.

For a few weeks the bookkeeping students loved to dissect their class experiences with me, until the class became simply too tedious to bother. They did only one activity in class: stand, read sentences from their textbook, be curtly corrected for their mistakes, then repeat. Teacher Zhu, unlike Teacher Yang at the Bridge School, focused entirely on phonetics and phonology, and their class consisted almost exclusively of him hectoring the students to clarify phonemes that are distinct in Mandarin but are indistinguishable in Nanjing dialect. The nasal sounds "n" and "l" are classic examples and in standard Mandarin are easy markers of Jiangsu natives; he made the students endlessly repeat sentences like "Grandma gave me a glass of milk" (*Nainai gei wo he yibei niunai*) to make them focus on the initial "n" sound. Eventually, the boredom of the class outweighed the entertainment value of teasing the teacher, and the students began to doze off.

Relations between Zhu and the students quickly soured and moved from jokes to outright insults. One day as Teacher Zhu nagged a student about one of her many errors, the student, unusually, stopped and asked him to explain why she was wrong. Teacher Zhu, annoyed at the interruption, said, "Turn to page 142. There's an explanation there of the theory behind this mistake. You can just read it yourself. I'm not going to bother to explain it to you because you won't understand it anyway. It's really all about the sense of the language, the rhythm, and the ways you're supposed to speak it to get it right, which none of you have. I don't think it's necessary for me to explain this, since you won't get it anyway." The students merely gazed back open-mouthed in astonishment. What the students had thought of as good-natured banter came to a stop, and Mandarin class, too, became a place to nap.

Teacher Zhu soon drifted off to his own studies and job hunting and simply stopped showing up for class. Mandarin class was canceled halfway through the semester, and the lessons in civilized behavior and communicating for the Olympics never materialized. Party Secretary Ji's goals of using the *Putonghua* class as a means to teach the students to behave properly backfired, and Mandarin for these students never became a proxy for the kinds of civilized habitus he wanted to develop. As with most of the Bridge School students, these students never learned to "serve," never learned the rigors of the standard dialect, and never learned to embody the right disciplines of high-end service labor.

Conclusion

Two kinds of disciplines operate simultaneously in the two vocational schools. One consists of the capitalist and socialist workplace regimes that manage teachers as employees; the other, of the multiple classroom disciplines that oversee the ways students are taught and behave in classrooms every day. These are deeply interconnected, helping demonstrate how two of the seemingly unrelated questions raised at the very beginning of the book are also deeply connected: Why do the students sleep in class all day? And how are the socialist and capitalist forms of production relevant in the lives of the schools and the students?

As the stories of life in the students' classrooms show, discipline in the two schools is partial, incomplete, and uneven. Although the bookkeeping course's Teacher Zheng may have tried to act like a jailer, unlike the panoptic discipline and surveillance Foucault (1977) described for industrial-model schooling, these young people are poorly disciplined, poorly behaved, and unruly (Zhan 2005). The schools are not the totalizing, homogenizing, and individuating systems that Foucault described in his early work. Teacher Zheng inspected her bookkeeping course girls for makeup and nail polish, yet the girls put on lipstick and earrings the minute the final bell rang at the end of the school day. They teased and taunted their other teachers. Students read comic books in class, played poker all night in the dorms, and slept in class all day. They were under only limited surveillance, including the discipline and surveillance of exams.

More extensive forms of discipline and surveillance were, in fact, unnecessary, because most of the production of these young people as subjects had already been accomplished at the moment of the HSEE, when they were sorted into vocational schools and made into working-class subjects. They were produced at that moment as "vocational students" with all the associated stigmas and limits on their upward mobilities. After that, there is little need for the schools to invoke additional discipline and surveillance.

For this reason, it is difficult to characterize their sometimes unruly behavior in school as resistance to the educational system, as in the case Paul Willis famously described in *Learning to Labor* (1977). Willis argued that the young working-class males he studied in England's industrial Midlands, the "lads," actively resisted the academic structures and cultures of schooling as part of a process of reproducing their gendered working-class culture. In Nanjing, however, these students are not products of an anti-education family culture nor an anti-school working-class culture. Of course they are clearly *not* striving to attain the "educational desires" of the kind Kipnis (2010) described—an active striving for grades, academic credentials, social "face" through educational achievement, and additional numeric capital—and in this respect they are indeed acting in contrast to the dominant Chinese academic culture. Although they passively resisted their teachers by sleeping through class and not studying for tests or participating in class, the vocational students in Nanjing were generally not actively producing a counterculture in opposition to their schools, and crucially, they did not have a *class* culture that they reproduced through resistance to school.

The more we observed classes and spoke with the students, their classroom behavior seemed less and less like resistance and more like a reasoned response to their educational situation. After they graduate, these students will be part of the working class, but they will not enter factory jobs. Yet both schools are structured on a model of funneling students into industry. The Bridge School is a holdover from the worker training schools of the era when China's industry was the focus of its urban economy, and *Dianda*'s vocational schools were originally designed on the same model. And while some of the course materials the students covered, such as the Bridge School's Mandarin class, was presented in an effort to prepare them for the kinds of service jobs they will eventually enter, there was very little actual instruction designed to teach them to be service workers. They were, in effect, being trained for neither the industrial nor the service economies.

Of course, this did not escape the notice of the students themselves. The students in the Canal School computer tech course explained this most eloquently just as they were getting ready to graduate after five years of classes. "Look," said Qian Ling, a soft-spoken young woman whom we interviewed just before she graduated, "during our first year, we all took studying seriously. In the second year, we started to talk in class, but it wasn't too bad. By the third year, we started to talk without worrying about anything. We just didn't care anymore. Every time a teacher yelled at us, we yelled back. We just started arguing with the teachers." Her classmate Tang Limei agreed: "We figured out by the second year that all that matters is the credential. It's just a piece of paper. We never learned anything in this program. We're supposed to have computer skills, but really we know almost nothing. I spent five years at the Canal School, and I don't have any confidence in really basic things, like making a good PowerPoint presentation or designing a simple website. So why should we bother paying attention in class? And the teachers they hire—they don't know much more than we do, or if they do, they have no idea know how to teach. So why should we respect them or listen to them?"

Indeed, over the course of the year, we noticed that the students at the Canal School were more defiant and disrespectful than their counterparts at the Bridge School. Their reasoning, they explained to us, had a logic. The students' inattention in class and mild rudeness to their teachers were natural reactions to their teachers' rudeness to them. If the teachers can't be bothered to show up on time, learn our names, and treat us politely, why should we be polite to them?

Sleeping in class, too, seemed less oppositional and more rational over the course of the year we observed classes. Recall that in the regime of numeric capital, schooling is part of an accumulative temporal regime, an ordering of time toward the future. Staying awake in class makes sense only when time spent on academic tasks is time invested toward accumulating more numeric capital (better test scores, more knowledge, academic advancement) for the future. For the vocational students, schooling is a nonproductive activity; they are not progressing toward anything except a credential that is not linked to their classroom performance. Time in school is not time invested. Studying is not time used toward a productive goal or personal progress. Why stay awake?

The problem of youth caught up in nonproductive temporal regimes—or, as adult observers frequently call it, "wasting time"—is not at all confined to vocational students in China. Many anthropologists have examined a growing gap between normative accumulation strategies and young people's ability to progress toward the future, particularly in countries where economic contraction and structural adjustment limit economic possibilities for youth. Michael Ralph (2008), for example, looked at how a generation of unemployed youth "kill time" in Senegal through ritualized tea-sharing ceremonies while they fruitlessly seek jobs. Craig Jeffrey (2010) examined a new temporal category in India called "timepass" that describes the ways unemployed and underemployed young men fill their days. Although in China the ideology of numeric capital means that any hint of young people "wasting time" is still considered deeply aberrant, Jeffrey points out that growing numbers of youth around the world are caught in "cultures of limbo" (2010, 2) where time is not accumulative and how it is spent does not progress youth toward the future. As he notes, refugees, asylum seekers, incarcerated youth, and the very poor may all spend years of their lives "just waiting" (Bayart 2007; Jeffrey 2010; Mains 2007).

The question of how the vocational students in Nanjing spend their time in school cannot be divorced from either their class position or the structural limitations of their schools. These, too, have analogies across the globe. In an insightful study of a working-class high school in Tokyo, anthropologist David Slater (2010) discussed the class-sorting process in postindustrial urban Japan and looked at similar issues among the students in the high school he studied. The Japanese system works somewhat differently from China's, because rather than use a high-stakes testing system to sort youth into different secondary streams (vocational and academic), Japan sorts youth by funneling them into differently ranked high schools. Economically, Japan is far ahead of China in moving to a postindustrial economy, so much so that the "economic miracle" there has already peaked and collapsed, leading Slater to question the ways that the "systematic sorting and socializing of their children to fill the shifting bottom of its economic miracle has [already] unravelled" (2010, 140). Yet in Japan the schools' "compromised and often contradictory role in this process of sorting and selective socialization" into the low-end urban labor market has many similarities to what I observed in Nanjing (141).

Slater analyzed this problem as the "virtual meaninglessness" of school. Elite schools, he says, grant teachers the institutional authority to control their classes, but in the case of the working-class schools,

> neither the instrumental value of grades nor the academic orientations of students apply in [this case]. By definition, these students are those who failed to demonstrate such abilities and orientations—otherwise they would not be at Musashino [the working-class school] in the first place. This is combined with the virtual meaninglessness of an academic curriculum, leaving working-class high schools without any coherent center. Missing is the primary mechanism that establishes daily routine, motivates students, and helps teachers establish their authority around some model of orderly social control, some pattern of legitimate governance. When students have no reason to be in school, making their time in school meaningful is quite difficult. (2010, 155)

Between lack of training in any real vocational skills, actual curricular content, or exams that matter, the Nanjing vocational schools have lost their coherent center. There are no grounds for disciplinary control and no meaning for students. Why not sleep all day?

The problem of poor learning in these schools thus cannot be laid at the feet of the students, the teachers, the curriculum, or the administrators of the schools. At both the Canal and Bridge Schools the teachers and administrators asked me regularly how I thought they could improve their teaching and the students' learning; they wanted their students to do better and were deeply concerned about their students' educational outcomes. But the issue of how to improve vocational education, to make it more relevant, and to get the students to wake up for their classes is not merely a matter of tweaking the pedagogy or the curriculum or of better classroom discipline. It is clearly a systemic problem. In fact, arguably in their current classes the students *are* learning important skills for their future jobs as workers in the precarious service economy: How to be flexible workers, ready to "jump" to new jobs when the opportunity arises. How to tolerate long hours of tedium and capricious authority. How to amuse themselves with very limited resources. These might be the best possible skills for the kinds of jobs they might get upon graduation.

Finally, and perhaps most acutely, there is the problem of jobs. Vocational schools, by definition, are supposed to solve the problem of the school-to-work transition by providing students with skills they should be able to take directly to the job market immediately after graduation. While the Nanjing students do get jobs after graduation, the transition to work is not nearly as smooth as the schools promise it will be because of the complex status of the Chinese labor market, which is also caught in the transition between the socialist and capitalist modes of production. I take this up in Chapter 5.

4 Creating Identities

In private conversations with us, many teachers shook their heads about their students and sighed about their futures. One longtime Bridge School teacher, Teacher Yao, told us, "These kids don't have a lot of choices for the future, so they haven't thought through what they're going to do. They're just wasting time, hanging out in school [*hun rizi*]. Even their parents don't know what to do [*fumu ye meiyou banfa*]. Maybe it's because they didn't study well in the past and failed their exams that they have this attitude now, but they're very lax, with no plans and no goals. They haven't thought about anything, just think that in the end their parents will take care of them, so even if they do make plans, it won't matter. This isn't always true, but it leads them to not know what they need to do now to prepare for the future. It's a big problem."

WHEN I BEGAN DESCRIBING the vocational students and their schools to different audiences, especially outside China, one of the first questions I was asked was, What are the students' identities? I initially hesitated to respond, thinking that this question meant more to the person who asked it than it did to the students. "Identity" is a topic that preoccupies far more people in the West than in China. While the word itself does have a Chinese translation (*rentong*), this is a recent neologism that only a few highly educated Chinese would recognize and that even fewer would employ in daily use.

Yet during the year of observing classes in the two schools, I found that something like the students' identity was of significant concern to their teachers. Although they did not use the word "identity" specifically, these adults, and potential employers, were deeply interested in how the students described themselves, especially how they articulated their dreams and plans for their futures. The teachers put particular effort into trying to get the students to narrate a story of themselves that included their interests, desires, and plans. To the teachers' exasperation, however, the students were not very good at generating these life narratives. The story of the subway prep students' Mandarin class, where the students had to describe their interests over and over until their narratives took precisely the form their teacher expected, is one example of the teachers' efforts to get the students to tell a tale of who they are.

This raises some interesting questions. Why did the teachers place such emphasis on the students' ability to narrate a story about themselves and their future plans? Why was the students' ability to create these narratives seemingly so fraught? And what kinds of identities are possible for the students today, and why? These questions seem simple at first glance, but the answers were far from obvious. I found that I could not merely assume that each student had an identity that he or she only needed the space to express; in other words, that each simply needed to be "given a voice" as much educational research in the West assumes. Instead, there was a question in the vocational schools over what the nature of the self was and how that self should be expressed.

As anthropologist Lisa Rofel points out, expressing identity in China today has not been simply a matter of casting off the strictures of socialism to reveal true, authentic selves (2007, 6). Nor was it merely a straightforward process of getting the students to tell me—or anyone else—who they think they are; if it were, the teachers would not have spent so many anxious hours worrying about this. I have explored some of the ways the students have been constructed in the Chinese national imaginary as failures: as bad students and immoral people who deserve their fate of limited futures. I now turn to the complex question of the students' identities and at some of the things they have to say about themselves. The discourse of numeric capital assumes a normative life course of accumulation, a progressive movement into a planned and rational future. This, however, is not the students' life course. Rather than own a fixed and stable core of identity that they saw as rationally progressing from the present into a planned future via ever-accruing accumulation, the students were constructing a counternarrative, one not based on accumulation, progress, or numeric capital.

This was linked to their class position. Across China, the emergence of new identities is a complex process that, in anthropologist Mei Zhan's words, is a "partially constituted, and open-ended project" that is "entangled in relations of production and labor practices" (2005, 34; see also Anagnost 2004, 2013; Pun 2003; Rofel 2007). Identities cannot be divorced from the changing labor market or the complex transformation in the relations of production in which the students are entangled. Their ongoing production of identity is connected to changing class formations in China and to the students' position in the new working classes.

I begin with an approach based in Foucault's concept of governmentality, which locates identity as part of a larger governmental project of regimes of the self. This requires two steps: destabilizing the concept of a fixed, authentic self and then discussing the emergence of new, neoliberal subjectivities in urban China today around discourses of desire and choice. I then explore other modes of constructing identity, including language and native place. Here, too, the VE students tend to confound predictions about identity formation in China, for reasons again linked to the sorting mechanisms that stream the students into vocational schools and position them in the working classes.

Projects of the Self

The challenge to our commonsense understanding of identity as something everyone has and that can and should be expressed through narrative comes from scholars who follow Michel Foucault's writing on governmentality (Foucault 1991; Burchell, Gordon, and Miller 1991), particularly Nikolas Rose's work on regimes of selfhood (1996, 1999). For Foucault, government is defined as the "conduct of conduct," or the rationalities and techniques that shape the "government of the self and others" (1982, 220–221). In this perspective, government is productive rather than repressive. Power operates to produce subjects who are socially normal and who govern themselves to act morally and rationally within social and legal norms (Dean 2010). These norms are determined both by the state and a wide range of nonstate experts, including teachers, medical experts, and psychologists, whose professional training provides the credentials that certify them to judge what normal conduct is and help everyday people achieve normality.

Nikolas Rose (1996, 1999) extended and elaborated this theory by tracing the historical genealogy of the concept of the private self in Western thought. He focused on what he calls "regimes of the self" as a historical (rather than individual) phenomenon and how the idea of a self became normative in the industrial West. Rose's conclusion is that rather than an inner core that exists in all people awaiting expression, the self is produced through the kinds of technologies of conduct that Foucault described. These technologies are embodied in particular technical practices that produce people as individuals who freely make appropriate choices. "In liberal and democratic regimes, the government of the self and others has always been linked to a certain way in which 'free' individuals are enjoined to govern themselves as subjects simultaneously of liberty and of responsibility—prudence, sobriety, steadfastness, adjustment, self-fulfillment, and the like" (Rose 1996, 12).

Many China scholars have found the concepts of governmentality and regimes of the self useful approaches for understanding transformations in the nature of Chinese state power since the reform era (Jeffreys 2009). This approach directly counters a prominent strain in recent Western analyses of China that see the reform era as the retreat of the Chinese state, one that has enabled formerly repressed Chinese subjects to be free to express their "real" and "authentic" selves. Instead, Elaine Jeffreys and Gary Sigley, seminal writers on this topic, argue that from a governmentality perspective, "the socialist market economy does not signal a retreat of the state; it requires a powerful government that simply intervenes in different ways" (2009, 10). Zhang and Ong label this different kind of state intervention as "government at a distance," which they define as "an interplay between the power of the state and the powers of the self" (2008, 3). Part of China's contemporary governing strategy has been "to set citizens free to be entrepreneurs of the self" (2).

Yet setting citizens free to become entrepreneurs of themselves does not imply that the state has freed people to do whatever they choose in any domain. Instead, as Zhang and Ong note, "neoliberal principles of private accumulation and self-interest—expressed in profit making, entrepreneurialism and self-promotion—are not allowed to touch key areas that remain firmly under state control" (2008, 1). Thus, while new regimes of the self encourage self-expression and entrepreneurialism in *some* domains, there are strict limits to self-expression in others. The new "self" constructed in China is constrained in what he or she can say and where.

This approach to state power and the nature of the self in China has been contentious. Both Foucault and Rose intended their theories as descriptions of neoliberal Western societies (Rose 1993). This has generated a controversial question: Is China neoliberal? Several scholars have argued that China is not neoliberal in the Western sense and that neoliberalism characterizes neither policy nor ideology across all of China's diverse terrain (Kipnis 2007; Nonini 2008). By extension, these scholars claim (or imply) that a governmentality approach is not applicable to China, since governmentality was intended by Foucault as the study of the production of neoliberal subjects. If China is not neoliberal, ergo, the approach is not relevant.

I do not argue that China is fully neoliberal. The two vocational schools I studied are places where a complex mix of socialist, capitalist, industrial, postindustrial, and neoliberal policies and modes of production intersect, overlap, and compete. The state has clearly not retreated. The case of the vocational schools shows how state policy has sorted students into different academic streams, manages different kinds of schools as well as public- and private-sector types of employees, and creates the discourse of numeric capital. These intersections, however, do not render a governmentality approach to the study of emergent subjectivities inapplicable. Instead, as the reforms deepen, there is pressure for new kinds of subjects to emerge, particularly in urban areas where social and economic conditions are changing rapidly.

Two previous studies by Lisa Rofel (2007) and Lisa Hoffman (2010) are useful to consider, for they looked ethnographically at ways that young people in urban China are being pressured to conform to new social norms: in other words, how they are being formed as new kinds of subjects. Both authors argue that the reform era requires the production of new kinds of individual subjects who can act in their own self-interest and become entrepreneurs of the self (cf. Zhang and Ong 2008). They focused on two dimensions around which new urban subjects are being produced: "desire" (Rofel 2007; see also Farquhar 2002) and "choice" (Hoffman 2010).

I examine some of the ways the teachers tried to incite the vocational students to understand and express themselves as desiring, choosing subjects, in Rofel and Hoffman's sense of the terms. For the teachers, this meant getting the students to narrate their lives in terms of wishes, dreams, and future accumulation, as well as their plans for taking future responsibility for themselves. These efforts, however, were largely unsuccessful, for the students saw themselves differently.

Desiring Subjects

In her influential book *Desiring China*, Lisa Rofel described an emerging form of subjectivity in China, which she called the "desiring" subject, defined as an individual "who operates through sexual, material and affective self interest" (2007, 3). Rofel was seeking to understand a key transformation in urban China during the reform era, as people she knew stopped speaking of themselves in terms of their class position and class consciousness and began to express themselves in terms of their desires: for material goods, professional achievement, sexual experiences, and love and romance. In contrast to their earlier forms of political consciousness, she found among her informants a new importance of having "wide ranging aspirations, hopes, needs and passions" (4). For Rofel, the "desiring subject" is a privileged new kind of urbanite in

China who understands him- or herself as a person who, through a "wide range of aspirations, needs and longings," will usher in a new era of Chinese cosmopolitanism, ending Chinese socialist-era backwardness and isolationism, and bringing the nation into global prominence (5–6 passim).

There are two important things to note regarding Rofel's concept of desiring subjects. First, this transformation was not a casting off of socialism to find "true, authentic selves" (2007, 6) that had been repressed by socialism but a technology of government in Foucault's sense of the term whereby new subjects were produced through the discourse of desire. This was not a freeing of the subject as socialist power ceased operating on individuals but a redirection of power: "postsocialist power operates on the site of 'desire'" (ibid.). Desires, in other words, were not automatic or natural but had to be produced, then expressed appropriately, and they had the constant possibility of social judgment. People became "normal" cosmopolitan urban citizens by experiencing and expressing the right desires. The state is involved in multiple ways, including producing the discourse of desire, credentialing a range of experts who certify which desires are appropriate, and limiting desires to particular realms. People thus do not necessarily develop their desires in opposition to the state (5). Indeed, as Zhang and Ong (2008) point out, the new neoliberal subject is strongly regulated so that while expressions of desire are strongly encouraged for new material goods and professional ambitions, there is no concomitant freedom of expression in the political realm.

A second important point concerns the ways Rofel shows how this desiring subject is being created. She ethnographically examined telenovelas, museum displays, gay bars, and other sites where desire is being produced, normalized, debated, and regulated in urban China today. Schools and education were not part of her research, but the discourse of numeric capital fits well into her broader argument. Numeric capital is a normative discourse of desire, which produces subjects who have ambitions for better futures that they plan for by investing today in academic credentials. The state helps produce and normalize this desire. The vocational students, by definition, do not fit appropriately into this temporal narrative, for they are not investing in the right credentials in the present. This produces a "novel form of class inequality through the improper embodiment of desire" (Rofel 2007, 5), another way to explain how their class positions are linked to the ways they are rationally investing for the future.[1]

The clearest example of this was an exercise where the vocational school homeroom teachers asked their students to express their desires in writing. Most had the students use colored markers to write their dreams (*mengxiang*), desires (*yuanwang*), or ideals (*lixiang*) onto pieces of construction paper that were cut into various shapes (hearts, stars, rainbows), and then they taped the responses to classroom bulletin boards. We encountered exercises like this in every classroom at some point in the year at both schools. This surprised us, because the two schools were administered by different bureaucracies, and they therefore did not follow the same curricula. The exercise seemed to be something the teachers and administrators came up with on their own and shared among themselves rather than as a directive from higher authorities.

The following list gives an idea of the responses from two of the classes at the Bridge School to the question about their desires. For example, one of the Bridge School's subway prep classes was given the prompt "Our Dreams" (*Women de Mengxiang*). Anonymous responses, written on heart-shaped pieces of construction paper, were taped to a bulletin board on the back of the classroom:

- find a good job
- always keep my good friends from school
- be happy (*kuaile zhe*)
- travel
- be happy, find a good job
- love myself
- I hope we'll all find good jobs.
- strive to enter the subway system
- I want all of us (teacher, students) to be happy and to find good jobs.
- I want to be happy every day and stay friends 4ever ("4ever" written in English).

Next door, the tourism class completed a similar exercise at about the same time. Their homeroom teacher, Teacher Xia, asked the students to write their "ideals" onto one large piece of construction paper that she taped to the wall at the front of the classroom. Teacher Xia started this off herself by writing in large characters at the top of the paper: "I love you and hope your studying keeps improving!" (*Wo ai nimen, xiwang nimen xuexi jinbu!*) We were surprised by this, both because few of the other Bridge School teachers had contributed their own dreams or ideals to this class exercise and because we found the tourism class to be particularly unlovable. A small and unusually surly group of students, the tourism course students were the only ones at the Bridge School who had not welcomed us warmly when we arrived as researchers. Instead, when we first entered their homeroom class, they glanced up from their prone positions on their desks, snarled briefly, and went back to sleep; they were also the only students who refused to talk with us during the school year. We were therefore very interested to read what their ideals for the future might be. Teacher Xia, we learned, felt the same way. "I asked them to do this because I wanted to know what they were thinking," she sighed. "I thought that telling them that I loved them as their teacher and that I encourage their success would push them to study harder [*duo xuexi*]." The students who did write responses to the prompt, however, showed that at least a few among those who did the assignment did so with about as much seriousness as they did the rest of their studies:

*My Ideals (*Wo de lixiang*):*
- forever [in English]
- friendship and unity
- be myself [*zuo ziji*]
- go go! [in English]
- happy [in English]
- tomorrow is another day [in English]
- be self-aware [*zijue*]
- be happy [*xingfu*]

At the Canal School, Teacher Zheng conducted a similar exercise, asking the bookkeeping students to write their desires (*yuanwang*) on heart-shaped pieces of colored construction paper that she then taped to the back wall. In keeping with her management style, Teacher Zheng assigned grades to their responses. Each student therefore assiduously completed a heart and signed it in order to receive a grade.

Zheng started off. Her heart was larger than the others and taped to the top of the wall: "My desire is that all accounting [*kuaiji*] class students learn how to feel gratitude, that they study well, and that they have beautiful lives." Below hers, we recorded twenty-one of the students' responses to the prompt "Our Desires." This is how some of the students expressed themselves in their own words:

1. everyone around me is happy
2. that my grades get better, that I learn a lot, and that I get to eat yummy things
3. a happy life, a smooth path to graduation, and health
4. study well and improve; get better at walking [from the disabled student in the class]
5. not be extravagant: live a happy and carefree [*ziyou de*] life
6. have a happy five years at this school

7. get good grades and a good internship; eat yummy things; leave my footprints everywhere I go
8. my dream is to become a lawyer
9. be happy every day and graduate smoothly
10. be happy every day and travel to lots of different places
11. that all my friends are happy, healthy, have good fortune, and that their lives don't have a lot of trouble
12. to live a life like Han Geng does in Korea![2]
13. own a Porsche [from one of the male students]
14. own a sports car [from the other male student]
15. remember the good times and forget the bad ones
16. be happy, have a great day every day, and improve in my studies
17. be happy and healthy and own a computer
18. live a happy life, be with my family every day, and get everything I ever want! (Haha! I'm so greedy!)
19. grow up faster, have fewer frustrations
20. be rich, happy, and healthy and pass my math tests
21. get a new laptop

We noticed several trends after reading dozens of these responses in both schools. The majority of the students said they dreamed of happiness, finding a good job, keeping their high school friends forever, and being able to travel to exotic places. A few were silly ("see the sun rise in the west"; "live and let die" and "you only live twice"—some classes stuck to a James Bond theme), and a few were more poignant ("for my parents to be healthy and happy"). What surprised us was that in spite of the increasing materialism evinced in everyday life in urban China, few of the students said they dreamed of becoming rich; only two said they dreamed of owning expensive cars, and only one admitted to dreaming of becoming a movie star. None said they dreamed of love or romance, of marriage or families, or buying expensive homes. Perhaps these topics were too personal or sensitive to post on classroom bulletin boards. Yet most of their desires were almost touchingly simple: to find a job, own a laptop computer, eat lots of delicious food, be healthy. Rather than dream of a future of ever-accumulating numeric capital in the form of educational credentials, rising income, and material possessions, a majority said their desire was happiness.

This did not escape their teachers' notice, nor their criticism. When we asked the teachers about these exercises, they just shrugged. Vocational students, the teachers said, don't have any idea what their future will be. They thought that by asking them to write down what their dreams were, maybe the teachers could push them to think more about their plans. When we asked them how well they thought the exercise had gone, some teachers snorted in response. "They have no idea what they want," one Bridge School teacher said. "Be happy. Eat good food. That's all they can think of. They're just like little children."

When we asked the students what they thought about this exercise, they, too, shrugged. Most said they did not find it particularly interesting or fun, except, perhaps, the part about cutting up the construction paper. They neither saw this as an opportunity to express their "real" selves or say what they "really think," nor did they think of their dreams as something they had to hide from the prying eyes of their teachers or classmates. It appeared to be just another task they were asked to do in school, as interesting (or meaningless) as anything else they did every day.

The Limits to Desire

I do not agree with the teachers that the students' limited expressions of desire should be dismissed so quickly. As does Rofel (2007), I see their expressions of desire—even ones as seemingly limited as these—as important indicators of identity. Given that desires—for material goods, new experiences, love and romance—loom so large in contemporary Chinese life (Farquhar 2002; Rofel 2007), the question is what the students are saying about both the limits and the potentials of their identities through their narrow statements about their dreams and ideals.

One problem may be the individualistic nature of the exercises. As Eileen Otis points out, managers at the elite Beijing hotel she studied had to put significant effort into teaching their working-class employees how to answer the question "Who are you?" (2011, 83). These workers, like the VE students, were reluctant to respond aloud, finding the question awkward and uncomfortable. Managers had to actively convince the workers that the modern self must be conceived as an individual apart from family, class, and other forms of social embeddedness. The hotel's foreign management believed that in order to become global and cosmopolitan, their workers had to learn to express themselves as an "I" in public, something the employees were deeply reluctant to do (ibid.).

For the vocational students, future possibilities may still not be imagined as individuals but as part of a family unit. Zhang Li notes this point in her discussion of the neoliberal self in China: "The search for a private self and the good life is still deeply entangled with larger social relationships, moral concerns, and traditional cultural practices. These two different orientations coexist and often are in friction with each other." A "complicated configuration of selfhood is emerging, in which the social and the collective remain important despite the rise of individualism" (2013, 663).[3]

There may be additional reasons the vocational students tended to limit their expressions of desire. Historically, vocational schools were originally intended to specifically teach young people to limit their desires; VE was designed to teach the working classes to be happy with their class position and find satisfaction in their working-class jobs (Schulte 2013). While today vocational schools may not actively be trying to rein in students' desires for their futures, many students' dreams had already been crushed by attending VE in the first place.

Several of the students told us stories of the dreams they had to give up when they failed the HSEE. Qian Ling, a student in the computer tech course at the Canal School, was a good example. She told us, "My dream was always to be an elementary school teacher. I love little kids. I would love to have been a Chinese teacher, or even an English teacher. I dreamed of that for as long as I can remember." She attended the Canal School computer tech course only because her parents selected it when she was offered a scholarship, an opportunity they thought was too good to turn down. She stayed through the five-year program, even after she realized she hated computers. Completing the course, she told us, was her duty to her family.

Qian was not alone. Her classmate Wei Ren said that as her graduation from the computer course approached, she spoke with her parents about how badly she regretted attending the Canal School. Her father encouraged her to attend night school after she graduated to gain more credentials, but Wei was deeply skeptical: "He said, 'Sure, go ahead!,' but then he said that he wouldn't pay for any more schooling. So I'd have to work full-time and go to school part-time. I know that work would be my first priority and school would be second, and it would all probably just be a waste of time and money. Night school is expensive, and I know I won't make a lot of money, so I won't even bother. Now I don't even think about going on and getting more education or taking more classes in some other area that might be more interesting for me."

Another sad example of crushed dreams was Li Tingting, in the Canal School bookkeeping class. Li had a disability that required her to use crutches. Although we never learned her diagnosis, she had significant difficulties walking and even sitting for the long school days. Li compensated for her physical limitations by being one of the only diligent students in her class; she got excellent marks on the tests that did not require fine motor skills (such as the abacus or money-counting tests), and Teacher Zheng praised her diligence. Over lunch one day she told us that attending the Canal School meant abandoning all of her dreams of academic success. "I was a good student in *chuzhong*," Li told us. "I planned to do well on the HSEE and enter an academic high school. My dream was always to go to university. I thought that because I was a good student and I studied hard, maybe I could do it." She sighed deeply. "But I couldn't keep up physically with the other students. I get tired a lot, and I didn't have the 'physical quality' [*tiyu suzhi*] necessary to pass the tests into a good high school. My father said that it would be too much trouble, so I should just give up and go to vocational school and then get a job as a cashier or a bookkeeper. That way I can sit at a desk all day and won't have to run around. It'll be the best I can do in the future. I guess I'm okay about it now."

Disciplining Desires

Trimming their dreams was more than simply a kind of functionalism on the students' part, where they were rational agents who limited their desires because they understood the futility of having big plans for the future. Instead, one of the many paradoxes of vocational education was that while they were exhorted to express their desires, the schools and teachers were simultaneously disciplining the students not to act on their desires in two key domains: romance and consumption. Just as the schools were working to incite the students to become desiring subjects, the students were also disciplined and surveilled to limit their desires. The irony of this contradiction did not escape the students, who resisted these disciplines whenever they could.

The teachers and administrators couched the issue of acting on desires as one of student morality. To them, vocational school posed a minefield of potentially immoral behavior for students because of the ways the temporalities of VE differed from regular high schools. The normative life course for youth in China includes spending every moment studying, memorizing, and preparing for the UEE. Time is a precious commodity and should be invested in studying in the present for future payoffs. Since time is to be used productively, teens are not supposed to have excess (i.e., leisure) time available for hanging out, spending their parents' money, or, most dangerously, getting involved with the opposite sex. This last issue, called "early dating" (*zaolian*), particularly worries teenagers' parents and teachers, for it is common knowledge in China that nothing will distract students from their studies more thoroughly than sex (Bakken 1993).

For the vocational students, however, studying and memorizing were largely irrelevant. They seldom took tests, and those they took did not matter much toward their degree or graduation. Since time for them was not productive or accumulative toward additional numeric capital, they had tremendous amounts of free time on their hands—after school, on weekends, and during the daily long lunch breaks—time that regular high school students spend studying. This greatly upset the VE teachers, who observed with dismay that the students slept late, stayed out late, and spent hours simply hanging out—on the school's basketball court, in the cheap snack bars near their campuses, and on nearby streets. Teachers thus spent a great deal of effort trying to shoo the students back to their desks to do more studying, efforts the students resisted every day. Why sit at a desk if there was nothing to do there? They already sat at their desks doing nothing during formal class time, so why spend any more time there than necessary?

In the same vein, teachers warned students about the moral perils of early dating. This, too, was based in an interesting paradox. Romantic relationships among high school students are very strongly censured in urban China, yet young people are endlessly encouraged to dream about love and romance, prodded by a vast media output that links love and romance to cosmopolitan modernity (Farquhar 2002). In the vocational schools, this paradox was even stronger, for if studying is irrelevant, why not find a boyfriend or girlfriend? Many of the students did, either among classmates or through introductions made by friends. Aware that this was transgressive, many hid these relationships from their teachers and parents; the intrigue of maintaining secrecy about dating was a central topic of lunch-table and after-school chat in both schools.

Because these relationships were so transgressive, the students were mostly reluctant to talk about them, so information was scarce. We did learn that at least some of these "relationships" were primarily virtual. Several of the bookkeeping students reported having a "boyfriend" whom they had barely met, with the entirety of the relationship conducted via text messages. (We discovered this during winter when some of the students knit scarves for boyfriends they had laid eyes on only once.) A few relationships were more open; for example, Xu Wenjuan, in the Canal School computer tech class, had been openly dating her classmate Su Xiaogang since they met in their first year of classes. A few of the students at the Bridge School were also openly couples, to their teachers' dismay.

The same moral and temporal logics held around the question of consumption. "Good" students are studying and therefore have little opportunity for casual consumption or to spend their parents' hard-earned money. The voc ed students' interest in shopping, fashion, and name-brand clothes and accessories was therefore deeply suspect and the cause of much nagging by homeroom teachers about wasting money.

The students ignored them. They assumed, rightly, that their teachers just didn't get it. After all, the teachers were in their fifties and from the Mao-era generation that never figured out brand recognition and did not fully understand the ways taste and fashion were central to the constitution of young people's identity (Bourdieu 1984). The students had their own counternarratives about shopping, which the teachers never heard. The girls in particular saw themselves as canny shoppers, keen hagglers, and eagle-eyed bargain hunters. They loved to compare clothes with each other and brag about how little they had spent to put together their fashionable outfits. They were incredulous that their middle-class age-mates in regular high schools spent outrageous amounts of money on brand-name fashions, when excellent fakes were available at a fraction of the price. In their own eyes, they were the morally superior consumers, who limited their desires to well-researched fakes and copies and consumed within their parents' very limited means. Frugal yet fashionable consumption was thus an essential part of their identity, especially—but not only—for the girls.

In spite of this, the overall tenor of the classes was that desires were immoral and wrong and needed to be monitored and controlled. It is perhaps no wonder that when the same teachers asked the students to express their dreams and desires, the students found it difficult to do so.

Self-Employment: Choice, Plans, and Connections

Desire, of course, is only one dimension around which contemporary urban identities are being formed today. As Lisa Hoffman (2010) notes, young people are also incited to demonstrate choice and responsibility as key aspects of their identity. Hoffman looked at the school-to-work transition just as the Chinese state was ending its policy of assigning lifelong state-sector jobs to university graduates. The transition to graduates to "seek self-employment" in the private labor market was fundamental to the transformations of the reform era. Hoffman noted that this transition made youth responsible for planning their own careers and, by extension, their own paths into the future: "In contemporary times, graduates must be well versed in what constitutes responsible choices; how to make these choices; and how to develop the self through the management of skills, knowledge and potential rather than through allegiance to a strict set of Party rules or state-directed welfare distribution." This transformation is producing a new kind of urban subject: the professional employee, who has emerged to replace the "assignee" (2010, 10).

Hoffman's work focused on university graduates and as such provides an excellent discussion of the ways new middle-class subjects are being produced through these changing labor regimes. Among vocational students this transition is still uneven; while the Canal School students must all seek self-employment, the Bridge School is still part of the workers' training school system that funnels some of its top students into state-allocated, public-sector jobs. Rather than commodify their labor on the open market, many of the subway prep students will be embedded in a socialist-style work unit after graduation. And instead of valorizing choice, knowledge, and planning for the future, these assigned jobs were the most highly coveted among the students for the stability and redistributive benefits they would bring. The subway students at the Bridge School were admired by the other students precisely because they will *not* have to become responsible, choosing subjects: they were able to avoid what they saw as the stresses of choosing a career, seeking a job, and figuring out how to be responsible for a lifetime of household income. While Hoffman describes the ways that for some middle-class youth, "late socialist neoliberal governmentality has cultivated active and enterprising subjects who are able to make choices about appropriate employment that develop the individual, the city and even the nation" (2010, 10), at the Bridge School, there were working-class subjects actively seeking to avoid this status.

To complicate the picture further, even some of the VE students who would have to seek self-employment in the private labor market were not necessarily becoming the "active and enterprising subjects" that Hoffman (2010) describes because they are entering a job market where in many cases choice, training, and skills are largely irrelevant.

Both the students and teachers told us that learning to make choices about future jobs was mostly a waste of time because many of the students would never actually exercise any choices about jobs or their careers. Instead, many students would gain jobs through family connections (*guanxi*) regardless of their interests, training, or job preparedness. Students with good *guanxi* took whatever job was available through their family connections. Those who chose a career and sought jobs in the private labor market had no family connections to turn to. "Choice" in their minds was something akin to a last resort.

The *guanxi* economy, we learned, was a primary reason for at least some of the students' poor planning for the future and may be why so many of them had problems expressing their *individual* desires for the future when asked. For example, I was struck by how difficult it was to get some of the Canal School bookkeeping students to tell me their future plans; they seemed impervious to conversations about the future. Eventually a few of them shrugged and told me,

"Look, my parents will get me a job. I'm not worried about it or thinking about it at all." When I expressed surprise at this response, the students were in turn surprised at me. They replied, "That's how my parents got *their* jobs. Of course it's how I'll get my job, too. Why should I be any different?"

This, understandably, did not please their teachers. One day at lunch we discussed this with Teacher Yao at the Bridge School, who had taught there for decades. She said,

> You know, I increasingly agree with a popular saying around here that I used to hate: "Studying well isn't as good as having good *guanxi*" [*Hao xuexi buru hao guanxi*]. But it's true. Even if you're a really great student, if you don't have good *guanxi*, you can't get anywhere. Especially for our voc ed kids. Look at how things work. When they graduate, a company [*danwei*] may ask us to recommend a few kids for jobs. So we look at their grades and their overall behavior and give them the names of a few top students. But then they don't pick those kids anyway—they select the students who have *guanxi* with the *danwei*. We don't recommend the students they do hire—their grades are low—but it doesn't matter.

In theory, because they have been sending graduates into the private labor market for so long, vocational schools should be sites par excellence for producing the kinds of active and enterprising subjects that Hoffman (2010) describes as being in the process of forming. But the class position of the students and their understanding that personal connections supplant skills, interests, and choice as the most important factors in job seeking have mitigated the ways that students are produced as choosing, desiring neoliberal subjects. They therefore do not describe themselves in a narrative of moving rationally from the present into a future of increasing accumulation toward a planned goal (Miyazaki 2006).

Their inability to articulate their identities in these terms, however, does not mean they have no identities. It only means that in this realm, as in so many others, they do not match the discourse of normative, middle-class youth. Morality, particularly frugality and filiality, is extremely important to them. Their temporal pathway is not accumulative, and in spite of their teachers' scorn they insist their future goal is happiness rather than the normative future path of accumulating ever more credentials, money, and career status. They do not have fixed, underlying identities that merely need to be revealed through narrative and voice, but instead are creating identities that are emerging in the contexts and through the opportunities available to them.

Identities of Place, Language, and Nation

Identity, of course, is more than the sum of an individual's desires and choices. Native place has long been assumed to be strong part of identity in China, and the question of place-based identity preoccupies the Chinese researchers who study second-generation migrants (see Zhongguo Gongyun Yanjiusuo 2011). We were therefore interested to learn whether the students had a strong localized identity, particularly since they came from so many different places and carried *hukou* documents from different localities. Did they see themselves as Nanjingers or as being from somewhere else? Did this identity matter to them on a day-to-day basis? Or, as Kipnis predicts (2012), were the state's efforts at creating a standardized national identity subsuming local identities so they were instead starting to think of themselves as being Chinese citizens?

Since we could not ask the students or their families to complete any surveys or questionnaires, my research assistants decided to try to ask each of the students at the Bridge School and in the two classes we followed at the Canal School one question: Where are you from (*ni shi nali de ren*)? We assumed that most of the students would reply with their *hukou* status, and we would get a fairly accurate count of how many students were urban, rural, or second-generation migrants. To the researchers' frustration, however, this seemingly simple question posed more difficulties than they had imagined. The more my research assistants—all sociologists in training—tried to gather systematic answers to this question, the more frustrated they became. "No two of them answer this the same way!" they complained to me after a day at the schools. "They all think it means something different!"

The range of responses was telling. Some students, who we knew from previous conversations had spent their entire lives in Nanjing, gave the name of their father's home village (*laojia*, ancestral home) when asked where they were from—even if they had never been to that place. This perplexed my graduate students, when they heard some of the students identifying themselves as being from a distant province while speaking local Nanjing dialect. A few students replied easily, saying, "Well, I've spent my life here, so I guess I'm from Nanjing," while another said, "I grew up in Nanjing, but my *hukou* is from Anhui, so I'm from Anhui." The student sitting next to her, however, offered the opposite response: "My *hukou* is from Anhui, but I grew up here, so I'm from Nanjing."

Others were more complicated. Some said that they had moved around frequently and, other than giving their *hukou* status, weren't entirely sure how to respond. Some students surprisingly gave the name of their mother's ancestral village as their home, in contrast to general Chinese practice that traces descent through the paternal line; they explained that their parents were divorced and they had had little contact with their fathers. Many students told us they were from large cities, including Yangzhou, Suzhou, and Jinan; only additional probing clarified that they had actually been born in small rural villages in the far hinterlands of these larger cities.

Further complicating the problem was Nanjing's recent expansion to include the two formerly rural counties on the city's outskirts, part of the state's project of urbanizing rural areas through the New Socialist Countryside movement (Bray 2013). Both the Bridge and Canal Schools recruited heavily among families in these two counties. Some students from these areas identified themselves as Nanjing residents; others, as county residents, or as rural residents, or sometimes as migrants—all indications of the complex status of these new peri-urban areas in the urban imaginary.

I raised the question of local identity over dinner one evening with some of the Canal School computer tech students. Su Xiaogang, a thoughtful young man who was quite popular among his classmates, was from a local family and carried a Nanjing *hukou*. I asked him if he thought of himself as a "Nanjinger" and if his family were "old Nanjing people" (*lao Nanjing*). After thinking about the question for a few moments, he replied that this was actually a difficult question. "During the war," he replied, "a lot of people who might have been *lao Nanjing* were killed or moved away, so a lot of people today who have Nanjing household registrations originally came from somewhere else. Maybe they came sixty years ago, or maybe last week."[4] In his view, because many current Nanjing *hukou* holders actually have backgrounds from somewhere else, the question of local identity was particularly fluid and open.

Thinking that we might perhaps gain more clarity on identity by focusing on language rather than strictly on location, we began to pay closer attention to how the students spoke every day, since dialect is closely associated with identity in China (Dong 2009). In his fieldwork in schools in rural Shandong Province, Kipnis (2012) found that students increasingly spoke standard Mandarin to each other inside and outside classrooms, and teachers he observed taught in Mandarin, as prescribed by the Ministry of Education. Kipnis concluded that this was part of the state's nation-building effort and that the next generation may be moving toward more national and possibly less regional or local identities. We were curious to learn whether or not this was occurring in the two schools we studied. Perhaps language would give us a more solid grasp on the students' identities than their localities.

Although both schools offered some classes on standard Mandarin, we found that we rarely heard Mandarin spoken in either school. The students tended not to use Mandarin to speak to each other or to address their teachers. Sometimes this was intentional; for example, the Canal School bookkeeping students took particular delight in using Nanjing dialect in their Mandarin class to annoy their teacher. In other classes, students in both schools used dialect naturally, and we never observed their teachers correct them or ask them to switch into standard Mandarin. More surprisingly, we found that many of the teachers taught using local dialect, in direct contravention of school policy. In general, we observed that the homeroom teachers, especially those who were former elementary school teachers, spoke precise, standard Mandarin. Some of the contract teachers who hailed from other provinces also used Mandarin as the lingua franca in class. Otherwise, local teachers seemed to switch between Mandarin and local dialect while teaching and in conversation with students, with dialect used far more frequently.

Thinking that their use of local dialect was an indication of a potentially strong local identity, I asked the students to teach me some Nanjing dialect. I thought this might give me a better sense of local identity, as well as enable me to better participate in their conversations (I speak only Mandarin so could not eavesdrop on them.) I simply assumed they were speaking Nanjing dialect with each other and that this conferred a local identity. I thought that their teaching me local dialect would be an opportunity for me to "give them a voice" about this identity and to tell me what it meant to them.

The students I asked, however, all begged off, telling me that their Nanjing dialect wasn't "standard" (*biaozhun*) enough for them to serve as appropriate teachers. "I'm from the suburbs," some students told me, refusing to tutor me; "you need a city person to get a real Nanjing accent." Others said, "I do speak Nanjing dialect at school, but I use a different dialect at home with my parents, and I get them mixed up sometimes. I'd be a bad teacher for you." I asked as often as I could, but the students seemed stumped to identify anyone among them whom they considered to speak pure or standard Nanjing dialect. Even those who lived in Nanjing and spoke Nanjing dialect at home with their parents said that their grandparents were originally from elsewhere, and they therefore didn't think of themselves as real speakers of standard Nanjing dialect.

Instead, the students communicated by speaking to each other using a variety of closely related, mutually intelligible Jiangsu and other Jiangnan dialects, particularly those from neighboring counties. When I pushed them to clarify for me exactly what they were speaking, most of the students just shrugged.

"I speak my home language," I was told by most. "I understand what everybody says and they understand me. It doesn't really matter, does it?"

Before giving up entirely, I tried to pin down the students on their broader Chinese identity by attempting to grasp their sense of patriotism. After all, I was living in China in the months leading up to the Beijing Olympics, and the Chinese media were in a nationalistic frenzy. I assumed they would have much to say on the topic, especially after extremely high-profile events like the tragedy of the Wenchuan earthquake in May and the demonstrations in Tibet.[5]

Here, too, the students confounded my expectations of their nationalism (Woronov 2007). The Olympics, they told me, were not all that interesting: "It's really just a big Beijing thing, so it doesn't have much to do with us," one student explained. They assured me that they did all plan to watch the Olympics on TV, but then added that as avid sports fans they would have watched the competition anyway. Because the Games were being held in China, they intended to cheer even harder than usual for the Chinese athletes, but they did not feel that the Games mattered that much to them personally. After months of following the Chinese media's frenetic lead-up to the Games, I had developed a strong personal interest in some of the Chinese athletes and was a bit crushed at the students' lack of enthusiasm.

The schools did try to get into the Olympic spirit, and both were required by their districts to carry out a range of Olympic preparation activities in class. These, too, were underwhelming. In one Bridge School class I observed, the homeroom teacher gave each student a mimeographed multiple-choice test sheet about the Olympics. After about fifteen minutes, she reviewed the answers. Three or four students practically jumped out of their seats to answer the questions, each of which they got right. I later learned that these students had been given the answers in advance. The entire exercise was administered so that all the students would be able to correct their answer sheets with the provided answers. At the end of the class the teacher collected all the test sheets. I never learned what was done with them afterward.

Although this short anecdote in no way adequately summarizes the students' patriotism or their attitudes toward their nation, it shows how the students continually confounded our preconceived ideas about the identities of Chinese youth. The processes of identity formation and subject construction among this group of young people—who combine urban and rural, first- and second-generation migrants, speakers of different dialects—is a complex and complicated process. I could not assume they each had an identity that they needed to express nor that their identity unproblematically resided in any one aspect of their lives.

Conclusion

Clearly, something like "the" identity of the vocational students was difficult to pin down; I have indicated the ways they could not simply be defined by where they were from, what they desired, what they planned for the future, or even which language they usually spoke together. Identity was not something I could assume each student already had or that I could document just by asking them who they thought they were. The common social categories that have commonly been used to define and sort people in China, such as *hukou*, native place, or dialect, do not easily apply to this group. Because they are not accumulating numeric capital, they are not moving into the future with ever-increasing test scores, educational credentials, and pathways into the professional middle classes. They cannot narrate themselves as desiring, choosing subjects on a normative middle-class path to the future. This was the cause of some anxiety on the part of the teachers, who pressed the students to create identities as desiring, planning, choosing subjects.

This does not mean that the students had no identities or sense of who they were. They certainly had friends. They formed social circles across groups that are generally assumed to be socially divided in China. Urban kids hung out with kids from the rural hinterlands. Children of migrant workers hung out with children of urban workers. They communicated across dialects. As we watched them socialize during the school year, we observed that their social groups were much like what we would expect from young people their age. They formed friendships based on proximity (they made friends with other kids in their classes), gender (girls tended to hang out with other girls, and boys with boys, although, as is typical in urban China, there were also mixed-gender friendship groups). Friends shared interests including sports, music, and fashion. These quotidian observations should not obscure our overall sense that something new might be happening in these classrooms. The students in these social groups might be starting to transcend the traditional social groupings that have been taken for granted in China. The issue may be less that they do not have an identity that they state out loud than that the categories and labels we assume should be used for their identities may no longer be relevant. Rather than judge their identities—or lack thereof—through the lenses we currently have, perhaps we need new ways to think about identity as these young people form social groups that are pushing social boundaries in China.

Along with the new social groups they were forming in their classrooms, the students were also deeply connected to their families. Not only were they filial children who obeyed and felt responsible for their parents; many families would also potentially be the ultimate sources of their future jobs. The project of trying to get the students to plan for their futures and identify their career interests flies in the face of the *guanxi* economy, where family connections are the link to employment. In the larger economy, *guanxi* challenges everything the vocational schools are theoretically trying to accomplish, including skills training and job preparation. Schools' efforts to create students' identities thus flounder in multiple dimensions.

I have highlighted the ways that their identity is an ongoing and contingent process rather than a fixed, preexisting condition. Unlike the middle-class youth who are increasingly constituted as desiring and choosing subjects, these young people do not see their lives as a narrative of ever-increasing accumulation of numeric capital, leading toward a rational, planned future. This is consistent with the many ways they are "other" or deviant to middle-class norms.

The issue of class raises another very interesting point. Rofel (2007) opened her discussion of the discourse of "desire" by arguing that it arose as a replacement for political consciousness. But if desires are not the way VE students are constituting their identities, is political consciousness, perhaps, still a possibility for *their* identities? Is class consciousness a way that they might start thinking about themselves and their identities as they move into their working-class futures? I address this question in the Conclusion.

Jobs, Internships, and the School-to-Work Transition

THE QUESTION OF JOB READINESS has been at the center of vocational education since it was first introduced to China. Early twentieth-century proponents of vocational education stressed technical skills and producing graduates willing to take on working-class jobs. After the founding of the PRC, vocational education focused on building national industrial capacity, which was targeted by PRC radicals starting in the late 1950s in the "red vs. expert" debates (Hoffman 2010; Pepper 1996). These debates were resolved after the Cultural Revolution, when reformers associated with Deng Xiaoping's "reform and opening" and "Four Modernizations" movements criticized radical policies that had focused on building students' revolutionary fervor and "love of labor" at the expense of developing specific job-related technical skills and national industrial and economic development (Thøgersen 1990).

Post–Cultural Revolution educational reforms included provisions to rapidly increase the vocational sector. One of the most important reforms was the introduction of "market mechanisms for job allocations after graduation" (Lewin and Xu 1989, 10; see also Hoffman 2010). By the mid-1980s, secondary vocational schools had begun to train students for jobs in the nascent private sector (Thøgersen 1990), and VE graduates increasingly faced a mixture of assignments to jobs in the state sector and self-employment in the new private job market (Hoffman 2010).

By the time I arrived in Nanjing in 2007–2008 to study vocational education, the private job market was very highly developed and urban vocational graduates faced the question of exactly what "job preparation" meant in the context of a rapidly changing urban economy. I have looked at the difficult question of skills teaching in the two vocational schools and how the teachers struggled with the knowledge that connections or social capital might be more valuable to the students' future employment than anything they might learn in school. I now turn to how the graduating classes in both schools prepared to enter the job market. The schools had sold their courses to students several years earlier by promising to turn graduates into "hot" commodities in the labor market. Now, three or five years later (depending on the course), they were left to figure out what that meant. How marketable were they? How were they supposed to sell themselves to potential employers? How should they construct narratives about themselves to make them sound like the right kinds of employees (Southwood 2011)?

Upon graduation the students had to turn themselves into a kind of commodity for employers, a process that was more complex and difficult than merely matching their supposed vocational skills to some employers' needs. My goal was to try to understand how students mediated between the various forms of capital they had to muster when looking for jobs; finding a job was not just a matter of having vocational skills that were packaged and labeled with a degree. Even for those who went to job fairs to seek employment in the private job market, the socialist system was still extremely relevant, as students tried to convert their experiences as class leaders, their membership in the Communist Youth League, and recommendations from teachers into social capital that could then be converted into jobs. Some had individual resources, traits such as initiative or confidence that allowed them to overcome the structural limitations of the vocational training system, while others did not. Some had family connections. One actually sought specialized training to learn how to be more outgoing. Most did not discover these issues until they were confronted head-on with the complexities of the job market: interviews, résumés, and presenting themselves—quickly, on demand—as the kinds of employees that employers want in the context of a job fair. Job hunting forced them to create a narrative of the self, to frame their lives as a form of personal development and accumulation, of moving toward the future in the right kinds of ways (Hoffman 2010; Southwood 2011).

The complexity of the job hunt and the students' production of themselves as the right kinds of employable service workers is buried in the Chinese employment statistics, which rightly indicate that employment opportunities in the service economy are quite good. Jobs in the tertiary (service) sector grew more than 30 percent between 2000 and 2010.[1] The odds of finding work in this sector are good, and the students did succeed in their job hunts. What these statistics do not show, however, is what kinds of jobs these young people get:

precarious, possibly short-term, likely dead-end. These new service-sector jobs link them to the new global precariat, which in turn helps define some of the contours of China's new urban working class.

Winning Friends and Influencing Employers

One Saturday afternoon in early 2008 we arranged to meet a group of the Canal School bookkeeping students for lunch. One of our favorite students, Zhang Zhi-gang, said he couldn't make it that day because he had enrolled in a "special class." He had been attracted by ads around town for a local branch of a national "success school," which promised to provide him with the concrete skills and confidence he would need in the job market, which he would face in another three years. He had purchased a set of "success classes" and would be attending one that coming weekend. Intrigued, Emma Wang and I asked if we could go along.

Zhang was a sweet-natured young man with the short, spiky haircut and thick accent frequently associated with migrants from rural China. Originally from a small village in northern Jiangsu Province, his parents migrated to Beijing as manual laborers when he was very young, and he was raised by his grandmother. After she died, he began boarding at various schools in and around Nanjing, and since grade 6 had seen his parents only once a year. As one of only two boys in the class, Zhang was the object of much teasing by his female classmates, which he tolerated with resigned good humor.[2]

Zhang met us that Saturday and led us to the top floor of a dingy downtown office building. There, a salesman named Li was waiting for us at the Nanjing branch of the China School for Winners (Zhongguo Yingzhe Xuexiao). This was a local branch of one of China's fastest-growing educational industries, known collectively as "success schools" (*chenggong xuexiao*): private, for-profit weekend and after-school self-improvement classes for Chinese youth and white-collar workers. This enormous industry exists online, in books, on DVD, and in formal classrooms and is often associated in China with popular Western motivational speakers such as Tony Robbins (2015), whose books and tapes sell there in the tens of millions.

Zhang, Emma, and I sat with Li at a small table in a noisy, crowded room filled with visibly nervous youth, all the targets of hard sells by other staff. A large poster of John D. Rockefeller hung on one wall, while a poster of another Western man, dating from the 1940s, dominated another side of the room. Li pointed to that picture and said, "That's our founder. We follow all his principles. He's one of the most famous Americans in history. His name is Jia-na-ji, and you of course know him and his work."

I was stumped. I didn't recognize the picture and had no idea whose name used that transliteration in Chinese. Kennedy? Obviously not. I mentally searched for midcentury names beginning with "J" or "K." Li was first visibly frustrated, then angry, assuming I was willfully toying with him by refusing to acknowledge one of the most famous Americans of all time.

It took several minutes before it finally clicked. Of course. Dale Carnegie. Jia-na-ji. *How to Win Friends and Influence People* ([1936] 1981). *That* most famous of Americans. The Winners School, I discovered, was not in fact associated in any way with the Dale Carnegie company, which has its own popular success schools and programs in China (Dale Carnegie Training 2015), but given lax copyright laws in China, this school felt free to appropriate his name and image. Most of the other existing success schools in Nanjing targeted university students and young white-collar workers who were anxious to learn how to win friends and influence people, but the Winners School had recently begun to sell classes to what it saw as a hot new market: secondary vocational students. Zhang was one of their first VE students, and as such he had been offered a special discount to enroll.

This new target made marketing sense, as vocational schools increasingly enrolled rural Chinese students, for whom the prospect of the urban job market was particularly daunting. Technical job skills were not the issue—these were (supposedly) being taught by the schools' vocational courses. The problem was a new set of skills that rural youth were particularly believed to lack: résumé preparation, job interview skills, and ability to speak confidently about their potential contributions to private companies. These were not skills required in rural areas or for jobs in the public sector. As Hoffman's (2010) exemplary work describes in detail, university-educated urban youth have been moving to the job market for well over a decade, and at least some have slowly been learning to transform themselves into the kinds of people who can confidently sell themselves to private employers. The rural youth who were now attending urban vocational high schools and colleges, however, were frightened by the prospect of the private job market, which seemed to require a mysterious new set of skills and personality traits. The most important of these, the success school informed them, were being "outgoing" (*waixiang*) and having confidence (*zixin*).[3] The success school industry supposedly sold classes to teach appropriate attitudes and demeanors for job hunting, as well as more specific job-searching skills. Zhang had already attended two classes on writing résumés and handling job interviews, both of which he thought were fairly useful.

Salesman Li told us that the Winners School offered three streams of classes. Zhang had signed up for the Excellence in Communication stream, which usually cost 500 RMB, but he had paid only 400 RMB.[4] This gave him a punch card that entitled him to attend up to twenty classes (actually, individual lectures), each ninety minutes long, during the year. There was no set curriculum for this stream or any course coordination at all. The school hired "teachers" who were available to teach on weekends and evenings and who provided the title of their class that same day. Li was extremely vague when we asked him about the background and credentials of the school's teachers.

The other two streams the school offered were Reaching the Peak of Success and Jewish Class (*Youtairen ke*), both of which were more expensive than the stream Zhang had selected; Wang did not tell us the specific costs, presumably because the sales staff offered different deals to different customers. The latter stream had caught my eye, largely because I assumed I'd misread the Chinese ad for the class. Li assured me that I had read it correctly; as everyone knows, he said, Jews are better than anyone at making money. That stream's lectures, he promised, would share the ancient secrets of the Jews for getting rich.

Li then led the three of us into the class Zhang had selected for that day, "Working for Success." The instructor, Teacher Ren, a young man in his early thirties, arrived breathlessly a moment before the class started. Dressed casually but expensively, Ren introduced himself vaguely as a "business consultant" to the group of about forty youth, the majority of whom were university undergraduates, although the class also included a few secondary and vocational secondary students. Rather than deliver a lecture, he announced, he would answer their questions about "working for success." With a bit of coaxing, the students raised some interesting and pertinent questions, including how they could go about finding jobs that were suitable for their interests, how they could find a job if they had no work experience, and how they could move into employment fields other than what they were studying in their degree programs. They seemed genuinely worried about how to face the job market and were seeking specific guidance. Teacher Ren nodded in encouragement, then launched into a completely unrelated monologue. He waved his arms, shouted, and switched in and out of English, presumably for my benefit. He apparently had memorized a number of popular self-help books, and his lecture consisted of a litany of their clichés as he paced the front of the room, including, "Believe in yourself." "Do what you love and the money will follow." "The selling begins when the customer says 'no.'" "Don't ask your boss what you can get from a job; ask yourself what you can give to your company." "What matters is self-confidence." "Be outgoing."

After ninety minutes of this the students' eyes were glazed, a few (including Zhang) were dozing, and many others were texting. Although there was clearly pent-up demand for specific information on how to navigate the job market, this class was not going to provide it. Afterward, when we asked Zhang what he had learned from the class, he sheepishly admitted he had not understood a word. This, he assumed, was his own fault; he believed the content was just too difficult for him to comprehend. We tried to console him, assuring him that in fact Teacher Ren had been largely incoherent, but were not sure that Zhang quite believed us.

We called the Winners School a few weeks later and learned that they had decided that vocational secondary students were deemed "too young" and "too inexperienced" to benefit from the school's lessons, and the sales staff were no longer targeting VE students for their courses. Perhaps not surprisingly, the inability of students like Zhang to understand Teacher Ren's incoherent message was blamed on the students, not the teacher, the school, or the success school industry model. Zhang later told us that after this experience he decided not to return to the Winners School. Instead, he planned to rely on skills he would eventually gain during his formal internship program to unlock the mysteries of the job market.

Internships: On-the-Job Training

Most job preparation in China's vocational schools consisted of internships in addition to the technical classes. During the students' final year of school (year 3 at the Bridge School; year 5 at the Canal School) little new course content was taught, while the students (ostensibly) completed year-long internships (*shixi*) in their vocational areas.[5] Although the schools promised that internships would provide on-the-job training in the students' vocational field, in practice they were a complex combination of public and private, socialist and capitalist, institutional and individual, and where promises made far exceeded actuality.

The Canal School

The Canal School's fifth-year computer tech's homeroom teacher, Teacher Fei, was in charge of students' final-year internships. By the time we caught up with her about halfway through the school year, however, she dismissed the entire idea of internships for the students. She said that none of the students she had placed in *shixi* positions had stayed in place for long, because they were bored, hated the work, and couldn't tolerate the hardships involved (*buneng chiku*). The students, however, told a different story.

The class president, Xu Wenjuan, seemed visibly uncomfortable when we asked her to confirm Teacher Fei's description. "Well, it's true that they're actually not doing that much," Xu admitted about her classmates. With her help we met many of her classmates and discovered that the majority had in fact spent most of their final year at the Canal School hanging out at home playing computer games, or they had simply found their own part-time jobs. When we talked with the students about their internships, they were quite articulate about what they had done for their final year of school and why.

Wei Ren, for example, had found a weekend job selling mobile phones at one of the large electronics stores in downtown Nanjing. Although she worked twelve-hour shifts and sold an average of seventy phones a day, she took home less than 400 RMB per month (approximately $58). "The regular, full-time employees write up the sales receipts, so they get all the sales commissions, while the part-timers like me do all the actual work of running around to get the phones out of stock, explaining the different models to the customers, installing the SIM cards, and setting up the phones," she explained. "They'd be happy if I worked there forever—workers like me do all the work, but they barely pay me anything." She quit after a few months, with several hundred yuan in savings and a renewed commitment to finding full-time work.

Others had found part-time work at KFC and McDonald's, earning 7 RMB/hour (about $1/hour). Classmate Tang Limei said, "It's actually a lot of fun to work at McDonald's, because you have to learn how to do everything when it's busy—not just make hamburgers. But it's so tiring there! They don't pay overtime wages, so the only way to earn more is to work more hours. Now whenever I eat at McD's, I throw away my own trash. People look at me like I'm crazy, but believe me, if you've ever worked there, you'd understand." Her friend Qian Ling nodded in agreement. "I worked in a small clothing store. It's a service job [*fuwu hangye*], and while people pretend to be nice to you, you can tell that they really look down on you. But no matter what they say to you or behind your back, you have to be nice to them. Wow, that's a lesson I never learned in school! People in society [*shehui shang de ren*] really aren't as pure as us students. I'm glad I had that experience." Several of the other female students worked part-time at supermarkets, doing promotional sales, or handing out flyers. They made 40–50 yuan (approximately $6.50) per day. "It's not bad work," said classmate Fang Bing. "You have to stand for a lot of hours, but it's not hard at all. People aren't rude; they just ignore you. You wear a uniform and hand out samples of stuff. It's easy money."

Wang Shui had no time for an internship but did part-time work as she was able to. Wang's mother sold vegetables in the market; her father is disabled and lives on a 500–600 RMB (approximately $73–87) monthly pension from his former employer, an urban factory. "Normally, I do all the housework at home," Wang told us. "I cook and do the laundry, so my parents can eat right after they get back from work and go to bed. I feel like I'm the one raising them! I also help my mom process some of the vegetables, like water chestnuts, that we have to peel before we sell. The good thing is that I don't need much money from them now." Wang was supposed to also be doing a full-time internship but had found time only to pick up part-time jobs in supermarkets and computer markets around town.

We eventually met three students from the computer tech course who had found formal internships. Xiao Gu had an internship at a computer company that paid him 700 RMB (approximately $100) per month. He hated the job, he told us in the spring, but the work was easy, and there was a chance of converting the internship into a regular job after he graduated. "It would only pay about 1,300 RMB [approximately $190] per month, but that's not bad for a starting job. And Teacher Fei found this gig for me. If I quit now, she'll lose face, and it'll make it hard for other students from the Canal School who want internships there in the future. So I have to stick it out until the end of the school year."

His best friend, Su Xiaogang, had made a different decision. He started a school-assigned internship at a small computer company but made only 500 RMB ($73) per month as a base salary. "They promised that we could make up to 2,000 RMB per month [$290] in commissions if the company had a good month, but they never had a good enough month to pay that kind of money. They hired a lot of us at the same time, almost sixty people, but lots of us have quit already. It's one of those companies that just can't last." Only one student in the Canal School computer tech course, Xiao Liu, had done well with his internship. Introduced by a friend to a small computer graphics company that worked with the advertising industry, Liu was having a terrific experience. "This is a great field to get into. I really like the graphic design part of the work, and advertising is a lot of fun. I'll definitely stay if they offer me a regular job and don't really care how much they pay me. I just want more experience and then can look for something better later."

The Bridge School

To learn about the Bridge School's internship program, Principal Huang suggested we call Teacher Guo, who was in charge of the internship programs for the school's graduating (third-year) students. He said that she would be very happy to introduce us to the students, who were all enjoying their internships immensely. He was wrong on both counts.

Teacher Guo avoided us for weeks. We eventually finally found her and some of the Bridge School students working in school-sponsored internships in a large construction company that was partly run by a graduate of the Bridge School. The company had been awarded a contract to widen a major highway near the center of the city, and approximately a dozen students from different Bridge School courses had been placed in internships there. We visited the students on-site several times during the final days of the 2008 Spring Festival (Chinese New Year) holidays while construction work was suspended. During the holiday the rural migrant workers who provide the actual construction labor leave town, so the students had time to chat.

One cold Saturday afternoon we gathered around a large table in an empty conference room in a temporary building erected on-site as the construction company's office space. Although usually a workday, the permanent office staff had taken the day off to attend a colleague's wedding, so the interns had the office to themselves. As we sat down, one of the young men, Fang Chao, snapped his fingers imperiously at one of his female classmates. "Chen Lu!" he called. "Bring us tea!" She responded by whacking him—hard—on the shoulder. "I was only joking!" he protested, rubbing his arm. "It's NOT funny," she replied through gritted teeth.

This small exchange summarized the problem with the construction site internship. The students explained that for the past few months, the girls had mostly been assigned to pour tea for the company managers. Occasionally, they were asked to type a document or file some papers, but they mostly sat around with little to do. They felt they were receiving no training, getting no real work experience, and learning little. The young men were even more frustrated. Although they had been recruited into the internship from several different third-year courses at the Bridge School, including construction management, wastewater treatment, and landscaping, all had been assigned to one task at the work site: directing traffic. For the months of their internship, the boys had each been issued orange vests, hard hats, and a stack of orange cones and were told to direct the flow of trucks, bulldozers, and cranes into and out of the construction site. They were livid. "Really," asked Fang Chao rhetorically, "how is this any different from any job they'd give to some migrant worker [*min'gong*]?"

This was the crux of the problem. As we got to know these students, over time they expressed a thoughtful critique of their vocational education: Did their degree adequately differentiate them from the masses of rural migrant workers in Nanjing? If so, how? If not, why had they spent three years and thousands of renminbi on their education?

Bright and loquacious Fang Chao explained it this way. Their internship was scheduled for about four months, from November until April or May (with a break for Spring Festival). They were paid 500 yuan per month, plus a small subsidy for daily transportation. Fang said, "I'm a single child [*dusheng de haizi*] and a city kid [*Nanjing hukou de*]. I know that I've been pretty spoiled. And I guess I knew that book learning is just theoretical, that it's not the same as real work. But I wasn't prepared to be standing outdoors all day, in the sun or out in the cold. None of us was prepared for that, to tolerate that kind of hardship. After this work I know I can do it [*neng chiku*], so I did learn something important, but doing this kind of migrant labor [*min'gong de gongzuo*] is really hard on all of us, physically and emotionally. What I've really learned from this internship is that I don't want to keep doing this." His classmates nodded in agreement.

When we finally reached Teacher Guo to hear her side of the story, she had little sympathy for the students' plight. First, she explained, the interns did not yet have a diploma, so there was very little actual work the company could give them to do. All they needed was a little more patience; if they proved themselves willing to work hard, some of them could convert the internships into regular, full-time jobs after they had actually graduated in a few months. These would pay better, and they might then have better, more interesting work to do. She then softened a bit. "Look," she said, "most of the third-year students don't even do internships if the work is this hard. They just give up. These kids are doing well. This is a kind of test for them. If they keep going, they might get something better and permanent out of it."

Guo also confirmed something we suspected: most of the Bridge School students located their own internships, and later their own jobs, through family connections (*guanxi*). Only those students whose families had absolutely no connections to draw upon had to rely on the school for internship placement. Principal Huang's description of the system—that the school had a fully functional internship program that placed students in meaningful positions that provided work experience leading to full-time employment after graduation—was an overstatement. In reality, the school's internships were more of a last resort for students whose families lacked the social capital to find placements for them on their own. It is therefore probably not terribly surprising that the school's internships resembled what the students saw as "migrant workers' work": gendered unskilled labor, like directing traffic and pouring tea, that appeared to lead nowhere. Students with alternative resources—sourced through family connections outside the school—used these resources to differentiate themselves from the rural migrants at the lowest levels of the service economy.

As China's demographics and the economy change—as more young people graduate from universities and place downward pressure on urban jobs, and as fewer rural people migrate to China's cities willing to perform dirty, degrading, and poorly paid urban work—young people with three-year vocational degrees may find there is indeed very little to differentiate them occupationally from rural migrant workers. Their urban resident status and their "spoiled" city backgrounds and identities notwithstanding, these Bridge School students might find they are distressingly in the vanguard of a new social group in the coming decade: urban Chinese workers whose employment increasingly overlaps work previously done by rural migrants. Earlier forms of social differentiation that may have been possible because they held an urban *hukou* and a graduation certificate from a secondary school may be breaking down. Just as classrooms already mix rural and urban students, *min'gong* and second-generation migrant children, after urban VE students graduate, they may no longer be able to take for granted that they differ professionally from rural migrants.

The boundaries between these social categories are bleeding—not just in the classrooms but occupationally as well—as the low-end urban service workers are increasingly indistinguishable from the higher ends of the migrant labor force. Current research indicates that urban jobs in retail and hospitality are becoming dominated by rural migrants (see Goodman 2014 for a review); for the moment we still know little about the overall constitution of the growing numbers of low-end "pink-collar" and other clerical workers in China's cities. The social outcomes of this remain to be seen. Chinese cities have a history of tightening residency laws precisely to reduce employment tensions among urban residents (by restricting rural migration into cities); this may be one possible outcome, but only time will tell (Chan K. 2012).

In the meantime, both schools set up internships that cover a range of the precarious work available to semiskilled urban labor in China today. One of the primary lessons that we—and the students—learned from internships is that these work arrangements are primarily an institutionalized site for the breakdown of schools' perceived moral obligations to their students (Hoffman 2010). When they entered voc ed in tenth grade, the schools promised to assign each student to a good internship, with the implicit promise that these would lead to good jobs. This implies that there is a relationship of care, patronage, and teacher-student relations based on love, tenderness, and nurturing—

precisely the kinds of relationships premised on the socialist work contract. Yet just as relationships between students and teachers are increasingly based on a commodity logic, so, too, are the ways internships are arranged. The pastoral care implicit in their relationship with their schools and teachers is breaking down, replaced with a commodified, commercialized relationship.

The graduates who will be worth the most are those who can draw upon the *guanxi* economy, which exists entirely outside the moral relationships set up inside the school. The *guanxi* economy is considered morally suspect at best, for it is not predicated on the love a school has for its students (and a naturalized reciprocal relationship of loyalty and patronage between students and teachers) or on the rational economic value of an exchange of job skills for salary. Instead, *guanxi* relations are potentially related to corruption, or "back door" (*houmen*) forms of cronyism.[6] The schools' internship programs are where these different moral economies become visible and marked and where the promised moral relationship between the schools and the students begins to fray upon meeting the contingencies of the new Chinese economy.

Internships and Exploitation: Slave Labor?

To our surprise, the Canal School graduating fifth-year students were not the only ones doing internship work. When we visited the school not long after the Spring Festival holidays in 2008, the second-year bookkeeping students were all absent. We later learned that they had been taken off-site for a two-week unpaid "internship" at one of the local universities, where they spent nine hours a day doing data entry for the admissions office. Secretary Ji justified pulling the students out of two weeks of classes as "good work experience" and "good discipline." To our even greater surprise, most of the students agreed with him, and only a few later grumbled about not being paid for the many hours of work they did or for missing two weeks of classes.

This was the only example we heard of students performing mandatory unpaid internship work arranged by their school, but it opens the question of just how exploitative the students' internships were. Since then, researchers Pun and Chan (2012) have argued that this practice is widespread in other parts of China, and claim that vocational students are a growing new form of forced labor in China's export factories. Focusing on Foxconn, the notorious manufacturer of Apple products in China, Pun and Chan state, "Foxconn's student internships are actually a way of implementing 'student labor' to help raise output and increase profits by paying sub-minimum wages during the busy season" (392). They argue that because the vocational student interns are not genuine employees, they are subject to "super exploitation" by the factory, including forced overtime and no breaks. This, they explain, occurs because the students are not protected by the nation's labor laws that require regular employees to earn at least a minimum wage and work a maximum number of hours a week, nor can the student interns quit if they are unhappy with their working conditions.

I cannot argue with their horrific findings. I did not study factories or factory labor anywhere in China. My concern is with the general assertion that vocational schools as a system are a pathway into highly exploitative factory-labor regimes (e.g., Chakrabortty 2013). Although Pun and her colleagues are not responsible for the ways their research has been sensationalized by the mainstream press, my research suggests that their findings need to be more specific in their claims about Chinese vocational schools and their internship programs. I suspect that it is rural vocational schools that are feeding students into these exploitative internships, for those are preparing students to enter the industrial economy as migrant workers. Pun and her colleagues have not yet provided detailed information about the students' original schools or the backgrounds, so it is impossible to assess and compare these students with the students I knew. On this basis, any claims about "Chinese vocational education" as a whole need to be assessed with a critical eye.

The Bridge and Canal School students were not being pressed into factory labor, for these urban schools were not linked to factories at all. The Nanjing students are preparing for the urban service economy, not the industrial economy; none of the graduates of the Canal or Bridge Schools plan to enter factory jobs. Although the internships they did complete were highly questionable in their usefulness as job training, they did not constitute super-exploitation by employers, because none of the students actually seemed to be doing much productive labor. Instead, the internships were largely a waste of time. Although a few students were reluctant to quit their internships because it might reflect badly on them or their schools, none said they were forced to stay.

The difference in my research findings from Pun and Chan's (2012) provides an interesting window into the ongoing production of social hierarchies in China today. Among the Bridge and Canal School students, the only ones who completed school-arranged internships in the first place were those whose parents did not have the connections (*guanxi*) to set up an internship on their behalf. A comparative study of internships might thus indicate the ways that well-connected urban youth are best positioned to enter the labor market. Urban youth without family connections are positioned below them, and they may increasingly have trouble distinguishing themselves from the migrant laborers who perform more menial labor in the cities. Rural vocational school students, on the other hand, may be forced into internships that track them into the industrial economy, and may be unprepared to enter the urban workforce force at all. These are still open questions.

Job Fairs

After the end of the Spring Festival holiday in 2008, six of the Canal School's graduating computer tech students invited us to join them as they started looking for full-time work at weekend job fairs organized by the Jiangsu provincial government and held in the vast Nanjing Convention Center (cf. Hoffman 2010). The students explained that the weeks following Spring Festival were considered prime job-hunting time: workers who were already employed but who were seeking to switch jobs wait to receive their New Year's bonuses and vacation time from their old jobs before looking for new ones, while graduating students would be close enough to finishing their degrees to begin serious job-hunting efforts. The job fairs were packed.[7]

We met at the entrance to the Convention Center on a rainy Saturday morning. The cavernous, unheated space had been divided into dozens of aisles, each lined with small booths that represented companies seeking workers. Signs, mostly handwritten, posted on the back of each booth listed the name and location of the company and the kind of work it did, the number of workers it was seeking in different job categories, and minimum employee requirements. This always included the gender, age limits, and educational credentials sought, but some listed additional requirements, such as minimum height, appearance (only for female applicants), language skills in standard Mandarin, and personality traits (e.g., "ability to tolerate hardships" [*chiku*], "outgoing" [*waixiang*], or "patient and willing to learn"). Because the job fairs we attended were designed for a broad, general group of companies and potential employees (rather than more-specialized, industry-specific fairs held later in the year), businesses represented included computer and technology companies, retailers, exporters, landscapers, insurance companies, and even a funeral parlor. Although it was impossible to count, we estimated that well over a thousand companies had booths at each of the four job fairs we attended in March 2008. By late morning on each of these days the Convention Center was so crowded that it was almost impossible to walk up and down the aisles or to get close enough to any of the booths to read the job descriptions clearly.

Each of the Canal School students arrived at the job fair clutching a plastic folder with a set of documents inside: their *dang'an* or personal dossiers (Dutton 1998), a record of their performance in school, as well as their attitudes, relationship with those in authority, and position in the Chinese Communist Party (i.e., proof of their membership in the Party Youth League, normal practice for high school–aged students across urban China [Woronov 2007]). The folder also contained a résumé that summarized their previous work experience and any additional credentials the students may have accrued. For example, Xu Wenjuan's dossier held documents attesting that she had served as the class president, an important position that indicated her potential for leadership and independent thinking. Other students had similar documents showing their service to their school and class. Because these positions are identical across all schools in China, these school-based job descriptions mark a relationship to peers and authority that are commonly understood and serve as a form of cultural capital that the Canal School students were supposed to deploy to their advantage at the job fair. It was up to each of them to construct a narrative from these familiar documents to use to sell themselves. This was particularly important because their dossiers did not yet include a formal graduation diploma, which they would not receive from the Canal School for another three months. The students told me they felt this put them at a significant disadvantage compared to other job seekers at the fair who had already finished school and had the diplomas to prove it.

One thing was immediately clear: the six Canal School students had no idea how to deal with the overwhelming choices available at the job fair. They did not think of the vast number of jobs on display as an opportunity to make a series of selections based on a rational assessment of their skills, balanced against their desires and dreams for their futures, nor had they worked out a game plan in advance about what kinds of jobs they wanted or even which part of the city they preferred. They did not act as rational agents, maximizers of their marginal utility, nor did they perceive themselves as owners of a quantifiable set of skills or human capital. They had not thought about how to summarize the contents of their résumés or *dang'an* to present themselves in the best possible light. Instead, when they entered the hall and saw the crowds, the number of booths, and the elaborate requirements listed on each booth's walls, the students staggered to a halt. They were, quite understandably, overwhelmed.

Over the next few weeks, each of the students worked out his or her own strategies for navigating the job fair. None of these, however, was a strategy of seeking work based on narratives of work as progress, development, or fulfillment. None saw work as a stepping-stone to the future or as a way of building a life of "meaning" (Southwood 2011). Instead, each student worked out short-term solutions to handle the crush of bodies, the pressures of the crowds, and the sheer amount of information available. When I interviewed them at the end of each day, the students tried their best to come up with largely ex post facto rationalizations of why they had made the choices they had at the job fair.

For example, after we first arrived, Wei Ren looked around at the entrance of the job fair, then took off at a run. A tiny young woman, Wei used her size as an advantage, squirming and elbowing her way through the crowds to get to the front of the lines at a few selected booths to shove a copy of her dossier at the interviewers. When we asked, she said that she moved so quickly because she wanted to cover as much ground as possible in a short time. She focused on companies seeking sales staff, reasoning that jobs that paid on commission might be most lucrative and that the pressure of doing sales for commissions might make for more stimulating and exciting work.

Her friend Xu Wenjuan decided to look solely at employer's locations and narrowed her search to companies in any industry located within five kilometers of her home. Unlike Wei, Xu and the others did wait patiently in the crowds to get to meet the interviewers. But when they finally reached the front of the unruly lines, the students often found it difficult to handle the questions they were asked. The interviewers had developed questions—and sometimes questionnaires—that were intended not only to help them differentiate among the thousands of potential applicants but also to serve as proxies for the right kinds of worker subjectivities (see Bauman 2008; Giddens 1991; Hoffman 2010). Interviewers asked questions that were supposed to enable applicants to display their individuality and their ability to narrate a life course of study, work, and progress (Hoffman 2010; McDowell 2012; Southwood 2011).

For example, the three boys in the group all decided to apply for one job with a computer gaming company, which required that they complete a special questionnaire. They huddled together to try to figure out what the company wanted for its answers. "It asks how many words I can type per minute," said Liu Yang. "Don't say 120!" advised his friend Xiao Gu. "You have to know a special system [wubi] to type that fast, and you don't! Say 60!" Together they brainstormed how to complete the sheet, but then discovered another problem: they had then completed three identical questionnaires. This led to a heated debate: Was it better to submit three identical sheets with what they guessed were the "right" answers or to tweak different answers so that the three sheets looked different? What, after all, were the employers looking for? What kinds of people were the "right" people for each company (Hoffman 2010; Southwood 2011)?

This same sense of mystification held across the entire job fair process. When Xu Wenjuan reached the front of the line for a customer service position, the interviewer said: "Take 30 seconds to tell me about yourself."[8] Xu said, "My name is Xu Wenjuan. I am a computer technology student at the Canal School in the 3+2 *dazhuan* degree program." The interviewer waited for her to continue, then said in surprise, "But that wasn't even 10 seconds!" Xu just shrugged in reply. We observed this repeatedly during the job fairs, where interviewers asked a question that was intended to give the students a chance to demonstrate that they "got it," that they understood the ideology of the new economy, the responsibilities of the capitalist system, the ways to present the self, what is and is not a real skill—and how mystified the Canal School students were at these tasks. We watched Wei Ren elbow her way to the front of one line and shove her résumé at one company's interviewer. Amused at her assertiveness, he asked her: "Do you like money?" Taken aback, she said nothing in reply. He asked again, and she merely stammered and blushed. The interviewer then softened and said: "The right answer to the question is to say, 'Yes, I really like money!' because then I know that you'd be willing to work hard!" Wei Ren brightened and replied that she was willing to work hard and really did want to make money. The interviewer then took her résumé and promised to call. Su Xiaogang, who had already held several part-time jobs selling computer supplies in various electronics stores in Nanjing, reached the front of the line at a software company. But when the interviewer asked him to describe how his work experience could be applied to a job at their company, Su just shook his head, said that he had no experience, and walked away.

These were examples of the students' demonstrating their low numeric capital, exposing the ways they had not invested their time appropriately or planned correctly for their future. Potential employers expected them to be able to narrate their current status as the outcome of a lifelong investment strategy in schooling, skills development, and planning and their job-seeking process as the first step in a rational move toward the future. Yet they did not perceive their lives in this way; as vocational students, they had already subverted the dominant temporal logics that assumed young people's lives were based on ongoing investments in the future. Their difficulty, however, is not an issue confined only to these students or only to China; the global economy dictates that rational moves to the future need to be narrated in life stories as a series of calculated moves (Jeffrey 2010; Miyazaki 2006). The narratives of progress from the past into the future that they were asked to perform at the job fair— and failed to do—are an aspect of global capitalism (Southwood 2011). Along with their vocational credentials, their inability to narrate their lives through the temporal logic of investment and return are precisely what marked these students as economically and socially marginal.

In general, the students responded to the mysteries of the job fair by lowering their expectations of what kinds of jobs they might get and the quality of the companies where they applied. At the third job fair weekend, I tried to interest Su Xiaogang in applying to a software design company. "Nah, why bother?" he replied. "They say they want creative people," he pointed out, "and I'm not creative." When I asked him why not, he had no answer. I suspect the company intended less to recruit genuinely "creative" employees than to use this requirement as a tactic to require applicants to explain why they're creative; in their view, the ability to narrate the self as creative served as a proxy for other forms of cultural and social capital. Su Xiaogang simply stopped applying for any jobs in the computer field and started leaving his résumé with some of the many companies in the home renovation business.[9] "I guess I could sell paint," he told me. "They don't care if I only have a voc ed degree." Tang Limei, who had started out looking for computer-related work, was, by the third weekend, not even stopping at booths that required basic computer skills. "What about this one?" I asked her, pointing to a company that required PC and PowerPoint skills. She scowled. "No, I'd be really scared about making a good PowerPoint presentation. It's not worth applying." The students thus self-limited their options; after five years of schooling in the computer field, and even after several years of part-time work, they felt themselves unqualified for even the most basic computer-related jobs.

To be fair to the students, it was not as if they were simply naïfs set adrift in a mysterious but rational labor system. The more we observed the ways the interviewers worked, the more we suspected that many of the companies— or the people representing them at the job fairs—were at least partly making up the rules as they went along. For example, Wei Ren tried to hand her résumé to a company to apply for a job doing phone sales but was told she wasn't tall enough. Height is an extremely important marker of physical beauty in China today, and the students all knew that some jobs (especially receptionists and sales staff) required applicants to be particularly attractive, and most of those jobs therefore had minimum height requirements. But phone sales? Another company, interviewing her for a file clerk job, asked her a few random questions about her background, then announced that her Mandarin wasn't standard enough. Presumably, height and standard Mandarin in both these cases serve as proxies for various forms of cultural capital (Otis 2011). What is unclear is why phone sales and file clerks require these forms of cultural capital in the first place.

At the next booth, however, Tang Limei was dismissed for speaking Mandarin that was *too* standard; the company's customers, she was told, were all local Nanjingers who would be put off by sale staff who spoke with very standard Mandarin accents. Tang was left tearing her hair in frustration, unable to discern what, specifically, employers really wanted in an applicant. There seemed to be no rational rules guiding the system. In other cases students did not seem to recognize some of the random questions posed by interviewers were opportunities to make themselves more attractive to employers. Xiao Gu, interviewing for sales jobs was asked: "Have you read any of Tony Robbins's books?" He simply replied, "Yes."

In spite of the students' limitations—their inability to generate the right kinds of narratives of progress, investment in the self, and diligence; their vocational degrees; and their radically lowered expectations over the weeks they attended the job fairs—eventually all of the computer tech graduates did find jobs. Indeed, several of them got calls back from interviewers they met at the job fairs and were hired for jobs they had first found in the Convention Center.

After Graduation: Jobs, Jumping, and Planning for the Future

In the weeks following the job fairs, we caught up with the same six students to find out how they were doing in their new jobs. We discovered that once they had broken the initial barrier of starting their first full-time jobs, the most important skill the new graduates needed following their graduation was learning how to "jump feeding troughs" (*tiaocao*), Chinese slang for rapidly moving from one job to another. We were stunned to learn that by July, some of the same Canal School computer tech students had already held three different jobs. Although they attended their first job fairs in early March with tremendous trepidation, unsure of how to sell themselves on the job market, they were very quick learners. Within only a few months their working worlds looked quite different.

The job fairs had initially been very intimidating, leading the students to greatly reduce their expectations and demands. But once they began their first jobs, the students discovered that they may have lowered their expectations too far. Calls to friends and classmates across the city to compare working conditions revealed small but important differences that led them each to quickly quit their first jobs. As soon as someone heard that another company provided free lunches or that there were jobs located several bus stops closer to home, they "jumped." Sometimes they jumped after perceived incidents of mistreatment.

For example, only two weeks after Xu Wenjuan was hired as a clerk at a small machine tools company, she was assigned to represent the business at another job fair. Instructed to wear high heels and a dress (which she loathed) so she would "look professional," Xu was told to stand at one side of the booth and "say nothing." She spent eight hours standing at the job fair in silence, without sitting down or talking to anyone once. She quit the next day.

Of course, this amount of jumping depended on a seemingly endless availability of entry-level jobs, another lesson the students learned almost immediately. In spite of the initial trouble they had breaking in to their first jobs, the enormous growth in the Chinese service economy at that time, combined with the rapid turnover of staff, meant that there was a huge demand for employees. There were retail, phone sales, and file clerk jobs, data entry and office staff work, entry-level computer and tech support jobs, and, increasingly in 2008, Internet-related work. Each job had its own characteristics and its own small strengths and weaknesses, any of which might be worth jumping into or out of. The students tried many of them. By July we had trouble locating and keeping up with them. Several of them told us they were already exhausted, after only four months of full-time work.

Flexible Labor and a New Generation of Young Chinese Workers

The students' experiences as job seekers and jumpers raise many issues that link them to other laborers in China—and the global economy. One is related to the flexibility of the kind of work they performed. On a regular basis the graduates changed not only the companies they worked for but the kinds of work they did, the conditions under which they worked, the nature of the tasks they performed, and the skills involved. Few found jobs in their area of vocational training. This kind of labor flexibility is a well-documented aspect of postindustrial economies around the globe (see, e.g., Dunk 2002; Harvey 1990; E. Martin 1994). To date, however, few have discussed that this is increasingly the way that young people in China are seeking and performing interactive service work in cities today, as industrial work moves out of cities and into periurban and formerly rural parts of China.[10]

These students are flexible workers, which is precisely what they learned in their vocational studies. Their contract teachers modeled labor flexibility every day. They learned that labor is not only commodified but is disposable and easily replaced. The students quickly demonstrated their ability to seek new opportunities and their willingness to grab them.

In this, the students closely resemble youth in other parts of the world. But this kind of labor flexibility is new for this generation of Chinese graduates and is specific to this particular moment of exponential growth in the Chinese economy, when service-sector jobs grew 30 percent in a decade (State Council of China 2012). In this the students were both similar to, and different from, their parents in some interesting ways. This was cause of some intergenerational tension. Many of the students' parents also had been "flexible" laborers who had migrated from the country to the city and worked in a series of jobs as manual laborers. Many of the urban *hukou*-holding parents had also changed work, as they were laid off from socialist-sector industrial jobs and moved through a series of low-end jobs in the private sector. Yet in spite of their parents' own flexible work histories, the students reported that their parents all pressed them to find stable, secure jobs and disapproved of their children's tendency to jump around. When we met in the early summer of 2008, the students told us that their parents were unhappy with their frequent job changing, but they were ignoring their parents' preferences.

For example, over dinner one evening, Tang Limei told us that at her most recent job, all the employees were expected to eat lunch together. She was always placed next to the company's accountant. He noticed that she had a nervous habit of tapping her foot and one day at lunch told her sharply to stop, saying that it's a very bad habit. Tang was mortified and felt that she'd been publicly humiliated. "What could I do?" she said. "He's the accountant. If I talked back to him, maybe he'd dock my pay." She told this to her father, who strongly advised her to ignore the criticism, stick it out for a year to gain some work experience, and save some money—and to stop tapping her foot. Tang quit anyway. My research assistant, aghast, asked, "You were willing to defy your father like that?" Tang replied, "My father adores me. Even if he disagrees with me, he'll go along with whatever I decide."

Wei Ren told us a similar story. After a few weeks scouting various options at the job fairs, she confirmed that she wanted to work in sales. Her parents objected, arguing that it was not an appropriate field for girls. They wanted her to get an office job, where she would stay safely in one place all day and not have to interact with strangers. To please her parents, she started an office job but was bored with the work, and she was in continuous conflict with her bosses and colleagues. She quit without telling her parents and took a sales job working on commission, where the work was faster paced and she had a chance to make significantly more money. Her parents had no choice but to concede that a job in sales was better than no job at all. Wei seemed much happier.

Although they were not always obedient to their parents, the students did keep their parents' experiences firmly in mind as they sought jobs. As several of them noted, even their entry-level service-sector jobs were generally better than what many of their parents did for a living. Tang reminded me that her father was a migrant worker on a construction site in Nanjing; as long as she continued to find work that was indoors and sitting down, he would be fine with her choices. Wang Shui's father was disabled and living on a meager state pension from his former industrial *danwei* in Nanjing; while her parents urged her to find something stable and reliable, her irregular work selling computer parts still brought in more money to the household than her parents' pension. The students' earlier filial obedience was thus tempered by their newfound economic power in their families.

Conclusion: Class Formations

The students' job jumps were by no means random; they were motivated and (mostly) reasoned. Yet even if there was a logic to each of their job jumps, their moving around to various different jobs was never couched in terms of a rational narrative of development, nor did they ever see their jumping as part of a linear process of developing the self (Miyazaki 2006). Job jumping did not add up to a long-term strategy that led to a professional end point. Work experience was not seen as cumulative, a form of investment in the self, or even résumé building. They did not construct narratives of the self with a trajectory into the future or narrate themselves as desiring, choosing subjects. They found jobs, then changed them, according to short-term, instrumental logics.

It is important to note a few things about their job jumping. While they had a lot of horizontal mobility, there was not a lot of vertical mobility in their job moves; job mobility did not equate to social mobility (McDowell 2012). Some of these limitations were structural, and some were limitations the students set themselves. Although they jumped for better conditions and treatment, they still settled for relatively low pay and jobs with little chance of advancement. Even a few years after graduating, they often continued to define "better conditions" by such things as the quality of air conditioning in their offices, the convenience of the workplace to their local bus line, and whether they had one day off every weekend. Additionally, none of their moves positioned them to begin to move into management positions or into the new middle classes. Finally, while their very high levels of job mobility gave the computer tech graduates the appearance of having power and autonomy, Tang Limei's story is telling. Once they are hired, they feel vulnerable to higher-ranking, professional staff, and if they experience conflict or problems, they exercise the only real power they have: the power to quit (S. Willis 1998).

Their working lives are thus categorized by high levels of horizontal job mobility, few opportunities for vertical mobility, and jobs based entirely within the service sector. What does this say about their futures, particularly about their future class positions?

I have argued that the HSEE was a moment of "class sorting" in China, whereby students who fail this exam are sorted into the working classes in two ways. One is a division whereby urban working-class families send their children to vocational schools because youth from wealthier families who failed the HSEE can buy their way out of the vocational system and into private academic high schools. The other is a class sorting that takes place after graduation, when vocational school students are locked out of middle-class, white-collar jobs because they lack the appropriate educational credentials. Now, having looked more closely at their school-to-work transition, the class-sorting process is clearer after the hurdle of the job fairs.

In the Conclusion I return to Nanjing to see how some of the vocational students fared a few years after their graduation. I explore there some of the characteristics of the urban working class the students are entering, including the ways the vocational youth increasingly resemble their age-mates around the world.

Conclusion

Precarious China

I CONCLUDE with two anecdotes, which occurred one year apart.

.   .   .

Nanjing. Summer, 2012. Although I recruited the help of Emma Wang and my former research assistants, when I returned to Nanjing, I had some difficulty setting up meetings with the voc ed students we used to know. We tried using social media, texting, mobile phones, and e-mail. But once the Canal and Bridge School students graduated, they scattered—across the city, the province, all across China. Unlike much existing research on China—and common sense—that predicts that connections among former classmates are important social links for young adults, it appeared that the voc ed students we knew well had not maintained very strong social connections after graduating. I had the sense that we had trouble connecting with them because they were not well connected with each other.

Eventually, one of my former research assistants tracked down Canal School computer tech course graduates Xu Wenjuan and Wang Shui. We arranged to meet for dinner at an upscale café in Nanjing where we had met before in 2007–2008. Yet when we rendezvoused on a humid July evening, the café no longer existed, and the only available place to eat was a hot and noisy Pizza Hut in the basement of a nearby shopping mall. We crowded into a booth there, and the two young women, formerly good friends in the Canal School computer tech class, eyed each other warily. They had not seen each other in almost two years.

Xu Wenjuan started off. After two years of jumping to different jobs after she graduated, she had settled into a permanent job in a customer service call center at one of China's largest online travel agencies. She worked six days a

week in an operations center on the far outskirts of Nanjing. The company provided employees with low-cost dormitory beds and cafeteria meals during the
week. She returned to her parents' home in central Nanjing every weekend. She
reported that the job was quite stressful, for customers called the service center
only when something had gone wrong with their travel plans; they called when
they were angry or dissatisfied with their flights or hotels or when they had
visa problems with international travel. She said that her job consisted almost
entirely of listening to people scream at her all day. When I shuddered with horror at this description of her daily work, she merely shrugged philosophically.

Three years earlier she had broken up with Su Xiaogang, her boyfriend
throughout vocational school. Somewhat ironically, her former boyfriend had
been hired as a technician by the Nanjing subway system—a job that many of
the Bridge School graduates would have coveted. Since their breakup Xu had
not had a boyfriend and was now reaching the potentially dangerous age of her
mid- to late twenties when she might be considered an "old maid" (*shengnü*)
and too old for marriage. She admitted that her parents were starting to get a bit
worried about her marriage prospects, although she was less concerned about
marriage than about her overall quality of life. She said that she had a pretty
good income, and her job was fairly secure, but she did nothing but work six
days a week, then return to her parents' house, and spend her one day off sleeping and watching TV. Her school friends had scattered, and because her workplace dorm had no Internet connection, she had poor social media connectivity
for keeping in touch with old friends during the week. She was too tired on her
day off every week to socialize much. Life, she said, was terribly boring. Since
graduating from the Canal School, she had saved enough money (with help
from her parents) to buy a small apartment of her own in Nanjing's distant suburbs across the Chiangjiang River but had not yet renovated the space so that it
was livable. She was waiting to see what would happen regarding her marriage
prospects before she did anything with the property. As is common in urban
China, Xu insisted that she would not date a man who did not already own his
own apartment, even though she already owned an apartment of her own.

Wang Shui snorted in response. As far as she was concerned, Xu's loneliness
was Xu's own fault, a result of her pickiness on the marriage and property markets. Wang stated flatly that she thought that Xu was being silly: since she owned
her own apartment, she should lower her standards and start dating men who
didn't own property. Wang herself had married two years earlier and arrived at
our dinner six months pregnant. Wang, a native of Nanjing, had made a most
unusual marriage decision: she married a migrant worker, a slightly younger

man from a very poor family in rural Anhui who had moved to Nanjing as a laborer. "He's a good guy," she assured me. "He's a little younger than me and a little fat, but it's okay with me." Wang explained that she and her husband, Xiao Zhu, had saved and scrimped until they could start their own business, a small stall in one of the computer retail marketplaces in Nanjing, where they sold low-cost computer supplies such as printers, toner, and USB flash drives. They worked ten hours a day, seven days a week, every day of the year except for a short break during the Spring Festival holiday when they visited her in-laws in the countryside. They had recently arranged for her husband's sister to move in with them from their village; she helped out with the business and would help care for the baby after it was born.

Wang's parents were still unwell. Her father was disabled, and her mother supported the family by selling vegetables in a local market. A source of pride today is that her small business enables Wang to contribute more money to support her parents, something her husband, atypically, strongly encouraged. "He has lots of siblings back in the countryside, and they help his parents, so he and his sister can help me care for my parents," she explained. "Even though I'm a daughter-in-law and technically I'm supposed to care for *his* parents, I'm an only child. He understands this and helps me take care of my family instead." She was pleased at the way her unorthodox decisions had enabled her to be a filial daughter to her impoverished parents.

Wang said that in spite of the relentless work hours, she enjoyed having her own business and liked working every day with her good-natured husband. They were currently renting a tiny apartment but were saving money to buy their own place. She said that she was grateful that she had married a man with whom she got along well, with whom she could build a business and family, and with whom she could work to build an independent life without having to rely on either set of parents. Xu, she said, was just being too picky—if she'd just consider broadening her criteria (*tiaojian*) for a boyfriend, she, too, could get married and start an independent life. Xu smiled wanly.

The evening was slightly uncomfortable. Xu, unhappy with Wang's criticism of her life choices, switched topics, and they began sharing gossip about their former classmates rather than talk more about themselves. Although Xu was the former class president, she did not have as much detailed news of many of her classmates as we had hoped. Most of the classmates she and Wang had information about were working in retail, staffing sales counters in various kinds of stores. A few others, they reported, had found jobs in Internet companies, while others, like Xu, were working as customer service reps. Some of the students who were originally from rural areas had left Nanjing and moved back to their home villages or to nearby county-level townships. There, some were trying to start Internet-based businesses on Taobao (an online marketplace) or had opened small computer shops. Detailed information was fairly limited, however, since neither had remained in very close contact with most of their former friends.

After dinner I left the restaurant with Wang to meet her husband, who was waiting patiently on the curb to take her home on the back of his heavy, socialist-era bicycle. She had indeed "married down" in the relentless, hypergamous Chinese marriage scheme that dictates that urban women should only marry men who are urban, taller, older, and better educated than themselves. Xiao Zhu was slightly shorter than Wang and a bit pudgy, especially next to her painfully thin frame. He had the plain clothes, dusky complexion, and spiky haircut that immediately identify a rural migrant in China's cities. But his smile shone with kindness, and he beamed with pleasure when he saw Wang approach; he clearly adored the down-to-earth, practical woman he had married. He shook my hand a bit shyly, for he had never met a foreigner before. As they pedaled away, he turned and waved good-bye to me again over his shoulder and smiled with genuine warmth. It seemed to me that if a prospect like Xiao Zhu were among the possible choices, Xu Wenjuan could do far worse than "marrying down" as Wang had.

Marriage may be the most salient issue in the voc ed graduates' lives today (cf. Osburg 2013).[1] The biggest question is how young people in working-class retail and other urban service-sector jobs will be able to raise enough capital to meet the stringent requirements of the marriage market. The problem is most acute for the men: If most women are like Xu Wenjuan and will only consider them as marriage partners once they own property, how will they be able to marry if they first must own an apartment? If their parents cannot afford to buy them a home, will marriage be out of the question? For some of the students, their best option may be to subvert the rigid social conventions about marriage partners. Since these students have already subverted so many of the formerly rigid social "rules" in China, this may be possible. Only a decade ago, for example, the idea of a young, single, working-class woman like Xu owning her own apartment would have been unthinkable, as would young people leaving a major city to seek work in a smaller city or township. Perhaps these youth will eventually be pathbreakers in the marriage market as well.

More concerning, however, is their relative lack of contact with each other. From what I could tell, the former classmates had not had a falling out, and I had the sense that the students I spoke with wished they were all closer. The graduates I met with suggested two causes for their relative lack of close connections with their former classmates. One was connectivity. Although they were all tech savvy, they said that lack of easy access to Internet connections, plus the expense of phone and Internet time, prevented them from using as much social media as they would have liked to stay in close touch. This is likely changing, for within a year of our meeting smart-phone use in China skyrocketed, and Internet connection costs lowered significantly. The more insidious problem was lack of time. Working six or seven days a week is not highly conducive to maintaining an active social life, regardless of access to social media. Even with better and more affordable connectivity, maintaining better connections among themselves may be difficult.

Presumably the graduates can and do draw upon each other for assistance as necessary; being former classmates creates life-long *guanxi* relations regardless of how actively they maintain their networks socially. But the sense I had was of atomized urban young people, increasingly disconnected from the kinds of social networks that once would have provided social stability and identity. The graduates I spoke to lived in tiny nuclear families; worked long, tiring days in stressful or repetitive jobs; and reported having little time or money for leisure activities. Many seemed to be finding their own ways through the new economy and the new urban landscapes, disconnected and somewhat alarmingly on their own.

. . .

Shanghai. Summer, 2013. I have given a talk about my vocational schools research to a group of Chinese graduate students in the social sciences. It has not gone well. Like the friends who questioned vocational schools as a research topic when I first arrived in China, these graduate students were similarly disinclined to believe the VE is worth studying. And, like my friends in 2007 (and many other highly educated Chinese in 2013), my audience that day was particularly concerned about the plight of the "ant tribes" (*yizu*), a slang expression sometimes used to describe the growing number of unemployed, impoverished university graduates in China's larger cities (Lian 2009). And as the audience also made clear during my talk, vocational schools and vocational students were just as socially disdained in 2013 as when I began my study in 2007.

My audience informed me that the ant tribes *deserve* to be studied, while vocational students do not. For these highly educated Chinese youth, there was an unspoken imperative for researchers to study a socially abject but deserving group and then offer applied, policy-based recommendations to solve the problems the research has identified. My work on vocational schools failed on both these counts. Voc ed students, they reminded me, end up in vocational school because they are bad students, unlike the ant tribes who studied well enough to complete both regular high school and university. Further, after graduation the vocational students *do* find jobs, which makes them much better off than the morally superior yet unemployed ant tribes. In fact, they continued, the newspapers had all published stories of vocational school graduates who struck it rich as entrepreneurs, which proved that my research findings were wrong: vocational school graduates are *not* becoming members of a new working class.

Some of these points were correct. According to information released by the Chinese government, vocational school graduates *are* doing well on the job market. Indeed, according to recent statistics, a vocational secondary degree is a better predictor of immediate employment after graduation than a BA. The Ministry of Education's 2012 *Report on Development and Employment of Chinese Secondary Vocational School Students* stated that vocational students have had employment rates over 95 percent since 2007, while university graduates' job rate in 2011 was only 90.6 percent.[2] This is largely because university enrollments increased very rapidly in the past fifteen years, much faster than the economy could absorb the new graduates.[3] As a result, the growing numbers of unemployed university graduates, many of whom have gone into significant debt for their education, are a serious social problem. At the moment, however, it is somewhat difficult to tease out what is actually happening to the ant tribes from the moral panic reported in the Chinese media and blogosphere.

In addition, the issue of unemployed educated youth is by no means restricted to China. Anthropologists have documented a growing crisis of under- and unemployed educated young people across the globe, including India (Jeffrey 2010), Morocco (Cohen 2004), Papua New Guinea (Demerath 1999), Senegal (Ralph 2008), and Ethiopia (Mains 2007). Yet because of the regime of numeric capital, the ant tribe issue had a particular moral urgency for these graduate students.

To counter the students' other arguments, I quoted Paul Willis, who pointed out that the success of a few individuals does not negate the structural forces that produce class formations for the vast majority:

> Opportunities are created only by the upward pull of the economy, and then only in relatively small numbers for the working class. The whole nature of

Western capitalism is also such that classes are structured and persistent so that even relatively high rates of individual mobility make no difference to the existence or position of the working class. (1977, 127)

Although he was specifically discussing Western capitalism, there are as yet no indications that the Chinese system is operating any differently. "Socialism with Chinese characteristics" and its unique blend of capitalism and socialism may have enabled a few working-class entrepreneurs with low levels of formal education to gain enormous wealth, but this does not mean that the vast majority have equivalent opportunities for class mobility.

I reminded the students that this is true at least partly because of state policy, which streams almost half of the nation's HSEE testers into VE, regardless of the students' efforts or moral probity. One of the graduate student bristled at my assertion. "Are you saying that this is wrong?" he demanded angrily. "Do you mean to suggest that anyone who wants to go to regular high school should be able to? And are you accusing the Chinese government of *intentionally* sabotaging the lives of half of the nation's youth?" The room grew quiet, for here the discussion took a potentially dangerous turn. With this question I potentially moved from the safe and familiar category of being a foreigner who simply doesn't understand China (by refusing to accept their commonsense moral categories), to possibly being a foreigner who is "anti-China" by openly criticizing the Chinese government. I tried to tread carefully.

The answer, of course, was both yes and no. In some ways, the Chinese government *is* intentionally sorting almost half of the nation's youth out of the academic stream and into the working classes through the mechanism of the HSEE. The Ministry of Education has a stated policy goal that around 50 percent of the nation's secondary students should enter vocational training. Current statistics show they are close to achieving this goal.[4]

But it is important to understand this in a global context. No nation educates all of its youth identically. *All* nations with formal education systems use these systems to sort young people, although different countries sort in different ways. Resources are allocated differentially; different students have different abilities and needs; labor markets absorb workers with different kinds of training. Many countries sort by class. One common class-sorting method, for example, is to underfund public education so that only wealthy students receive a decent education through private schooling. Others sort by region, where students from one part of a nation (i.e., cities) are privileged over others. These decisions are usually framed as a problem of resource allocation, not as a policy of class sorting, but the overall effect is one of class (re)production (see Slater 2010; Khan 2011). Gender, race, language, and ethnicity are also categories for which some educational systems may sort—and eliminate—students.

With this response, my hapless interlocutor's frustration rose at my seeming refusal to answer a question directly. What, he demanded, did I advocate as vocational educational policy for China? What were my policy recommendations to improve VE? Sadly, I had none to offer; this was not the goal of my research, nor did I see it as my position to advise the Chinese government on how to run its affairs.

Nor, in fact, do I need to. Educational researchers in China, including officials of the Ministry of Education itself, are already deeply critical of the vocational education system and have offered far more trenchant criticisms of the system than I have. Most of the criticisms I have implicitly or explicitly leveled against the schools—that schools throw educational "products" at students without teaching them to specialize in any particular skill; that some teachers are not properly trained; that the students don't want to be there; that assessment tools are poor or nonexistent—all of these and more have already been pointed out in Chinese- and English-language studies that seek ways to improve Chinese vocational education (e.g., Shi 2013; Luo 2013; Ministry of Education 2011; Yi et al. 2013; Zhou 2008). My goal instead has been to think about vocational schools as places to understand changing regimes of value in contemporary urban China and as sites of incipient class formation.

My audience, however, was deeply frustrated. To my dismay, one young woman appeared to be on the verge of tears. "If you can't give us any suggestions about how to improve our schools, then tell us how vocational education works in your country!" she wailed. "If your research isn't applied, then it at least should be comparative to be of any use!"[5] This was a good point, although from my perspective, the most useful comparison that I could offer was not a study of any particular foreign vocational education system. The Chinese Ministry of Education and Chinese educational researchers already publish detailed comparative studies of China's vocational schools with their global counterparts to seek ways to improve China's education system (e.g., Lei and Jiang 2013; Yan Hao 2010).

My goal has been to use a comparative approach to move away from assumptions of Chinese cultural exceptionalism in education and to utilize vocational schools as a platform for a comparative study of class formations. How are urban Chinese youth similar to their age-mates elsewhere? How is the new Chinese working class linked to the global economy?

Class Formations

This project began as an implicitly comparative study, for it was inspired by Paul Willis's *Learning to Labor* (1977). When he carried out his groundbreaking research in industrial England in the early 1970s, Willis asked, Why do young working-class males choose to enter the working classes? After all, he noted, the English government did not hold a gun to young people's heads to force them into dead-end factory jobs. Why, then, did so many young males continue to choose this work? Willis found that the working-class young men in his study, the "lads," waged a continual battle against the authority of the school, a battle he called "counter-school culture," which served as a kind of "cultural apprenticeship" to the realities of working-class life. This resistance to school rules and learning was not, he argued, because the lads lacked academic ability, for "the complex and subtle skills of their counter-school culture were equal to the intellectual skills required in the classroom" (1977, 128). Yet the lads' resistance to school, classes, and teachers "ultimately cemented their own subordination in the labor market" and relegated them to a lifetime of industrial-sector labor (ibid.).

Willis argued convincingly that the lads' classrooms were spaces of incipient working-class formations. What, then, is being produced at the Bridge and Canal Schools? If vocational schooling in urban China is partly an exercise in class formation, what kind of class is forming, and how does this compare globally?

Unlike Willis's lads, the vocational school students are not moving into an industrial economy but instead are finding job in the lower ends of a new urban service economy. Otis (2011) and Hanser's (2008) exemplary ethnographic studies of interactive service workers in China are among the few studies of this sector so far, so little is yet known about low-end service work as a growing form of labor. This is surprising, given that this is the fastest-growing sector of China's economy.[6] So far, there is little research on how workers in these jobs constitute a new segment of the working class.

The contours of this segment of the working class are also difficult to define. On the one hand, it is defined by what it isn't. Low-end service labor is defined partly as not being middle-class employment.[7] After graduation the vocational school students are not going to enter the "shiny new middle classes" (Slater 2010) that have drawn significant scholarly attention in the past few years, both in China and internationally (see, e.g., Goodman 2008; Li Chunling 2010; Tomba 2009; Zhang L. 2010). There are currently contentious debates about how to define the new Chinese middle classes, including definitions based on income, occupation, social strata, and political power (see Li Cheng 2010 for a review). There is consensus, however, that a university degree is a minimal requirement for entry into the middle class, for analysts agree that at the very least, membership in China's new middle classes requires a white-collar job and tertiary credentials. The vocational students, of course, do not meet these requirements. Whatever the specific definition of "middle class" may be, scholars all agree that the process of middle-class formation in China is exclusionary; vocational school graduates are among those who are excluded.[8]

Yet if they are excluded from the growing new middle classes, neither will the urban vocational students become members of the new *industrial* working class that some scholars argue is now forming in China's export factories (Pun and Lu 2010; Pun and Smith 2007). These workers have also drawn significant attention from Chinese and foreign researchers, partly because of the shocking working conditions in their factories (e.g., Lee 1998; Pun 2005; Pun and Chan 2012). Pun and Smith (2007) in particular have worked to theorize this group as a new class formation. Yet this is an industrial workforce, forming out of a rural population that has come together to form a new factory labor force; they are a very different group of workers who live in a different setting and who have different working lives, backgrounds, and life course trajectories than the students from the urban vocational secondary schools.

A Chinese Precariat?

As in so many areas of their lives, the urban vocational school students seem to fall between the cracks. In this case, they fall between the new middle classes and an incipient industrial working class. The VE youth I knew in Nanjing will form a segment of the urban working class, but the nature of this segment— what it will be like, what its future holds, and whether or not it will form a class "in and for itself" in Marx's definition—is exceptionally hard to pin down. This is precisely the point.

Their futures in uncertain service-sector jobs and their tenuous class positions link the vocational graduates to youth in other parts of the postindustrial world who have sometimes been called the new "precariat" (Allison 2012; Bourdieu 1998; Cross 2010; Mitropoulos 2006; Molé 2010; Muehlebach 2012; Neilson and Rossiter 2008; Southwood 2011; Standing 2011). The term "precariat" originated in Italy, where it was coined to describe a "lack of secure, work based identity" (Standing 2011, 9). Today the term is generally used to describe a growing group of mostly young workers, largely in Europe, who work in low-skilled, frequently part-time jobs with few benefits, little security, and no future. This kind of work is spreading globally, particularly in the postindustrial economies (Standing 2011).

Of course, unlike the situation scholars and the media describe in Europe, where a surplus of young workers is super-exploited by employers (Southwood 2011; Standing 2010), in China's larger cities today there is a very different situation: at the moment, there appears to be a surplus of low-end service-sector jobs, with young people jumping among them. Yet while this sector now provides multiple job opportunities for urban Chinese youth, these jobs offer low salaries with high turnover, low upward mobility, and few benefits. This resembles the employment situation for millions of postindustrial youth worldwide. But unlike international youth who are described as facing massive insecurity because of informal, irregular, and casual work (Cross 2010), the vocational school graduates in China appear to be facing a possible future of plenty of jobs yet with nowhere to go but sideways.

To date, the term "precariat" has rarely been used to describe labor in China, except to describe the industrial labor performed by rural migrants in export-zone factories (Lee and Kofman 2012; Pun 2004; Pun and Lu 2010). The fact that little work has been done on urban precariousness in China, in my opinion, is less because the concept it is not applicable or translatable to China (Neilson and Rossiter 2008) than because so few people are studying urban working-class youth.[9] Yet indications are that the urban service-sector work has many of the hallmarks of precarious labor. The VE graduates' service-sector jobs require relatively little skill or training. They have no job protection or security and are easily replaced. Their salaries are low. None of the graduates I knew reported any mechanisms at their jobs for moving out of the lower rungs of employment into management tracks. Their entry-level jobs may, perhaps, become their permanent jobs.

What this precarious group of workers at the lower ends of the urban service sector may look like as a segment of China's urban working classes over time is still an open question. If the number of unemployed university graduates (the ant tribes) continues to grow, they will likely put downward pressure on the urban labor market, possibly pushing vocational school graduates into ever-lower-paid work with ever-less security and status. Squeezed between rural migrant workers on one side and university and high school graduates on the other, vocational school graduates may find their options, and their lives, increasingly tenuous. If increasing numbers of vocational secondary graduates find that their *zhongzhuan* credentials are not enough to distinguish them from rural migrant workers in the urban labor market, then social precarity among this group can be expected to spread. The final outcomes are, of course, still unknown.

Class Consciousness?

This raises important questions about class consciousness and whether or not there may be a growing class identity associated with the graduates' new structural position in the changing economy. After all, for decades in China an individual's class designation was foundational to his or her identity, and throughout the Mao era, class was a foremost way of defining the self.[10] Since then, class as a concept and as a social category of analysis has been attenuated (Anagnost 2008a). Yet there are still many unresolved questions about what may constitute the grounds of individual and collective identity for this new segment of the working class. Could class become a relevant category of individual experience, meaning, and identity?

Others have made this claim for the new class formations in China. Pun and Lu (2010) argue that second-generation migrant factory workers are beginning to form an identity as a new, "semi-proletarian" class in China's export factories. Pun and her colleagues have looked at "dormitory regimes," where factory workers, particularly second-generation migrant workers, live and work together under very difficult and exploitative conditions (Pun and Chan 2013; Pun and Smith 2007). They argue that the conditions for a new proletariat are forming as a result of the government's *hukou* regulations. These workers are unable to make a decent living wage in the factories, yet because of *hukou* regulations they are prohibited from legally moving to the nation's cities and cannot gain full urban citizenship; at the same time, as second-generation factory workers they have no identity as ruralites and no home in the countryside to which they can return. The factory dormitories where these workers live are therefore sites of simmering anger and resentment. This is increasingly channeled into new forms of self-representation, such as worker poetry and literature (Sun 2012) and new forms of collective action. These grievances and these activities, Pun and Lu (2010) argue, may be precursors to a growing class consciousness.

At the other end of the socioeconomic spectrum, a new middle-class identity is coming into being through lifestyle practices and new forms of (conspicuous) consumption (Osburg 2013; Tomba 2009; Wang J. 2008; Zhang L. 2010). While this identity is still fragile, labile, and, in some cases, morally compromised (Osburg 2013), a nascent form of class consciousness around middle-class lifestyles is beginning to grow across China. The middle classes and the "new rich" are thus starting to form class identities separate and distinct from those of the working-class masses below them (Goodman 2014; Zhang L. 2010).

The vocational school graduates once again seem to fall in between. Neither are they consuming their way into new lifestyle middle-class identities, nor are they living in confined worker dormitories where expressions of resentment and despair can be concentrated and focused against employers and the factory system, leading perhaps to nascent forms of class consciousness. Instead, I suggest that the labor conditions under which the voc ed graduates are working, as well as the structural and ideological systems that funneled them into the urban service sector in the first place, currently constrain the emergence of class consciousness (cf., Chan and Siu 2012; Woronov 2012).

Again, a comparison with global youth helps illustrate this point. One of the most useful aspects of the global theorizing on precarious labor today is the way this work can help us understand not only the labor conditions of these uncertain jobs but the ontological condition that working in a state of ongoing mobility and insecurity produces (Allison 2012; Southwood 2011; Cross 2012; Molé 2010; Sennett 1998). Anthropologist Anne Allison, studying Japan, calls this a state of "social precarity," which she defined as an outcome of "being consigned to unstable or insecure work" (2102, 349), while Southwood (2011) describes his experience of endlessly cycling through dead-end jobs in the UK as a kind of "non-stop inertia." Bourdieu, discussing the effects of long-term casual employment, says that it "profoundly affects the person who suffers it: by making the whole future uncertain, it prevents all rational anticipation and, in particular, the basic belief and hope in the future that one needs in order to rebel, especially collectively, against present conditions, even the most intolerable" (1998, 82). Bourdieu was referring to the ways that job insecurity and frequent job changes in the West hamper both collective consciousness and possible political consciousness, causing only atomization and individuation.

Precarity, in this view, is a labor process and ontological state closely related to larger neoliberal processes of individuation in the contemporary world (Beck 1992; Comaroff and Comaroff 2000; Giddens 1991). As Giddens notes, in today's world, young people's identities are understood to be generated as the sum product of the choices they have made. This concept of individuation— the ideology of responsibilization and of each young person bearing the burden of her or his own decisions—mitigates against collective actions and identities.

In the case of the vocational students, individuation is linked to the ideology of numeric capital, which holds individual young people responsible for their futures through their studying and test scores. The testing regimes place responsibility for the future on the shoulders of the individual child, who, by studying badly, is understood to be responsible for his or her future in vocational school and in the working class, while obscuring the structural forces that sort youth by class. In this model, state power is invisible and structural forces are erased. Each student bears individual responsibility for his or her future in the working class.

This individuation is reinforced as other forms of collective identity are shifting. The VE students seem to be increasingly detached from forms of collective identity that would have been unquestioned only a decade ago, including residency status, locality, and even dialect. The social connections possible when they were students—the friendships they made across *hukou*, family background, and geographic differences—may not withstand the stresses of adult life in the new economy. The strains of jumping jobs, saving money to buy apartments, and working out what their parents call the "marriage problem"—might supersede the relationships forged in the classrooms. They have to find new ways to build social connections that will be very different from those of their parents' generation. New collective identities, which may possibly be linked to their class status, are yet to emerge.

Yet the future may not be entirely grim, consisting only of free-floating anomic individuals drifting in and out of dead-end jobs. The ontological insecurities described among the precariat in Europe and Japan are exacerbated in those place by comparisons with their elders, who were the beneficiaries of postwar prosperity and Fordist labor regimes. There, the current generation is depressingly downwardly mobile. Yet for many of the Nanjing students' families, a move into the urban service economy and the urban working class is still a form of upward mobility. Although the vocational students will be locked out of the growing middle classes, they are fully aware that the jobs they do find in the urban service sector—as cashiers, sales clerks, call center operators, subway system security guards—are better than many of their parents' occupations. Recall that the students' parents worked all night to make tofu for the local market, lived on construction sites as security guards, or moved from city to city seeking work cleaning hotel rooms. For these youth, an urban job that is indoors, perhaps in a setting that includes heat in the winter and air conditioning in the summer, or a job that entails sitting down most of the day, is a distinct improvement in their generation. The new precariat that may be forming at the lower ends of the service sector should not obscure the possibilities and potentials these new opportunities may bring for individual youth.

. . .

The idea of promise and potential brings the story of these young people full circle, back to the image at the opening of this book: classrooms full of students sprawled on their desks, sleeping through class. I have shown that there is more behind this image than indicated by the stereotypes of vocational school students. The students, and their schools, are full of paradoxes and contradictions. The stereotypes of vocational students present them as academic and moral failures, yet they see themselves as moral and filial youth, even when they defied their parents to take a job they wanted. The state promises that vocational education will be a pathway to full participation in the modern urban economy, yet students and their families see it as a last resort. The ideology of numeric capital blames the students for their own fate, while obscuring the state's role in sorting the students by class. The schools promise skills training, yet the students learn few useful skills; even their teachers acknowledge that family connections are a better pathway into employment than their vocational degrees. The students seem to be breaking down a range of social barriers while they're in school—*hukou*, social background, place of origin—to form new friendships and connections, but our limited contact with them after graduation seems to point to adult lives of increasing fragmentation and precariousness.

Yet so much of who these students are and what they do are already so unlikely, according to our current predictions and stereotypes of Chinese youth, that the future may hold many surprises. Among this small group of youth there are already single women buying their own apartments and urban women marrying migrants from the countryside. Urban graduates are moving from a large city to a smaller ones to seek work. These are highly unusual and creative solutions to the challenges the students face in the changing economy.

Perhaps returning once again to Paul Willis for guidance may help clarify some of these paradoxes. Willis argued that the young working-class males he studied in England's industrial Midlands actively resisted the academic structures and cultures of schooling as part of a process of (re)producing their gendered working-class culture. In contrast, there is little culture of active resistance in the Nanjing vocational schools. There is, however, a strong culture of passive resistance, as students sleep through classes for days at a time. With a few exceptions, such as the bookkeeping class students' behavior around some of their teachers, the voc ed students stopped short of outright confrontation, choosing instead to disengage from school. Could this passive resistance form the grounds for a new kind of collective culture?

Anthropologist Pun Ngai has posited a "minor genre" of resistance in the factories she studied, a genre "capable of articulating a personal itinerary into a historical narrative and analysis" (2005, 166). From this perspective, perhaps the vocational students' passive resistance to their schools and their teachers might be the seed of a minor genre of resistance, leading to new modes of being in the working class. Pun suggests seeking new "terrain[s] of resistance" (167), which set the grounds to challenge existing social relations. The students' mode of being may not yet lead to collective action or conscious collective identity, but they are already open to new possibilities and to new kinds of lives. In the tentative and hesitant process of coming to class consciousness (Sun 2012), perhaps their moves into their adult lives may be a first step.

.   .   .

Today, the Western media inundates readers with stories of extremes in China. Salacious tales of abuse and exploitation in export factories are matched by stories of outrageous displays of conspicuous consumption by the new rich. Endless stories of cram schools where students study twenty hours a day feature next to tales of punk rockers. The unglamorous millions of urban youth who staff sales counters, restaurants, offices, and call centers are invisible in the discourse of the new urban China, yet these young people may be at the cutting edge of new social relations and new class formations. Although they are little seen, their futures will surely be as creative and interesting as their lives have been so far.

Notes

Introduction

1. Primary enrollment was estimated at 99.5 percent in 2007; junior middle school rose from 36.7 percent in 1985 to 98.0 percent in 2007 (Yan Hao 2010, 2). This figure is lower in poorer, far western, and minority areas, but today enrollment in grades K–9 is universal in larger, urban areas.

2. The name "regular" (*putong*) further indicates the ways that studying and high educational achievement are normative in China and that educational failure is stigmatized and unnatural.

3. This goal has been repeated regularly since then. For example, the Ministry of Education's "Work Priorities" for 2012 stated that "it will be ensured that regular high schools account for a ratio roughly same [*sic*] as that of vocational schools in the education of this stage" (Ministry of Education 2012, 9).

4. As Shi (2013) notes, vast differences in labor markets, levels of development, and training needs across the different parts of the country make it difficult to gather and produce national-level statistics. Although there are national-level goals that call for equal relative enrollment in regular high schools and vocational schools, officials also recognize that they have to take local conditions into account when setting targets and passing rates.

5. See Ministry of Education (2013a). Presumably, if 55 percent of students are enrolled in regular high schools (those who passed the HSEE), 45 percent must have failed, but that must be inferred from the enrollment data. A close look at the figures on this site shows the totals and relative percentages of vocational, technical, adult ed, and regular secondary enrollments have fluctuated significantly in the past fifteen years. This is more a reflection of changing policies than enrollment anomalies or demographic variations. Since 2000, the government has vigorously promoted voc ed (and then retreated from its initial vigor; see Lewin and Xu 1989; Yan Hao 2010), added vocational programs into regular high schools, converted some regular schools into vocational schools (and converted them back again), and changed the definition of what counts as a "vocational" or "technical" school. Luo refers to this as "disorderly management" (2013, 24).

6. See Ministry of Education (2013a). This number includes technical schools, vocational schools, and adult education.

7. Secondary vocational school graduates do have a few options to continue their education. Some vocational tertiary institutions are open to vocational secondary graduates (although most tertiary vocational institutions today serve graduates of regular high schools who fail the UEE and do not gain entry into regular universities). There is also a self-study version of the UEE for students who did not complete regular high school, but passing rates for these tests are exceptionally low. (A Jiangsu Province Educational Office official we spoke with in 2008 estimated the passing rate on the provincial "self-study UEE" was less than 5 percent.) Students who do pass the self-study UEE are admitted into separate programs on university campuses, where it is widely believed that they receive a second-rate education and are poorly positioned in the job market after graduation.

8. In spite of these limitations, a few vocational secondary graduates have become quite wealthy as entrepreneurs. The Chinese media frequently use the example of these few exceptions to make the case that the vocational stream does not foreclose class mobility. Yet, as Osburg (2013) notes, entrepreneurial wealth is morally suspect in China, and people are generally skeptical of those whose wealth is not clearly derived from white-collar employment.

9. Song, Loyalka, and Wei (2013) have completed one of the very few studies in English or Chinese that measured the ambitions and intentions of graduating ninth-graders against their actual educational outcomes after taking the HSEE, although it is based on a study of rural students.

10. These assumptions and discourses are increasingly mirrored globally around middle-class ethnic Chinese and their parenting styles; for example, the recent "Tiger Mother" (Chua 2011) phenomenon in the United States is an example of the way class is muted in the cultural naturalization of global "Chinese mothering," which supposedly focuses on pressuring children to study and high academic achievement.

11. The term—and concept—"economism" originated with a 1916 article by Lenin, later published in *Bolshevik* magazine, in which he refuted the possibility that socialist reforms can be purely economic and without a political dimension (Lenin [1916] 1929). For a discussion of the history of use of the term "economism" in China, see Wu (2014).

12. This is particularly stressful for families, because they are aware that sometimes their investments will not pay off. For example, because of the very rapid growth in Chinese tertiary education since 2000, increasing numbers of university graduates are finding that their (and their families') enormous investment in their education has not paid off, for the job market has been unable to absorb them. This is creating a well-publicized social and moral crisis of impoverished, unemployed young university graduates who have clustered in some of China's largest cities, a phenomenon known to sociologists there as the "ant tribes" (Lian 2009).

13. The value of students who excel at nonacademic tasks, such as athletes or musicians, is also produced through testing regimes that condense their abilities into test scores (Chumley 2013).

14. There are, of course, exceptions. See, e.g., Hanser (2008); Hsu (2007); Lee (2007); Otis (2011).

15. I cannot stress strongly enough that I am discussing *urban* schools, urban students, and labor markets in China's larger cities. The situation for rural schools, students, and labor markets is markedly different. This book does not discuss rural education or compare urban and rural vocational education. For an excellent discussion of rural secondary education, see Hansen (2014).

16. Western sources at the time romanized the city's name as "Nanking."

17. Note that all Chinese names are listed surname first, according to standard Chinese usage.

Chapter 1

1. Conservative approaches to vocational education during the Republican era dominated official educational policy, but they were not the only forms in existence. Radical anarchists, for example, also experimented with a kind of vocational education at the same time; see Chan and Dirlik (1991). There have been extensive studies of Republican-era education, particularly vocational schools and Huang Yanpei's role in Republican politics; see Gewurtz (1978); Schulte (2012, 2013); Schwintzer (1992); and Yeh (2008).

2. Education at all levels was complex and fraught during the Mao era, and at some times schools were literal battlegrounds for the ideological struggles of the CCP leadership. Many excellent sources cover these years, including Pepper (1996); Thøgersen (1990); and Unger (1982).

3. As many historians point out, the ascendency of the red faction did not end competition in education. Instead, competition over test scores and educational advancement transformed into competition among students over revolutionary ideology and the revolutionary purity of their family backgrounds. See A. Chan (1985); Hoffman (2010); Shirk (1982); and Wu 2014..

4. See Hoffman (2010) for an excellent and detailed discussion of how this transition worked for university graduates in the 1990s.

5. Interview, December 12, 2007, anonymous official, Jiangsu Department of Education.

6. Roughly US$435 and $100 at 2008 exchange rates.

7. Most regular high schools charged roughly the same amount for tuition at the time, but students enrolled in regular high school must pay higher fees for books, tutors, extracurricular activities, special preparation classes for the UEE, and other ancillary fees that bring the total cost of their education much higher than that of the vocational schools.

Chapter 2

1. The *China Development Brief* was an influential, Beijing-based, English-language monthly online newsletter about nongovernmental organizations (NGOs) and development in China. See Kahn (2007) regarding the closure.

2. The Chinese government implemented the *hukou* system in the mid-1950s to monitor and control population movement. Residence permits were assigned at birth, inherited from the mother, and divided the population into two broad categories: agricultural and nonagricultural. Holders of nonagricultural (i.e., urban) residence permits

were entitled to *danwei* work assignments and a bundle of socialist-era state benefits, particularly subsidized food rations. While it was possible to convert an urban *hukou* to a rural one (which was common during the Cultural Revolution, when millions of urban youth were relocated to the countryside), converting a rural *hukou* to an urban one was exceptionally difficult. As the private labor market began in the mid-1980s, however, increasing numbers of rural people began to move into China's cities without holding a legal residence permit for their new place of work. Called "rural migrant laborers" (*nongmin'gong or min'gong*), these workers now number in the hundreds of millions across China. Research on the *hukou* system and on migrant workers is voluminous; classic introductions include Chan K. (1996, 2012); Cheng and Selden (1994); Potter and Potter (1990); Solinger (1999); Zhang L. (2001).

3. Wet markets are covered but mostly outdoor street markets that sell food (as opposed to supermarkets or to outdoor street-stall markets that sell other things, like household goods or clothes).

4. Chinese sociologists have recently begun studying the *min'gong di'er dai* phenomenon in China's cities and generally conclude that as a group, these young people are not assimilating well into urban civil society, at least partly because they are largely excluded from taking the UEE and gaining tertiary education credentials. Researchers have also concluded that these second-generation migrant youth are isolated, lonely, and unsettled and have no sense of belonging in the cities where they live (see Zhongguo Gongyun Yanjiusuo, 2011). Based on my small-scale, qualitative research, I generally disagree with these findings, which tend to be based on large-scale, quantitative research. Anthropologist Pun Ngai has also looked at the "second-generation migrant" phenomenon, but her research has focused on factory workers, not urban dwellers (see Pun and Lu 2010).

5. It is important to stress that I by no means suggest that the HSEE is the only class-sorting mechanism in Chinese education. The UEE may also function to sort students into different classes; how this works requires further research.

6. This was not their only finding; the authors also found a strong correlation between HSEE scores and students' overall grades in junior middle school. Students with overall poorer grades did not score as well on the HSEE as the better students; performance on the HSEE is not correlated solely with income for this rural group. In addition, other factors contributed to the students' decision to attend vocational schools, including whether or not their parents were migrant workers and their parents' overall educational levels (Song, Loyalka, and Wei 2013).

7. There are presumably exceptions in urban areas, where children from wealthy families may opt for vocational schooling rather than private academic education, but this has not been the general trend. Rural families seem to opt for their children to repeat grade 9 and to then retake the HSEE. See Hansen (2014); Hansen and Woronov (2013); Song, Loyalka, and Wei (2013).

8. Osburg's recent (2013) work on China's new rich demonstrates that the entrepreneurial nouveaux riches may be admired for their wealth, but if their riches are not clearly linked to white-collar employment, there are deep social suspicions of this group's morality. Osburg, however, is vague on the specifics of the educational background of his entrepreneur informants.

9. These anxieties were not entirely without merit. Students in vocational courses have little reason to study diligently and may indeed be a disruptive influence on students for whom studying for the UEE was an extremely serious task.

Chapter 3

1. My Chinese surname is Wu, and the students at both schools all called me Teacher Wu (*Wu Laoshi*) as a polite form of address.

2. At both the Bridge and Canal Schools the curriculum was divided into two parts: basic classes (including Chinese, English, math, and politics) that were identical for all students and specific vocational classes that differed for each vocational course. The basic classes in both schools were watered-down versions of the regular secondary Nanjing curriculum, using materials specifically designed for vocational schools.

3. About US$4.35/hour at 2008 exchange rates.

4. Emma Wang, the graduate student research assistants, and I were also provided with free lunches every day we attended classes at the Bridge School. The food was hearty and healthy, and we all quite enjoyed it, which the Bridge School teachers adamantly refused to believe, accusing us of just being polite.

5. *Banzhuren* are also assigned to university students, but their responsibilities and power over tertiary-level students are limited compared to students in K–12.

6. *Tiaocao*, the common Chinese slang for rapidly changing jobs to seek better opportunities.

7. The equivalent of tenth grade in the American or Australian systems.

8. *Shehui qingnian* is a widely used term for both males and females who have completed school and begun working full-time, and implies young people who are no longer bounded or protected by the disciplines of schools and studying. In this particular context the term also implies a young person who is sexually active, although none of the students were willing to discuss this with me openly.

9. Teacher Zheng might have had a valid point. Otis, for example, points out that female job applicants who appeared too sexualized were not employable at the high-end luxury hotel she studied, and employees at the midrange hotel she studied had to put tremendous effort into deemphasizing their sexuality so they were not mistaken for the prostitutes who frequented the premises (2011, 79). How the sexualization of women's appearance influences employment opportunities and workplace culture in industries other than the hotel business remains to be studied.

10. Sent-down youth were urban youth relocated from urban areas to the countryside during the Cultural Revolution. See Zhou and Hou (1999) for a review.

11. It is important to note that this campus was about to close its doors, which surely affected the quality of its teaching and programs.

12. Because the largest cash denomination in China is a 100 RMB note, large transactions may require many hundreds of notes. In 2007–2008 debit and credit cards were rarely used.

13. We were never able to confirm who, precisely, administered these tests and the concomitant credentials.

14. Sociolinguists have recently begun to study different language ideologies

(Kroskrity 2000; Schieffelin et al. 1998) regarding standard Mandarin use in different social contexts in China, including ideologies that assume that lower-class status is linked to less-standard Mandarin skills. See, e.g., Dong (2009, 2010).

Chapter 4

1. This is not a phenomenon restricted to China. Scholars working with marginalized youth around the globe show that marginality is marked and evinced by challenging or subverting the dominant temporal logics of parents and the state (Jeffrey 2010, 2; Mains 2007; Ralph 2008; Shoshan 2012).

2. Han Geng is a Chinese K-pop star.

3. This is not just Chinese; young people around the world imagine future possibilities and constitute their identities in terms other than radical individualism. See, e.g., Mains (2007); Weiss (2002).

4. Su is referring to the 1937 Nanjing Massacre, or the "Rape of Nanking" (Chang 1997).

5. The year 2008 was eventful in China. Beijing's hosting of the Summer Olympics prompted demonstrations around the world against China's policies in Tibet and massive antigovernment uprisings across Tibet. For a detailed discussion of these events, see Smith (2010). Then on May 12, a catastrophic earthquake struck Wenchuan in Sichuan Province. The 7.9 quake was so powerful we felt it in Nanjing, almost 1,700 kilometers (1,050 miles) away. The tragedy of the earthquake, particularly the number of children killed, led to an outpouring of grief and national solidarity. Yin and Wang (2010) examine some of the ways the earthquake was represented in the Chinese media and its effect on the national psyche.

Chapter 5

1. This is a rough estimate, based on statistics released by the Chinese State Council's (Guowuyuan) National Development and Reform Commission, which claims that employment in service-related industries (the tertiary sector, *disan chanye*) grew from 198.23 million in 2000, to 230.11 million in 2004, 234.39 million in 2005, to 263.32 million in 2010. See Central People's Government of the People's Republic of China (2013).

2. The other male student in the bookkeeping class was surly and irritable and hated the girls' bantering. The girls in the class generally ignored him, and Zhang Zhigang patiently took the brunt of all their teasing.

3. This is not only true in China. Elizabeth Dunn (2004), for example, documented how the transition from socialism to capitalism in Poland involved pressuring workers to become more outgoing, confident, and self-motivated, all qualities associated there with the capitalist mode of production.

4. Zhang paid approximately $58, while the usual cost was about $72.

5. Internships are very common in China, even at the university level. For more on internships among vocational students, see Pun and Chan (2013).

6. Scholarly research on the moral ambiguities of *guanxi* is voluminous. Classic references in anthropology include Kipnis (1997); Yan Y. (1996); and Yang (1994).

7. Secretary Ji at the Canal School told us that 480,000 students were expected to

graduate from university in Jiangsu Province in 2008, and approximately 50,000 people would go to the first spring job fair seeking work. Today (2013), job hunting is increasingly done online rather than at job fairs.

8. See Otis (2011) for discussion of employers' use of a similar system to teach new employees how to present a narrative of themselves as appropriate employees.

9. In early 2008 there was an explosion in housing construction. Because new homes in China are sold without any interior fixtures and lack plumbing, electrical wiring, or any appliances, there was concomitant job growth in fields related to home decorating, including sales of furniture, plumbing and kitchen fixtures. These jobs were plentiful at the job fairs we attended, were considered very low prestige, paid low salaries, and had very low barriers to entrance.

10. Exceptions are discussed in Hanser (2008) and Otis (2011).

Conclusion

1. These youth are not alone. Anthropological research has documented marriage crises in India (Jeffrey 2010; Chowdhry 2009) and across Africa (Masquelier 2005; Cole 2014), as working-class youth across the world are increasingly unable to follow normative pathways to adulthood and marriage in the face of neoliberal economic transformations and structural adjustment policies.

2. See Ministry of Education (2012b). See also Wang and Ross (2013).

3. According to the Ministry of Education, passing rates on the UEE (and concomitant admissions into university) have skyrocketed in the past fifteen years. Ministry data indicate that while only 46.1 percent of graduating twelfth-graders passed the UEE in 1998, that rate had risen to 87.6 percent in 2013. See Ministry of Education (2013b).

4. See Ministry of Education (2013a), which indicates that 55 percent of the nation's youth attend regular high schools.

5. As Schulte (2012) points out, vocational education in China has been a comparative project since its inception in the early Republican era. In the broader sense, Chinese intellectuals have long been acutely aware of China's educational status relative to other nations. Pepper (1996) reviews the history of this comparative project; Anagnost (2008b) and Woronov (2006) explore some of the contemporary ideological aspects of the search for China's position on an educational global stage.

6. Recent statistics indicate that the tertiary sector has been growing at over 10 percent per year annually since 2000 and in 2012 was almost as large as the industrial sector (industry that year made up 45.3 percent of GDP; the service sector, 44.6 percent). See http://www.ce.cn/xwzx/gnsz/gdxw/201401/20/t20140120_2162354.shtml (accessed April 15, 2015) [in Chinese].

7. Service-sector work is highly stratified, covering a very wide spectrum of employment from hotel cleaners and retail sales clerks to lawyers, IT experts, and financial traders (Sassen 2012). Statistics on the growth of the tertiary labor sector include all forms of service employment; the voc ed graduates will enter only the lowest levels of this economy.

8. There are some exceptions, particularly where middle-class status is defined exclusively by personal wealth and consumption patterns. In those cases, wealthy entre-

preneurs may be defined as "middle class" regardless of their educational background (cultural capital). Many Chinese sociologists therefore tend to avoid defining middle-class status exclusively by income and consumption. See Li Chunling (2010).

9.　Some of the existing research on the urban service sector (e.g., Yan Hairong 2008; Sun 2009) looks specifically at migrant workers from the countryside. Because of China's *hukou* regulations, these studies understandably tend to focus more on the precarity of the workers than the work itself. In their studies of urban service workers, both Hanser (2008) and Otis (2011), however, noted that female interactive service workers in the sites they studied (department stores and hotels) are often pressured or forced to quit their jobs when they get married, pregnant, or reach their thirties. This relationship between gender, precarity, and age is a question open to much further research.

10.　The classic study of the essential role of classes and class labels in China during the Mao era is Billeter (1985); see also Meisner (1989); and Wu (2014).

References

Allison, Anne. 2012. "Ordinary Refugees: Social Precarity and Soul in 21st Century Japan." *Anthropological Quarterly* 85 (2): 345–370.

Anagnost, Ann. 1997. *National Past-Times: Narrative, Representation and Power in Modern China.* Durham, NC: Duke University Press.

———. 2004. "The Corporeal Politics of Quality." *Public Culture* 16 (2): 89–208.

———. 2008a. "From 'Class' to 'Social Strata': Grasping the Social Totality in Reform-Era China." *Third World Quarterly* 29 (3): 497–519.

———. 2008b. "Imagining Global Futures in China: The Child as a Sign of Value." In *Figuring the Future: Globalization and the Temporalities of Children and Youth,* edited by J. Cole and D. Durham, 49–72. Santa Fe, NM: SAR Press.

———. 2013. "Life-Making in Neoliberal Times." In *Global Futures in East Asia: Youth, Nation and the New Economy in Uncertain Times,* edited by Ann Anagnost, Andrea Arai, and Hai Ren, 1–28. Stanford, CA: Stanford University Press.

Andreas, Joel. 2009. *Rise of the Red Engineers: The Cultural Revolution and the Origins of China's New Class.* Stanford, CA: Stanford University Press.

Bailey, Paul. 1990. *Reform the People: Changing Attitudes towards Popular Education in Early 20th Century China.* Edinburgh: Edinburgh University Press.

Bakken, Borge. 1993. "'Never for the First Time': 'Premature Love' and Social Control in Today's China." *China Information* 7 (3): 9–26.

Baum, Richard. 1994. *Burying Mao: Chinese Politics in the Age of Deng Xiaoping.* Princeton, NJ: Princeton University Press.

Bauman, Z. 2008. *Work, Consumerism and the New Poor.* Buckingham, UK: Open University Press.

Bayart, Jean-François. 2007. *Global Subjects: A Political Critique of Globalization.* Cambridge, UK: Polity Press.

Beck, Ulrich. 1992. *Risk Society: Towards a New Modernity.* London: Sage.

Becker, Gary. (1964) 1993. *Human Capital: A Theoretical and Empirical Analysis with Special Reference to Education.* 3rd ed. Reprint, Chicago: University of Chicago Press.

Bettie, Julie. 2003. *Women without Class: Girls, Race and Identity*. Berkeley: University of California Press.

Biermann, Horst. 1999. "China's Vocational Education System Facing the Twenty-First Century." *International Journal of Sociology* 29 (1): 21–41.

Billeter, Jean-François. 1985. "The System of 'Class Status.'" In *The Scope of State Power in China*, edited by Stuart Schram, 127–169. London: St. Martin's Press.

Bourdieu, Pierre. 1984. *Distinction*. Cambridge, MA: Harvard University Press.

———. 1991. *Language and Symbolic Power*. Cambridge: Cambridge University Press.

———. 1998. "Job Insecurity Is Everywhere Now." Translated by Richard Nice. In *Acts of Resistance: Against the New Myths of Our Time*, edited by Pierre Bourdieu, 81–87. Cambridge, UK: Polity Press.

Bourdieu, Pierre, and J. C. Passerson. 1977. *Reproduction in Education, Society and Culture*. London: Sage.

Bray, David. 2005. *Social Space and Governance in Urban China: The Danwei System from Origins to Reform*. Stanford, CA: Stanford University Press.

———. 2013. "Urban Planning Goes Rural: Conceptualising the 'New Village.'" *China Perspectives* 2013 (3): 53–62.

Burchell, Gordon, Colin Gordon, and Peter Miller, eds. 1991. *The Foucault Effect: Studies in Governmentality*. Chicago: University of Chicago Press.

Carnegie, Dale. (1936) 1981. *How to Win Friends and Influence People*. Rev. ed. Reprint, New York: Simon and Schuster.

Central People's Government of the People's Republic of China. 2013. Accessed July 1, 2013. http://www.gov.cn/gzdt/2012-12/28/content_2301131.htm.

Chakrabortty, Aditya. 2013. "Forced Student Labour Is Central to the Chinese Economic Miracle." *The Guardian*, October 14, 2013. Accessed April 15, 2015. http://www.theguardian.com/commentisfree/2013/oct/14/forced-student-labour-china-apple.

Chan, Anita. 1985. *Children of Mao: Personality Development and Political Activism in the Red Guard Generation*. London: Macmillan.

Chan, Anita, and Kaxton Siu. 2012. "Chinese Migrant Workers: Factors Constraining the Emergence of Class Consciousness." In *China's Peasants and Workers: Changing Class Identities*, edited by Beatriz Carrillo and David Goodman, 79–101. Cheltenham, UK: Edward Elgar.

Chan Kam Wing. 1996. "Post-Mao China: A Two-Class Urban Society in the Making." *International Journal of Urban and Regional Research* 20:134–150.

———. 2012. "Migration and Development in China: Trends, Geography and Current Issues." *Migration and Development* 1 (2): 187–205.

Chan Ming K. and Arif Dirlik. 1991. *Schools into Fields and Factories: Anarchists, the Guomindang, and the National Labor University in Shanghai, 1927–1932*. Durham, NC: Duke University Press.

Chang, Iris. 1997. *The Rape of Nanking: The Forgotten Holocaust of World War II*. New York: Basic Books.

Cheng, T., and M. Selden. 1994. "The Origins and Social Consequences of China's Hukou System." *China Quarterly* 139:644–678.

Chowdhry, Prem. 2009. "'First Our Jobs Then Our Girls': The Dominant Caste Perception on the 'Rising' Dalits." *Modern Asian Studies* 43 (2): 437–479.

Chua, Amy. 2011. *Battle Hymn of the Tiger Mother.* New York: Penguin.

Chumley, Lily. 2013. "Evaluation Regimes and the Qualia of Quality." *Anthropological Theory* 13 (1–2): 169–183.

Cohen, Shana. 2004. *Searching for a Different Future: The Rise of a Global Middle Class in Morocco.* Durham, NC: Duke University Press.

Cole, Jennifer. 2014. "Producing Value among Malagasy Marriage Migrants in France: Managing Horizons of Expectation." *Current Anthropology* 55 (S9): S85–S94.

Comaroff, Jean, and John L. Comaroff. 2000. "Millennial Capitalism: First Thoughts on a Second Coming." *Public Culture* 12:291–343.

Connell, Raewyn. 2009. "The Work of Teaching." *History of Education Review* 38 (2): 9–16.

Cross, Jamie. 2010. "Neoliberalism as Unexceptional: Economic Zones and the Everyday Precariousness of Working Life in South India." *Critique of Anthropology* 30 (4): 355–373.

Culp, Robert. 2007. *Articulating Citizenship: Civic Education and Student Politics in Southeastern China, 1912–1940.* Cambridge, MA: Harvard University Asia Center.

Dahlman, Carl J., and Jean-Eric Aubert. 2001. "China and the Knowledge Economy: Seizing the 21st Century." Washington, DC: World Bank.

Dale Carnegie Training. 2015. Accessed April 15, 2015. http://www.dalecarnegie-china .cn/.

de Kloet, Jeroen. 2010. *China with a Cut: Globalisation, Urban Youth and Popular Music.* Amsterdam: Amsterdam University Press.

Dean, Mitchell. 2010. *Governmentality: Power and Rule in Modern Society.* 2nd ed. London: Sage Publications.

Demerath, Peter. 1999. "The Cultural Production of Educational Utility in Pere Village, Papua New Guinea." *Comparative Education Review* 43 (2): 162–192.

Donald, Stephanie. 2009. "Education, Class and Adaptation in China's World City." *Chinese Journal of Communication* 2 (1): 25–35.

Donald, Stephanie, and Yi Zheng. 2008. "Richer Than Before: The Cultivation of Middle-Class Taste." In *The New Rich in China*, edited by David Goodman, 71–82. London: Routledge.

Dong Jie. 2009. "'Isn't It Enough to Be a Chinese Speaker': Language Ideology and Migrant Identity Construction in a Public Primary School in Beijing." *Language & Communication* 29 (2): 115–126.

———. 2010. "The Enregisterment of Putonghua in Practice." *Language & Communication* 30 (4): 265–275.

Dunk, Thomas. 2002. "Remaking the Working Class: Experience, Class Consciousness, and the Industrial Adjustment Process." *American Ethnologist* 29: 878–900.

Dunn, Elizabeth. 2004. *Privatizing Poland: Baby Food, Big Business, and the Remaking of Labor.* Ithaca, NY: Cornell University Press.

Dutton, Michael. 1998. *Streetlife China.* Cambridge: Cambridge University Press.

Farquhar, Judith. 2002. *Appetites: Food and Sex in Postsocialist China.* Durham, NC: Duke University Press.

Feher, Michel. 2009. "Self-Appreciation; or, The Aspirations of Human Capital." *Public Culture* 21 (1): 21–41.

Fong, Vanessa. 2004. *Only Hope: Coming of Age under China's One-Child Policy.* Stanford, CA: Stanford University Press.

Foucault, Michel. 1977. *Discipline and Punish and the Birth of the Prison.* New York: Vintage Books.

———. 1982. "The Subject and Power." In *Michel Foucault: Beyond Structuralism and Hermeneutics,* edited by H. L. Dreyfus and P. Rabinow, 208–226. Chicago: University of Chicago Press.

———. 1991. "Governmentality." In *The Foucault Effect: Studies in Government Rationality,* edited by G. Burchell, 87–104. Chicago: University of Chicago Press.

———. 2008. *The Birth of Biopolitics: Lecture at the Collège De France, 1978–1979.* Edited by Frederic Gros. New York: Palgrave Macmillan.

Gewurtz, Margo. 1978. "Social Reality and Educational Reform. The Case of the Chinese Vocational Education Association 1917–1927." *Modern China* 4 (2): 157–180.

Giddens, Anthony. 1991. *Modernity and Self-Identity: Self and Society in the Late Modern Age.* Stanford, CA: Stanford University Press.

Gold, Thomas, William Hurst, Jaeyoun Won, and Qiang Li, eds. 2009. *Laid-Off Workers in a Workers' State: Unemployment with Chinese Characteristics.* New York: Palgrave Macmillan.

Goodman, David, ed. 2008. *The New Rich in China: Future Rulers, Present Lives.* London: Routledge.

———. 2014. *Class in Contemporary China.* Cambridge, UK: Polity Press.

Gordon, Colin. 1991. "Government Rationality: An Introduction." In *The Foucault Effect,* edited by Graham Burchell, Colin Gordon, and Peter Miller, 1–52. Chicago: University of Chicago Press.

Greenhalgh, Susan, and E. Winckler. 2005. *Governing China's Population: From Leninist to Neoliberal Biopolitics.* Stanford, CA: Stanford University Press.

Guo Yingjie. 2012. "Classes without Class Consciousness and Class Consciousness without Classes: The Meaning of Class in the People's Republic." *Journal of Contemporary China* 21 (77): 723–739.

Hannum, Emily. 2005. "Market Transition, Educational Disparities, and Family Strategies in Rural China: New Evidence on Gender Stratification and Development." *Demography* 39 (1): 95–117.

Hansen, Mette Halskov. 2014. *Educating the Chinese Individual: Life in a Rural Boarding School.* Seattle: University of Washington Press.

Hansen, Mette Halskov, and T. E. Woronov. 2013. "Demanding and Resisting Vocational Education: A Comparative Study of Schools in Rural and Urban China." *Comparative Education* 49 (2): 242–259.

Hanser, Amy. 2008. *Service Encounters: Class, Gender and the Market for Social Distinction in Urban China.* Stanford, CA: Stanford University Press.

Harvey, David. 1990. *The Condition of Postmodernity.* Oxford: Blackwell Publishers.

Hertz, Ellen. 1998. *The Trading Crowd: An Ethnography of the Shanghai Stock Market.* Cambridge: Cambridge University Press.

Hochschild, Arlie Russell. 2003. *The Managed Heart: Commercialization of Human Feeling.* Berkeley: University of California Press.

Hoffman, Lisa. 2010. *Patriotic Professionalism in Urban China.* Philadelphia: Temple University Press.

Hsu, Carolyn. 2007. *Creating Market Socialism: How Ordinary People Are Shaping Class and Status in in China.* Durham, NC: Duke University Press.

Huang Quanyu. 2014. *The Hybird Tiger: Secrets of the Extraordinary Success of Asian-American Kids.* New York: Prometheus.

Hubbert, Jennifer. 2006. "(Re)Collecting Mao: Memory and Fetish in Contemporary China." *American Ethnologist* 33 (2): 145–161.

Jacka, Tamara. 2006. *Rural Women in Urban China: Gender, Migration and Social Change.* Armonk, NY: M. E. Sharpe.

Jacka, Tamara, and Sally Sargeson, eds. 2011. *Women, Gender and Rural Development in China.* Cheltenham, UK: Edward Elgar Publishing.

Jeffrey, Craig. 2010. *Timepass: Youth, Class and the Politics of Waiting in India.* Stanford, CA: Stanford University Press.

Jeffery, Lyn. 2000. "Selling Selves: The Cultural Construction of a Market in the PRC." PhD diss., University of California, Santa Cruz.

Jeffreys, Elaine, ed. 2009. *China's Governmentalities: Governing Change, Changing Government.* Abingdon, UK: Routledge.

Jeffreys, Elaine, and Gary Sigley. 2006. "China and Governmentality: A Special Issue." *Economy and Society* 35 (4): 487–593.

———. 2009. "Governmentality, Governance and China." In *China's Governmentalities: Governing Change, Changing Government*, edited by Elaine Jeffreys, 1–23. London: Routledge.

Judd, Ellen. 2002. *The Chinese Women's Movement between State and Market.* Stanford, CA: Stanford University Press.

Kahn, Joseph. 2007. "China Shuts Down Western-Run Newsletter." *New York Times*, July 11, 2007. Accessed April 15, 2014. http://www.nytimes.com/2007/07/11/world/asia/11cnd-china.html?_r=0.

Katz, Cindi. 2008. "Childhood as Spectacle: Relays of Anxiety and the Reconfiguration of the Child." *Cultural Geographies* 15: 5–17.

———. 2011. "Accumulation, Excess, Childhood: Towards a Countertopography of Risk and Waste." *Documents d'Analisi Geografica* 57 (1): 47–60.

Khan, Shamus Rahman. 2011. *Privilege: The Making of an Adolescent Elite at St. Paul's School.* Princeton, NJ: Princeton University Press, 2011.

Kipnis, Andrew. 1997. *Producing Guanxi: Sentiment, Self and Subculture in a North China Village.* Durham, NC: Duke University Press.

———. 2001. "The Disturbing Educational Discipline of 'Peasants.'" *China Journal* 46:1–24.

———. 2006. "Suzhi: A Keyword Approach." *China Quarterly* 186: 295–313.

———. 2007. "Neoliberalism Reified: Suzhi Discourse and Tropes of Neoliberalism in the People's Republic of China." *Journal of the Royal Anthropological Institute* 13 (2): 383–400.

———. 2010. *Governing Educational Desire: Culture, Politics and Schooling in China.* Chicago: University of Chicago Press.

———. 2012. "Constructing Commonality: Standardization and Modernization in Chinese Nationbuilding." *Journal of Asian Studies* 71: 731–755.

Kohrman, Matthew. 2005. *Bodies of Difference: Experiences of Disability and Institutional Advocacy in the Making of Modern China.* Berkeley: University of California Press.

Kroskrity, Paul, ed. 2000. *Regimes of Language: Ideologies, Polities, and Identities.* Santa Fe, NM: School of American Research Press.

Lee Ching-Kwan. 1998. *Gender and the South China Miracle: Two Worlds of Factory Women.* Berkeley: University of California Press.

———. 2007. *Against the Law: Labor Protests in China's Rustbelt and Sunbelt.* Berkeley: University of California Press.

Lee Ching-Kwan and Yelizavetta Kofman. 2012. "The Politics of Precarity: Views beyond the United States." *Work and Occupations* 39 (4): 388–408.

Lemke, Thomas. 2002. "Foucault, Governmentality, and Critique." *Rethinking Marxism* 14 (3): 49–64.

Lenin, V. I., ed. (1916) 1929. *Lenin Collected Works.* Vol. 23, *The Nascent Trend of Imperialist Economism.* Reprint, Moscow: Progress Publishers.

Lewin, Keith, and Hui Xu. 1989. "Rethinking Revolution: Reflections on China's 1985 Educational Reforms." *Comparative Education* 25 (1): 7–17.

Li Cheng, ed. 2010. *China's Emerging Middle Class: Beyond Economic Transformation.* Washington, DC: Brookings Institution Press.

Li Chunling. 2010. "Characterizing China's Middle Class: Heterogeneous Composition and Multiple Identities." In *China's Emerging Middle Class: Beyond Economic Transformation,* edited by Cheng Li, 135–156. Washington, DC: Brookings Institution Press.

Lian Si. 2009. *Yizu: Daxue Biye Sheng Juju Cun Shiji* [Ant tribes: A true record of university graduates living in villages]. Nanning: Guangxi Shifan Daxue Chubanshe.

Luo Yan. 2013. "Crisis in the Restructing of China's Vocational Education System, 1980–2010." *Chinese Education & Society* 46 (4): 22–29.

Mains, Daniel. 2007. "Neoliberal Times: Progress, Boredom, and Shame among Young Men in Urban Ethiopia." *American Ethnologist* 34 (4): 659–673.

Martin, Emily. 1994. *Flexible Bodies: Tracking Immunity in American Culture from the Days of Polio to the Age of AIDS.* Boston: Beacon Press.

Martin, Randy. 2002. *Financialization of Daily Life.* Philadelphia: Temple University Press.

Marx, Karl. (1867) 1978. *Capital, Vol. 1.* In *The Marx-Engels Reader,* edited by Robert Tucker, 294–438. Reprint, New York: Norton.

Masquelier, Adeline. 2005. "The Scorpion's Sting: Youth, Marriage and the Struggle for Social Maturity in Niger." *Journal of the Royal Anthropological Institute* 11 (1): 59–83.

McDowell, Linda. 2012. "Post-crisis, Post-Ford and Post-gender? Youth Identities in an Era of Austerity." *Journal of Youth Studies* 15 (5): 573–590.

Meisner, Maurice. 1989. *Marxism and the Chinese Experience: Issues in Contemporary Chinese Socialism.* Armonk, NY: M. E. Sharpe.

———. 1996. *The Deng Xiaoping Era: An Inquiry into the Fate of Chinese Socialism.* New York: Hill and Wang.

Ministry of Education, People's Republic of China. 2011. "Jiaoyubu Guanyu Tuijin Zhongdeng He Gaodeng Zhiye Jiaoyu Xietiao Fazhan De Zhidao Yijian" [Guiding views of the Ministry of Education on advancing the coordinated development of secondary and higher vocational education]. In *Document no. jiaohicheng[2011]9 hao.* Beijing. Accessed July 30, 2013. http://www.gov.cn/zwgk/2011-09/20/content_1951624.htm.

———. 2012a. "Ministry of Education—2012 Work Priorities." Beijing. Accessed July 30, 2013. https://internationaleducation.gov.au/International-network/china/PolicyUpdates-China/Pages/ArticleChineseMinistryofEducation2012WorkPriorities.aspx.

———. 2012b. "Ministry of Education. *2012 Zhongguo Zhongdeng Zhiye Xuexiaosheng Fazhan yu Jiuye Baogao* [2012 Report on development and employment of Chinese secondary vocational school students].* Beijing: Foreign Language and Teaching Research Press.

———. 2013a. "Composition of Students in Senior Secondary Schools." Accessed December 29, 2014. http://www.moe.gov.cn/publicfiles/business/htmlfiles/moe/s8493/201412/181722.html.

———. 2013b. "Promotion Rate of Graduates of Regular School by Levels." Accessed December 29, 2014. http://www.moe.gov.cn/publicfiles/business/htmlfiles/moe/s8493/201412/181725.html.

———. 2015. "National Outline for Medium and Long-Term Education Reform and Development (2010–2020)." Accessed April 12, 2015. http://www.moe.gov.cn/publicfiles/business/htmlfiles/moe/info_category_query/index.html.

Mitropoulos, Angela. 2006. "Precari-Us." *Mute* 1 (29). Accessed January 19, 2011. http://www.metamute.org/editorial/articles/precari-us.

Miyazaki, Hirokazu. 2006. "Economy of Dreams: Hope in Global Capitalism and Its Critiques." *Cultural Anthropology* 21 (2): 147–172.

Molé, Noelle. 2010. "Precarious Subjects: Anticipating Neoliberalism in Northern Italy's Workplace." *American Anthropologist* 112 (1): 38–53.

Muehlebach, Andrea. 2012. *The Moral Neoliberal: Welfare and Citizenship in Italy.* Chicago: University of Chicago Press.

Narotzky, Susana, and Niko Besnier. 2014. "Crisis, Value, and Hope: Rethinking the Economy: An Introduction to Supplement 9." *Current Anthropology* 55 (S9): S4–S16.

Neilson, Brett, and Ned Rossiter. 2008. "Precarity as a Political Concept, or Fordism as Exception." *Theory, Culture and Society* 25 (7–8): 51–72.

Nonini, Donald. 2008. "Is China Becoming Neoliberal?" *Critique of Anthropology* 28 (2): 145–176.

Osburg, John. 2013. *Anxious Wealth: Money and Morality among China's New Rich.* Stanford, CA: Stanford University Press.

Otis, Eileen. 2011. *Markets and Bodies: Women, Service Work, and the Making of Inequality in China.* Stanford, CA: Stanford University Press.

Patico, Jennifer. 2008. *Consumption and Social Change in a Post-Soviet Middle Class.* Stanford, CA: Stanford University Press.

Pepper, Suzanne. 1996. *Radicalism and Education Reform in 20th-Century China: The Search for an Ideal Development Model.* Cambridge: Cambridge University Press.

Potter, Sulamith, and J. Potter. 1990. *China's Peasants: The Anthropology of a Revolution.* Cambridge: Cambridge University Press.

Pun Ngai. 2003. "Subsumption or Consumption? The Phantom of Consumer Revolution in 'Globalizing China.'" *Cultural Anthropology* 18 (4): 469–492.

———. 2004. "Women Workers and Precarious Employment in Shenzhen Special Economic Zone, China." *Gender and Development* 12 (2): 29–36.

———. 2005. *Made in China: Women Factory Workers in a Global Workplace.* Durham, NC: Duke University Press.

Pun Ngai and Jenny Chan. 2012. "Global Capital, the State, and Chinese Workers: The Foxconn Experience." *Modern China* 38 (4): 383–410.

———. 2013. "The Spatial Politics of Labor in China: Life, Labor and a New Generation of Migrant Workers." *South Atlantic Quarterly* 112 (1): 179–190.

Pun Ngai and Huilin Lu. 2010. "Unfinished Proletarianization: Self, Anger, and Class Action among the Second Generation of Peasant-Workers in Present-Day China." *Modern China* 36 (5): 493–519.

Pun Ngai and Chris Smith. 2007. "Putting Transnational Labour Process in Its Place: The Dormitory Labour Regime in Post-socialist China." *Work, Employment and Society* 21 (1): 27–45.

Qvortrup, Jens. 1995. "From Useful to Useful: The Historical Continuity of Children's Constructive Participations." *Sociological Studies of Children* 7: 49–86.

Ralph, Michael. 2008. "Killing Time." *Social Text* 26 (4): 1–30.

Ren Hai. 2013. *The Middle Class in Neoliberal China: Governing Risk, Life-Building, and Themed Spaces.* New York: Routledge.

Robbins, Tony. 2015. Anthony Robbins. Accessed April 15, 2015. http://www.tonyrobbins.com.

Rofel, Lisa. 2007. *Desiring China: Experiments in Neoliberalism, Sexuality and Public Culture.* Durham, NC: Duke University Press.

Rose, Nikolas. 1993. "Government, Authority and Expertise in Advanced Liberalism." *Economy and Society* 22: 283–299.

———. 1996. *Inventing Ourselves: Psychology, Power, and Personhood.* Cambridge: Cambridge University Press.

———. 1999. *Governing the Soul: The Shaping of the Private Self.* 2nd ed. London: Free Association Books.

Sassen, Saskia. 2012. *Cities in a World Economy.* 4th ed. London: Sage.

Schieffelin, Bambi, Katherine Woolard, and Paul Kroskrity, eds. 1998. *Language Ideologies: Practice and Theory.* Oxford: Oxford University Press.

Schram, Stuart. 1984. "'Economics in Command?' Ideology and Policy since the Third Plenum, 1978–84." *China Journal* 99: 417–461.

Schulte, Barbara. 2012. "Webs of Borrowing and Lending: Social Networks in Vocational Education in Republican China." In *World Yearbook of Education: Policy Borrowing and Lending in Education*, edited by Gita Steiner-Khamsi and Florian Waldow, 95–117. New York: Routledge.

———. 2013. "Unwelcome Stranger to the System: Vocational Education in Early Twentieth-Century China." *Comparative Education* 49 (2): 226–241.

Schwintzer, Ernst Peter. 1992. "Education to Save the Nation: Huang Yanpei and the Educational Reform Movement in Early Twentieth Century China." PhD diss., University of Washington.

Sennett, Richard. 1998. *The Corrosion of Character: The Personal Consequences of Work in the New Capitalism*. New York: W. W. Norton.

Shao Jing. 2006. "Fluid Labor and Blood Money: The Economy of HIV/AIDS in Rural Central China." *Cultural Anthropology* 21 (4): 535–569.

Shi Weiping. 2013. "Issues and Problems in the Current Development of Vocational Education in China." *Chinese Education & Society* 46 (4): 12–21.

Shirk, Susan. 1982. *Competitive Comrades: Career Incentives and Student Strategies in China*. Berkeley: University of California Press.

Shoshan, Nitzan. 2012. "Time at a Standstill: Loss, Accumulation and the Past Conditional in an East Berlin Neighborhood." *Ethnos* 77 (1): 24–49.

Sigley, Gary. 2009. "Suzhi, the Body, and the Fortunes of Technoscientific Reasoning in Contemporary China." *positions* 17 (3): 537–566.

Slater, David. 2010. "The 'New Working Class' of Urban Japan: Socialization and Contradictions from Middle School to the Labor Market." In *Social Class in Contemporary Japan: Structures, Sorting and Strategies*, edited by Hiroshi Ishida and David H. Slater, 139–169. London: Routledge.

Smith, Warren W. 2010. *Tibet's Last Stand? The Tibetan Uprising of 2008 and China's Response*. Plymouth, UK: Rowman and Littlefield.

Solinger, Dorothy. 1999. *Contesting Citizenship in Urban China: Peasant Migrants, the State, and the Logic of the Market*. Berkeley: University of California Press.

———. 2009. "Xiagang and the Geometry of Urban Political Patronage in China: Celebrated State (once-) Workers and State Chagrin." In *Laid-off Workers in a Workers' state: Unemployment with Chinese Characteristics*, edited by Thomas Gold, William J. Hurst and Jaeyoun Won, 39–60. NY: Palgrave Macmillan.

———. 2012. "The New Urban Underclass and Its Consciousness: Is It a Class?" *Journal of Contemporary China* 21 (78): 1011–1028.

Song Yinguan, Prashant Loyalka, and Jianguo Wei. 2013. "Determinants of Tracking Intentions, and Actual Education Choices among Junior High School Students in Rural China." *Chinese Education & Society* 46 (4): 30–42.

Southwood, Ivor. 2011. *Non-stop Inertia*. Winchester, UK: Zero Books.

Standing, Guy. 2011. *The Precariat: The New Dangerous Class*. London: Bloomsbury Academic.

State Council, People's Republic of China. 1993. "Zhongguo Jiaoyu Gaige He Fazhan Gangyao" [Outline of China education reform and development]. Beijing: State Council of the PRC. Accessed July 30, 2013. http://www.moe.gov.cn/publicfiles/business/html files/moe/s6986/200407/2484.html. [in Chinese]

———. 2012. "Fuwuye Fazhan 'She Er Wu' Guihua" [Service sector employment development "Ten Two Five" plan]. Beijing: National Development and Reform Commission. Accessed July 30, 2013. http://www.gov.cn/zwgk/2012-12/12/content_2288778 .htm. [in Chinese]

Sun Wanning. 2009. "Suzhi on the Move: Body, Place, and Power." *positions* 17 (3): 617–642.

———. 2012. "Poetry of Labour and (Dis)Articulation of Class: China's Worker-Poets and the Cultural Politics of Boundaries." *Journal of Contemporary China* 21 (78): 993–1010.

Taussig, Michael. 1980. *The Devil and Commodity Fetishism in South American.* Chapel Hill: University of North Carolina Press.

Thøgersen, Stig. 1990. *Secondary Education in China after Mao: Reform and Social Conflict.* Aarhus, Denmark: Aarhus University Press.

Tomba, Luigi. 2004. "Creating an Urban Middle Class: Social Engineering in Beijing." *China Journal* 51: 1–26.

———. 2009. "Of Quality, Harmony, and Community: Civilization and the Middle Class in Urban China." *positions* 17 (3): 592–616.

Tsang, Mun C. 2000. "Education and National Development in China since 1949: Oscillating Policies and Enduring Dilemmas." *China Review* 2000: 579–618.

Unger, Jonathan. 1982. *Education under Mao: Class and Competition in Canton Schools, 1960–1980.* New York: Columbia University Press.

United Nations Development Programme. 2013. *2013 Human Development Report.* Accessed April 15, 2015. http://hdr.undp.org/en/2013-report.

Walder, Andrew. 1986. *Communist Neo-traditionalism: Work and Authority in Chinese Industry.* Berkeley: University of California Press.

Wang Dewen. 2010. "Reform and Development of Vocational Education." In *The China Population and Labor Yearbook,* edited by Fang Cai, 93–116. Leiden, Netherlands: Brill.

Wang Jing. 2008. *Brand New China: Advertising, Media, and Commercial Culture.* Cambridge, MA: Harvard University Press.

Wang Lei and Dayuan Jiang. 2013. "Chinese Vocational Education: Borrowing and Reforming." *Chinese Education & Society* 46 (4): 92–99.

Wang Lei and Heidi Ross. 2013. "Vocational Education (I): Current Issues and Challenges." *Chinese Education & Society* 46 (4): 3–11.

Weber, Max. 1978. *Economy and Society.* Vol 1. Berkeley: University of California Press.

Weiss, Brad. 2002. "Thug Realism: Inhabiting Fantasy in Urban Tanzania." *Cultural Anthropology* 17 (1): 93–124.

Whiteside, Tom, and Minxuan Zhang. 1992. "Recent Developments in Technical and Vocational Education in the Chinese Senior Secondary System." *Vocational Aspect of Education* 44 (3): 283–294.

Willis, Paul. 1977. *Learning to Labor: How Working Class Kids Get Working Class Jobs.* New York: Columbia University Press.

Willis, Susan. 1998. "Teens at Work: Negotiating the Jobless Future." In *Generations of Youth,* edited by Joe Austin and Mike Willard, 347–357. New York: NYU Press.

Woronov, T. E. 2003. "Transforming the Future: 'Quality' Children and the Chinese Nation." PhD diss., University of Chicago.

———. 2004. "In the Eye of the Chicken: Hierarchy and Marginality among Beijing's Migrant Schoolchildren." *Ethnography* 5 (3): 289–313.

———. 2006. "Chinese Children, American Education: Globalizing Child-Rearing in Contemporary China." In *Generations and Globalization: Youth, Age, and Family in the New World Economy*, edited by J. Cole and D. Durham, 29–51. Bloomington: Indiana University Press.

———. 2007. "Performing the Nation: China's Children as Little Red Pioneers." *Anthropological Quarterly* 80 (3): 647–672.

———. 2008. "Raising Quality, Fostering 'Creativity': Ideologies and Practices of Education Reform in Beijing." *Anthropology and Education Quarterly* 39 (4): 401–422.

———. 2009. "Governing China's Children: Governmentality and 'Education for Quality.'" *positions* 17 (3): 567–589.

———. 2011. "Learning to Serve: Urban Youth, Vocational Schools, and New Class Formations in China." *China Journal* 66: 1–26.

———. 2012. "Class Consciousness, Service Work: Youth and Class in Nanjing Vocational Secondary Schools." *Journal of Contemporary China* 21 (7): 779–791.

Wu Yiching. 2014. *The Cultural Revolution at the Margins: Chinese Socialism in Crisis.* Cambridge, MA: Harvard University Press.

Yan Hairong. 2008. *New Masters, New Servants: Migration, Development, and Women Workers in China.* Durham, NC: Duke University Press.

Yan Hao. 2010. *China's Vocational Education and Training: The Next Key Target of Education Promotion.* Singapore: East Asia Institute.

Yan Yunxiang. 1996. *The Flow of Gifts: Reciprocity and Social Networks in a Chinese Village.* Stanford, CA: Stanford University Press.

Yang, Mayfair. 1994. *Gifts, Favors and Banquets: The Art of Social Relationships in China.* Ithaca, NY: Cornell University Press.

Yeh Wen-Hsin. 2008. "Huang Yanpei and the Chinese Society of Vocational Education in Shanghai Networking." In *At the Crossroads of Empire: Middlemen, Social Networks and State-Building in Republican Shanghai*, edited by Nara Dillon and Jean C. Oi, 25–44. Stanford, CA: Stanford University Press.

Yi Hongmei, Linxiu Zhang, Chengfang Liu, James Chu, Prashant Loyalka, Maani May, and Jianguo Wei. 2013. "How Are Secondary Vocational Schools in China Measuring Up to Government Benchmarks?" *China and World Economy* 21 (3): 98–120.

Yin Liangen and Haiyan Wang. 2010. "People-Centred Myth: Representation of the Wenchuan Earthquake in China Daily." *Discourse and Communication* 4 (4): 383–398.

Zhan Mei. 2005. "Civet Cats, Fried Grasshoppers, and David Beckham's Pajamas: Unruly Bodies after SARS." *American Anthropologist* 107 (1): 31–42.

Zhang Li. 2001. *Strangers in the City.* Stanford, CA: Stanford University Press.

———. 2010. *In Search of Paradise: Middle-Class Living in a Chinese Metropolis.* Ithaca, NY: Cornell University Press.

———. 2013. "Afterword: Flexible Postsocialist Assemblages Form the Margin." *positions* 20 (2): 659–667.

Zhang Li and Aihwa Ong, eds. 2008. *Privatizing China: Socialism from Afar.* Ithaca, NY: Cornell University Press.

Zhang Zhen. 2000. "Mediating Time: The 'Rice Bowl of Youth' in Fin de Siècle Urban China." *Public Culture* 12: 93–113.

Zhongguo Gongyun Yanjiusuo (All-China Federation of Trade Unions Research Institute), eds. 2011. *Xin Sheng Dai Nongmin'gong: Wenti, Yanpan, Duiceianyi* [The new migrant worker generation: Problems, research evaluations, solutions and recommendations]. Beijing: Zhongguo Gongren Chubanshe.

Zhou Xueguang and Liren Hou. 1999. "Children of the Cultural Revolution: The State and Life Course in the People's Republic of China." *American Sociological Review* 64 (1): 12–36.

Index

Page references followed by "*f*" refer to figures.

science and rationality in, 9–10
tertiary (service) sector increase, 19,
    64, 132–133, 158n1 (Ch. 5)
economism, 10, 12, 14, 16, 68, 154n11
education
    aspiration management in, 44, 77,
        101, 130–131
    class reproduction in, 57–60,
        143–145, 151
    class sorting by HSEE, 23, 57–60, 62,
        86, 135, 156nn5–7
    class sorting by UEE, 156n4
    class sorting by underfunding,
        143–144
    complexity of system, 42f, 53–54
    "counter-school culture" in, 145, 151
    as human capital accumulation, 1,
        10–13, 54
    in the Maoist era, 31, 155nn2–3
    private academic high schools, 5, 23,
        59, 62, 135, 156n7
    progression in, 2–3, 42f, 154n7
    social mobility through, 33–34,
        55–56, 61, 142–143
    success classes, 115–118
    suzhi and, 17–18
    tuition in, 39, 51, 155n7
    universal, through grade nine, 4, 34,
        153n1
educational failures
    in Chinese culturalist view, 6–7
    Chinese exceptionalism and, 8, 18
    class-based discourse on, 7, 141–142
    vocation education students as, 2–3,
        6, 36, 44, 50, 141–142
Education Commissions (Jiaowei), 34–35
Education Reform Law (1986), 34
English (ESL) classes, 75, 83–84, 157n2
entrepreneurs
    perceived morality of newly rich,
        154n8, 156n8
    of the self, 94–95
    in the working class, 59, 140,
        142–143, 154n8

factories moved out of cities, 19, 146,
    155n15
factory-labor regimes, 125–126, 146
families
    filial piety of students, 24, 51, 55,
        61–62, 101, 139
    internships through, 122–123
    investing in child's education, 12–13,
        154n12
    in obtaining jobs (guanxi), 105–106,
        112, 122–124
    students disobeying parents in job
        search, 133–134, 151
    See also guanxi; parents of students
Fang Bing (pseudonym), 119
Fang Chao (pseudonym), 121–122
Fan Li (pseudonym), 53
Farquhar, Judith, (24, 95, 100, 103)
Fei, Teacher (pseudonym), 118–119,
    120
feibianzhi. See contract teachers
fetish of the number, 14–15, 28
flexible workers, 23, 72, 90, 132–134
Foucault, Michel, 7, 12, 74, 82, 86,
    93–94, 96
Foxconn, 124–125

gaokao. See University Entrance Exams
    (UEE)
gender
    appearance requirements for jobs,
        74, 126, 130, 157n9
    course choices by, 52
    gendered disciplines, 73–74
    home ownership and, 138, 140, 151
    internships and, 121, 122–123
    job choices and, 52, 77, 123, 133
    place-based identity and, 107–108
    working when married, pregnant, or
        older, 160n9
Gewurtz, Margo, 76
Giddens, Anthony, 149
global capitalism, narratives of progress
    in, 129–130, 134

Yang Juan, 21
Yang Minglu (pseudonym), 53
Yao, Teacher (pseudonym), 91, 106
Yeh Wen-hsin, 29
youth
    after elementary school, 1–2
    becoming enterprising subjects, 105,
        106, 115–118
    capital accumulation in, 11–13
    civility of rural vs. urban, 80–81
    factory-labor regimes, 125–126, 146
    filial piety in, 24, 51, 55, 61–62, 101,
        139
    identity formation in, 107–112
    limited economic possibilities for,
        88–89
    mandatory education through grade
        nine, 4, 34, 153n1
    normative behavior in, 13–14, 56

as numeric capital, 14–15
sent-down, 75, 157n10
service sector jobs for, 19, 123–124
studying by, 54, 60–61, 102–103
Unemployed (see "ant tribes")
See also class sorting; global youth;
    "precariat"; urban working class;
    vocational students

zaolian ("early dating"), 102–103
Zhang Li, 94, 100–101
Zhang Zhigang (pseudonym), 48, 55,
    79, 115–118, 158n2 (Ch. 5), 158n4
    (Ch.5)
Zhan Mei, 92
Zheng, Teacher (pseudonym), 72–75, 78,
    86, 98–99, 101
zhongzhuan degree, 37, 41, 42f, 147
Zhu, Teacher (pseudonym), 84–86

The authorized representative in the EU for product safety and compliance is:
Mare Nostrum Group
B.V Doelen 72
4831 GR Breda
The Netherlands

www.ingramcontent.com/pod-product-compliance
Lightning Source LLC
Chambersburg PA
CBHW030843270326
41928CB00007B/1198

* 9 7 8 0 8 0 4 7 9 6 9 2 7 *